Combat Leader's Field Guide

Code of Conduct

**FOR MEMBERS OF THE ARMED FORCES
OF THE UNITED STATES**

1. I am an American, fighting in the forces which guard my country and our way of life. I am prepared to give my life in their defense.
2. I will never surrender of my own free will. If in command, I will never surrender the members of my command while they still have means to resist.
3. If I am captured I will continue to resist by all means available. I will make every effort to escape and aid others to escape. I will accept neither parole nor special favors from the enemy.
4. If I become a prisoner of war, I will keep faith with my fellow prisoners. I will give no information or take part in any action which might be harmful to my comrades. If I am senior, I will take command. If not, I will obey the lawful order of those appointed over me and will back them up in every way.
5. When questioned, should I become a prisoner of war, I am required to give name, rank, service number, and date of birth. I will evade answering further questions to the utmost of my ability. I will make no oral or written statements disloyal to my country and its allies or harmful to their cause.
6. I will never forget that I am an American, fighting for freedom, responsible for my actions, and dedicated to the principles which made my country free. I will trust in my God and in the United States of America.

FOR THE GOVERNMENT OF THE UNITED STATES

The U.S. government also has responsibilities under the code. The Nation has pledged itself:

- To keep faith with you and stand by you as you fight for its defense;
- To care for your family and dependents; and should you be captured,
- To use every practical means to contact, support, and gain release for you and all other prisoners of war.

Combat Leader's Field Guide

13th Edition

Sgt. Maj. Brett A. Stoneberger,
USA (Ret.)

STACKPOLE
BOOKS

Combat Leader's Field Guide
Copyright © 2005 by Stackpole Books

Published by
STACKPOLE BOOKS
5067 Ritter Road
Mechanicsburg, PA 17055
www.stackpolebooks.com

Printed in the United States of America

10 9 8 7 6 5 4

First edition, 1956, © Military Service Publishing Company
Second edition, 1960, © The Stackpole Company
Third edition, 1961, © The Stackpole Company
Fourth edition, 1962, © The Stackpole Company
Fifth edition, 1964, © The Stackpole Company
Sixth edition, 1966, © The Stackpole Company
Seventh edition, 1967, © The Stackpole Company
Eighth edition, 1973, © The Stackpole Company
Ninth edition, 1980, © The Stackpole Company
Tenth edition, 1987, © Stackpole Books
Eleventh edition, 1994, © Stackpole Books
Twelfth edition, 2000, © Stackpole Books
Thirteenth edition, 2005, © Stackpole Books

Library of Congress Cataloging-in-Publication

Stoneberger, Brett A., 1962–
  Combat leader's field guide / Brett A. Stoneberger.—13th ed.
    p. cm.
  Includes bibliographical references and index.
  ISBN 0-8117-3195-2
  1. United States. Army—Field service—Handbooks, manuals, etc. I. Title
UD433.S76 2005
355.4—dc22
                                        2004024007
ISBN 978-0-8117-3195-9

Contents

Preface

This guide is designed to assist leaders or prospective leaders of combat infantry units or other groups that, in an emergency, must fight as infantry. The content is tactical and logistical, administrative matter mostly being omitted. When in the field, especially under stress of combat or simulated combat, the combat leader cannot instantly recall everything he has been taught. Rapid changes in the situation may cause him to assume a position for which he has not yet been trained. He will then appreciate some brief reference material to guide him. He cannot carry a "five-foot shelf" of field manuals, and unlike the staff officer or higher commander, he does not have ready access to organizational files or a library when in the field. What he needs he must carry in his pocket, condensed yet in a form approximating at-a-glance capability. This field guide has been compiled from current doctrine and field manuals with those requirements in mind.

You will note that much of the reference material is in fact a comprehensive checklist to ensure that you have not overlooked some important consideration of troop leading.

As with the prior edition, the material in this edition is in two parts, unit combat operations and soldier combat skills. The material in Part I focuses on dismounted infantry operations at the platoon and squad levels, including battle drills—those collective actions rapidly executed without applying a deliberate decision-making process. Indeed, a small unit's ability to accomplish its mission often depends on soldiers and leaders executing key actions quickly. Part II focuses on critical individual soldier skills necessary for battlefield effectiveness and survival.

This guide also includes the considerations applicable to how U.S. Army doctrine addresses the range of "full-spectrum operations" across the spectrum of conflict. When conducting full-spectrum operations, commanders combine and sequence offensive, defensive, stability, and support operations to accomplish the mission.

Acknowledgments

Hidden between the lines of any good piece of work is the idea and source for that work. The *Combat Leader's Field Guide* was originally published as the *Junior Leader's Field Notebook* in 1956; since that time, it has gone through eleven revisions, and this one will be the twelfth making it the 13th edition. In the profession of arms our doctrine comes from research and experience, and our experience usually comes from the sacrifices of those people who train and fight for our great nation. I'd like to take a moment and thank all of those people both in and out of uniform—for without their experience, doctrine would fail to stay current. Even as I write this revision, many of our countrymen and allies are fighting the war on terrorism in Afghanistan, Iraq, and other dangerous places of the world. They fight for freedom and for the hope of providing a better way of life for the oppressed. I cannot help but feel a great sense of admiration and pride for their many military victories and for the sacrifices of their families.

Additionally, I would like to acknowledge the information managers in the U.S. armed forces who formulate our fighting doctrine. Without these writers, historians, and soldiers who compile and share our many lessons learned, we would not have the *Combat Leader's Field Guide*.

Brett A. Stoneberger
SGM, U.S. Army (Ret.)

PART ONE

Unit Combat Operations

1

The Battlefield

ARMY DOCTRINE

Small unit leaders must understand the concepts and fundamentals of Army doctrine to effectively lead in combat.

The U.S. Army's current operational doctrine holds warfighting as the Army's primary mission. It recognizes the ability of Army forces to dominate land warfare across the full spectrum of conflict from large-scale operations to military operations other than war (MOOTW). Full-spectrum operations include offensive, defensive, stability, and support operations. Army commanders may combine different types of operations either simultaneously or sequentially to accomplish the missions of war. For each mission, the joint force commander and Army component commander determine the emphasis Army forces place on each type of operation. Offensive and defensive operations normally dominate.

The foundations of full-spectrum operations are: *fundamentals, battle command*, and *conduct*.

FUNDAMENTALS

The fundamentals of full-spectrum operations are: the *elements of combat power*, the *principals of war*, the *tenets of Army operations*, and the *operational framework*.

The Elements of Combat Power

The elements of combat power are building blocks that underlie the Army's ability to dominate land warfare. Commanders combine and apply the elements of combat power to produce overwhelming effects.

Maneuver. Maneuver is the employment of forces, through movement combined with fire or fire potential, to achieve a position of advantage with respect to the enemy. Maneuver is the means by which commanders concentrate combat power to achieve surprise, shock, momentum, and dominance.

Firepower. Firepower provides the destructive force essential to overcoming the enemy's ability and will to fight. Firepower and maneuver complement each other. Firepower magnifies the effects of maneuver by destroying enemy forces and restricting his ability to counter friendly actions; maneuver creates the conditions for the effective use of firepower. The threat of one in the presence of the other magnifies the impact of both. One without the other makes neither decisive.

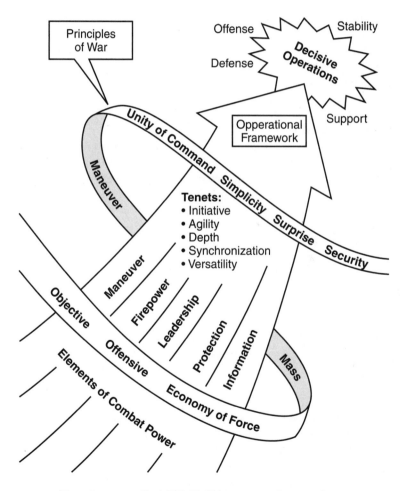

Fundamentals of Full-Spectrum Operations

Leadership. Because it deals directly with soldiers, leadership is the most dynamic element of combat power. Confident, audacious, and competent leadership focuses available combat power and creates the conditions for success. Leaders who embody the warrior ethos inspire soldiers to succeed. They provide purpose, direction, and motivation in all operations, especially in small units.

Protection. Protection is the preservation of the fighting capacity of a force so that the commander can apply it at the decisive time and place. Protection consists of force protection, field discipline, safety, and fratricide avoidance.

Information. Information enhances leadership and magnifies the effects of maneuver, firepower, and protection. Today, Army leaders use information collected by manned and unmanned systems to increase their understanding of the common operational picture (COP) before engaging the enemy.

The Principles of War

The nine principles of war provide general guidance for conducting war and military operations other than war at the strategic, operational, and tactical levels. They do not apply in the same way to every situation. Rather, they summarize the characteristics of successful Army operations.

Objective

Direct every military operation toward a clearly defined, decisive, and attainable objective. The ultimate military purpose of war is the destruction of the enemy's armed forces and its will to fight. In operations other than war, the ultimate objective might be more difficult to define, but it must be clear from the beginning.

Offensive

Seize, retain, and exploit the initiative. Offensive action is the most effective and decisive way to attain a clearly defined common objective.

Mass

Mass is the act of bringing overwhelming combat power to bear at the decisive place and time. Synchronizing all the elements of combat power where they will have decisive effect on an enemy force in a short time is to achieve mass.

Economy of Force
Economy of force is the judicious employment and distribution of forces in order to achieve mass elsewhere. Allocate minimum essential combat power to secondary efforts.

Maneuver
Place the enemy in a position of disadvantage through the flexible application of combat power. Maneuver is the movement of forces in relation to the enemy to secure or retain positional advantage.

Unity of Command
For every objective, seek unity of effort under one responsible commander. At all levels of war, employment of forces in a manner that masses combat power toward a common objective requires unity of command and unity of effort.

Security
Never permit the enemy to acquire unexpected advantage. Security results from the measures taken by a commander to protect his forces.

Surprise
Strike the enemy at a time or place or in a manner for which he is unprepared. The element of surprise can allow forces to achieve success well out of proportion to the effort expended.

Simplicity
Prepare clear, uncomplicated plans and concise orders to ensure thorough understanding. Other factors being equal, the simplest plan is preferable.

The Tenets of Army Operations
The fundamental tenets of Army operations describe characteristics of successful operations, which build on the principles of war. The U.S. Army asserts that the five basic tenets are the keys to victory. In and of themselves, they do not guarantee victory, but their absence makes victory difficult and costly to achieve.

Initiative
Initiative means setting or changing the terms of battle by action. Infantry forces attempt to maintain their freedom of action while limiting the enemy's. This requires an offensive spirit in all operations. Decentralized

operations in which small units aggressively fight through enemy resistance with the immediately available resources support the seizure or retention of the initiative. Individuals act independently within the framework of their commander's concept. Leaders and soldiers must understand the intent of commanders two echelons above. Commanders use mission-type orders and clear, concise instructions to ensure that subordinates understand the concept and how they fit within it.

Agility

Infantry forces seize or retain the initiative by acting and/or reacting faster than the enemy. This begins with the commander, who must have the mental agility to rapidly analyze tactical situations, thinking through many possible courses of action and the enemy's likely reaction to them, and determining the most effective and least costly course. Standing operating procedures (SOPs) and drills enable the unit to rapidly execute assigned missions without long, detailed orders.

Depth

Depth is the extension of operations in time, space, and resources. A commander seeks to fight the enemy throughout the depth of the enemy's formations by properly positioning his forces or by skillfully maneuvering his unit. This allows the unit to seek out and concentrate against enemy weaknesses. By swiftly concentrating against first one, then another enemy weakness, a skilled commander can begin to seize the initiative on a local level, allowing a higher commander to then exploit the opportunity.

Synchronization

Synchronization is the arrangement of battlefield activities in time, space, and purpose to produce maximum combat power at the decisive point. A commander synchronizes his subordinates' actions on the battlefield by assigning clear missions, making understood the timing required in the operation, and focusing all actions toward achieving overwhelming combat power at a decisive point. Issuing orders, identifying the main effort, and assigning each subordinate element clear tasks and purposes are the best means of maintaining synchronization in a fast-paced, fluid environment.

Versatility

Versatility is the ability of tactical units to adapt to different missions and tasks. In a force-projection army, the demands for versatility increase. Forces must be prepared to move rapidly from one region to another, one type of warfare to another, and one form of combat to another. This was admirably displayed in the war with Iraq, when U.S. forces switched from a conventional combat mode to a counterinsurgency mode in a matter of days.

The Operational Framework

The operational framework consists of the arrangement of friendly forces and resources in time, space, and purpose with respect to each other and the enemy or situation. It consists of the *area of operations, battlespace*, and the *battlefield organization*. The framework establishes an area of geographic and operational responsibility, and provides a way for commanders to visualize how to employ forces against the enemy. Commanders design an operational framework to accomplish their mission by identifying and arranging its three components. They use the operational framework to focus combat power.

BATTLE COMMAND

Battle command is the leadership element of combat power. It is principally an art that employs skills developed by professional study, constant practice, and considered judgment. Commanders, assisted by the staff, visualize and describe the operation in terms of intent and guidance, and direct the actions of subordinates within their intent. Commanders direct operations in terms of the battlefield operating systems (BOS). They directly influence operations by personal presence, supported by their command and control (C^2) system.

Full-spectrum operations generally follow a cycle of *planning, preparation, execution*, and *continuous assessment*. Battle command, however, is what drives the operations process. Army forces design and conduct operations to win on the offensive; dictate the terms of combat and avoid fighting the enemy on his terms; seize and retain the initiative; and build momentum quickly to win decisively. For more information on full-spectrum operations and battle command, one should review Army Field Manual (FM) 3-0 *Operations*.

BASIC RULES OF COMBAT

These rules appeared in Army doctrine for a short time but are no longer included in recent publications. At the small-unit level, however, they encompass the essence of the above fundamentals.

Secure

- Use cover and concealment.
- Establish local security and conduct reconnaissance.
- Protect the unit.

Move
- Establish a moving element.
- Get in the best position to shoot.
- Gain and maintain the initiative.
- Move fast, strike hard, and finish rapidly.

Shoot
- Establish a base of fire.
- Maintain mutual support.
- Kill or suppress the enemy.

Communicate
- Keep everybody informed.
- Tell soldiers what is expected.

Sustain
- Keep the fight going.
- Take care of soldiers.

2

Command and Control

Command and control (C^2) refers to the process of directing, coordinating, and controlling a unit to accomplish a mission. C^2 implements the commander's will in pursuit of the unit's mission. The two components of C^2 are the commander and the C^2 system. The command and control system includes all collective tasks associated with supporting the exercise of authority and direction by a properly designated commander over assigned and available forces in the accomplishment of the mission. Leadership is what gets these tasks done effectively.

LEADERSHIP

Military leadership is the process of influencing people—by providing purpose, direction, and motivation—to accomplish the mission and improve the organization. Leaders must motivate their soldiers and give direction to their efforts. They must know their soldiers, their profession, and the tools of war. Only this kind of leader can direct soldiers to perform difficult tasks under dangerous and stressful conditions.

Today's Army has a leadership framework that recognizes leaders of character and competence who act to achieve excellence. The model begins with what the leader must BE and spells out the values and attributes that shape the leader's character. It may be helpful to think of these as internal qualities; they define who you are and give you a solid footing. Skills are those things you KNOW how to do, your competence in everything from technical know-how to people skills. But character and knowledge—though absolutely necessary—are not enough. You cannot be an effective leader until you apply what you know, until you act and DO what you must. Be, know, do is a clear, concise statement of the Army's leadership doctrine. Under these headings are all the knowledge and guidance you need.

9

Infantry Leaders
The infantry leader is closest to the fight and must be a resourceful, tenacious, and decisive warrior as well as a tactician. Leaders in other branches must also on occasion act as infantry leaders. The leader must understand and use initiative in accomplishing a mission; he cannot rely on a book to solve tactical problems. He is expected to lead by example, be at the point of decision to maintain control, understand the situation, and issue orders when required. This means that he must know how to quickly analyze a situation and make decisions in light of the commander's intent. He must be prepared to take independent action if necessary. The art of making quick, sound decisions lies in the knowledge of tactics, the military estimate process, and platoon and squad (small-unit) techniques and procedures. Infantry leaders are physically tough, technically knowledgeable, mentally agile, and have a firm grasp of how to motivate soldiers to fight in the face of adversity.

MISSION-ORIENTED COMMAND AND CONTROL
The mission-oriented C^2 (or mission control) both encourages and helps subordinates to act within the intent and concept of both the battalion and company commanders. Mission-oriented C^2 requires that subordinate elements clearly understand the purpose and intent of their commanders two levels up. This allows them the freedom to respond, with disciplined initiative, to the changing situation without further guidance. With mission-oriented C^2, the combat leader must:

Expect Uncertainty. Understand that the impact of combat and dynamic battle conditions may challenge the leader's ability to know what is happening, even in his immediate area of operations (AO).

Reduce Leader Intervention. Adopt the principle that trained subordinates with a clear understanding of the mission will accomplish the task when subordinates must act without leader guidance or intervention.

Optimize Planning Time for Subordinates. Ensure that the timelines you develop for mission planning and preparation allow adequate troop leading time for the subordinate leaders.

Allow Maximum Freedom of Action for Subordinates. Given the expected battlefield conditions, avoid unnecessary limits on soldiers' freedom of action. Soldiers win battles; place them where they can seize the opportunity to do so.

Encourage Cross Talk. In some instances, because of their position on the battlefield, two or more subordinates working together may have on-site information that enhances the leader's understanding of the situation, thus providing a clearer view of what is happening. Encourage this.

Lead Well Forward. The leader positions himself where he can best employ his unit and make critical decisions to influence the outcome of the fight. This is normally a position with the main effort.

Battlefield Environment. The framework of the battlefield can vary, ranging from one extreme of front and rear (linear) to a dispersed, decentralized (noncontiguous) structure with few secure areas and unit boundaries. To visualize the battlefield accurately, the leader must know the friendly situation at least one level higher. The leader must also know the enemy situation and continuously analyze and reform his strategy based on how he sees the operational picture.

Troop-Leading Procedures

TLPs begin when the unit leader receives the first indication of an upcoming mission and continue throughout the operations process (plan, prepare, execute, and assess). TLPs comprise a sequence of actions that help leaders use available time effectively and efficiently to issue and execute tactical operations. TLPs are not a hard and fast set of rules, but a guide that must be applied consistently within the situation as influenced by the experience of the leader and his subordinate leaders. The tasks involved in some actions (such as initiate movement, issue the warning order, and conduct reconnaissance) may recur several times during the process. The last action, supervising and refining the plan, occurs continuously throughout TLP.

Step 1. Receive the Mission

The leader may receive the mission in a warning order (WARNO), an operation order (OPORD), or a fragmentary order (FRAGO). He immediately begins to analyze it using the factors of METT-TC:

- What is the MISSION?
- What is known about the ENEMY?
- How will TERRAIN and WEATHER affect the operation?
- What TROOPS are available?
- How much TIME is available?
- Are there CIVILIAN considerations?

The leader should use no more than one-third of the available time for planning and for issuing his OPORD. The remaining two-thirds is for subordinates to plan and prepare for the operation. Leaders should also consider other factors such as available daylight and travel time to and from orders and rehearsals. In scheduling preparation activities, the leader should work

Troop-Leading Procedures

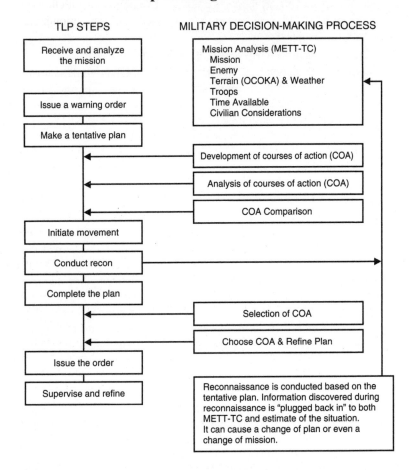

backward from the line of departure (LD) or defend time. This is reverse planning. He must allow enough time for the completion of each task. The leader should not become involved in a detailed METT-TC analysis. This will occur after he issues the initial WARNO.

Step 2. Issue a Warning Order (WARNO)

The leader provides initial instructions in a warning order. The warning order contains enough information to begin preparation as soon as possible. Unit SOPs should prescribe who will receive all warning orders and the actions they must take upon receipt, such as drawing ammunition, rations, and water and checking communications equipment. The warning order has no specific format. One technique is to use the five-paragraph OPORD format. The leader issues the warning order with all the information he has available at the time and provides updates as often as necessary. If available, the following information may be included in a warning order:

- The mission or nature of the operation
- Who is participating in the operation
- Time of the operation
- Time and place for issuance of the OPORD

Most importantly, by issuing a WARNO as quickly as possible, the leader enables his subordinates to begin their own planning and preparation while he begins to develop the unit operation order. This is called parallel planning.

Step 3. Make a Tentative Plan

After receiving the company order (WARNO, OPORD, or FRAGO), the leader develops a tentative plan. The process of developing this plan in a time-constrained environment usually has four steps: mission analysis, course of action development, course of action analysis, and course of action selection. Typically, a platoon leader will develop one course of action (COA). If more time is available, he may develop more than one COA; however, these will be limited in nature. If he develops more than one COA, he will then need to compare these COAs and select the one that best accomplishes his assigned purpose. Selection of a course of action represents the tentative plan. The leader updates the estimate continually and refines his plan accordingly. He uses this plan as the start point for coordination, reconnaissance, task organization (if required), and movement instructions. He works through this problem-solving sequence in as much detail as time allows. As the basis of his estimate, the leader considers the factors of METT-TC:

(M) Mission. The leader considers the mission given to him by his commander and analyzes it in light of the *commander's intent* two command levels higher. He derives the specified task, essential tasks, implied tasks, and limitations and/or constraints of the mission.

(E) Enemy. The leader considers the type, size, organization, tactics, and equipment of the enemy he expects to encounter. He identifies the greatest threat to his mission and the enemy's greatest vulnerability.

(T) Terrain and Weather. The leader considers the effect of terrain and weather on enemy and friendly forces using the guidelines below (OCOKA):

- *(O) Observation and fields of fire.* The leader considers ground that allows him observation of the enemy throughout his area of operation. He considers fields of fire in terms of the characteristics of the weapons available to him; for example, maximum effective range, the requirement for grazing fire, and the arming range and time of flight for antiarmor weapons.

- *(C) Cover and concealment.* The leader looks for terrain that will protect him from direct and indirect fires (cover) and from aerial and ground observation (concealment).
- *(O) Obstacles.* In the attack, the leader considers the effect of restrictive terrain on his ability to maneuver. In the defense, he considers how he will tie in his obstacles to the terrain to disrupt, turn, fix, or block an enemy force and protect his own forces from enemy assault.
- *(K) Key terrain.* Key terrain is any locality or area whose seizure or retention affords a marked advantage to either combatant. The leader considers key terrain in his selection of objectives, support positions, and routes in the offense and in the positioning of his unit in the defense.
- *(A) Avenues of approach.* An avenue of approach is an air or ground route of an attacking force leading to its objective or key terrain in its path. In the offense, the leader identifies the avenue of approach that affords him the greatest protection and places him at the enemy's most vulnerable spot. In the defense, the leader positions his key weapons along the avenue of approach most likely to be used by the enemy.

In considering the effects of weather, the leader is most interested in visibility and trafficability.

(T) Troops Available. The leader considers the strength of subordinate units, the characteristics of his weapon systems, and the capabilities of attached elements as he assigns tasks to subordinate units.

(T) Time Available. The leader refines his allocation of time based on the tentative plan and any changes in the situation.

(C) Civilian Considerations. The leader identifies any civilian considerations that may affect the mission. These factors may include refugees, humanitarian assistance requirements, or specific considerations related to the applicable rules of engagement (ROE) or rules of interaction (ROI).

Step 4. Initiate Movement
The platoon may need to begin movement while the leader is still planning or forward reconnoitering. The platoon sergeant or a squad leader may bring the platoon forward usually under the control of the company executive officer or first sergeant. This step could occur at any time during the TLP.

Step 5. Reconnoiter

If time allows, the leader makes a personal reconnaissance to verify his terrain analysis, adjust his plan, confirm the usability of routes, and time any critical movements. When time does not allow, the leader makes a map reconnaissance. The leader must consider the risk inherent in conducting reconnaissance forward of friendly lines. Sometimes the leader must rely on others (for example, scouts) to conduct the reconnaissance if the risk of contact with the enemy is high.

Step 6. Complete the Plan

Completion of the plan includes several actions that transform the commander's intent and concept and the platoon concept into a fully developed platoon OPORD. These actions include preparing overlays, refining the indirect fire list, completing combat service support (CSS) and C^2 requirements, as well as updating the tentative plan as a result of the reconnaissance or information updates. Completing the plan allows the platoon leader to make final coordination with other units or the commander before issuing the OPORD to his subordinates and it enables him to prepare his briefing site and materials for the briefing.

Step 7. Issue the Complete Order

Platoon and squad leaders normally issue oral OPORDs. To aid subordinates in understanding the concept of the mission, leaders should issue the order within sight of the objective or on the defensive terrain. The OPORD must not contain unnecessary information that could obscure what is essential and important. Whenever possible, the leader issues the order in person, to ensure each leader and soldier understands the mission and what his element must achieve. When this is not possible, they should use a terrain model or sketch. Leaders must ensure that subordinates understand the mission, the commander's intent, the concept of the operation, and their assigned tasks. Leaders may require subordinates to repeat all or part of the order or demonstrate on the model or sketch their understanding of the operation. They should also quiz their soldiers to ensure that all soldiers understand the mission. The section on precombat inspections (PCIs) provides a list of questions that leaders can ask to determine whether soldiers understand the mission.

Step 8. Supervise and Refine

Leaders surpervise the preparation for combat by conducting confirmation briefs to ensure subordinates know the mission, the commander's intent, the concept of the operation, and their assigned tasks. Confirmation briefs can be conducted face-to-face or by radio.

Rehearsals

Rehearsals are an important part of plan refinement. During the rehearsals, leaders practice sending tactical reports in accordance with the unit's SOP. Reporting before, during, and after contact with the enemy is rehearsed in detail starting with actions on the objective. Rehearsals are not intended to analyze a COA. Rehearsals should accomplish the following:

- Practice essential tasks (improve performance)
- Reveal weaknesses or problems in the plan
- Coordinate the actions of subordinate elements
- Improve soldier understanding of the concept of the operation (foster confidence in soldiers)

Rehearsals include having squad leaders brief their planned actions in execution sequence to the platoon leader. The leader should conduct rehearsals on terrain that resembles the actual ground and in similar light conditions. The platoon may begin rehearsals of battle drills and other SOP items before the receipt of the OPORD. Once the order has been issued, the platoon can rehearse mission-specific tasks. Some important tasks to rehearse include:

- Action on the objective
- Assaulting a trench, bunker, or building
- Actions at the assault position
- Breaching obstacles (mine or wire)
- Using specific weapons or demolitions
- Actions on unexpected enemy contact

Precombat Inspection

Squad leaders should conduct initial inspections shortly after receipt of the warning order. The platoon sergeant spot-checks the unit's preparation for combat. The platoon leader and platoon sergeant make a final inspection of the following:

- Weapons and ammunition
- Uniforms and equipment
- Mission-essential equipment
- Soldiers' understanding of the mission and their specific responsibilities
- Communications
- Rations and water
- Camouflage
- Deficiencies noted during earlier inspections

COMBAT ORDERS
Operation Order

An OPORD is a directive issued by the leader to his subordinate leaders to effect the coordinated execution of a specific operation. The leader briefs his OPORD orally from notes that follow the five-paragraph format below.

Task Organization.

Explain how the unit is organized for the operation. If there is no change from the previous task organization, indicate "no change."

Paragraph 1. Situation.

Provide information essential to the subordinate leader's understanding of the current situation. Subparagraphs include:

    a. *Enemy Forces.* Refer to overlay or sketch. Include pertinent intelligence provided by higher HQ and other facts and assumptions about the enemy. This analysis is stated as conclusions and addresses enemy disposition, composition, strength, capabilities, and most probable course of action.

    b. *Friendly Forces.* Provide information that subordinates need to accomplish their tasks, such as verbatim statements of the missions of the higher unit, left unit, right unit, forward unit, the unit in reserve or following, and units in support or reinforcing the higher unit. Be sure also to include any units attached or detached from the platoon, together with the effective times.

Paragraph 2: Mission.

Provide a clear, concise statement of the task to be accomplished and the purpose for doing it (who, what, when, where, and why). The leader derives the mission from the mission analysis. The platoon leader uses the mission statement to summarize the upcoming operation. This brief paragraph (sometimes a single sentence) describes the type of operation, the unit's tactical task and purpose, the actions to be taken, and the reasons for these actions. It is written based on the five "Ws," and the leader must ensure that the mission is thoroughly understood by all leaders and soldiers two echelons down. When developing the mission statement, leaders consider the following:

    (1) *Operations.* Operations are groupings of related activities in four broad categories: offense, defense, stability, and support.

    (2) *Tasks.* Tactical tasks are specific activities performed by the unit while it is conducting a tactical operation or a form of maneuver. (The title of each task can also be used as an action verb in the unit's mission state-

Operation Order Format

TASK ORGANIZATION
(Explain how the unit is organized for the operation.)

1. SITUATION:
    a. Enemy Forces
    b. Civilians/Noncombatants
    c. NGOs/PVOs, and Neutral Nation Observers, as applicable
    d. Friendly Forces
    e. Attachments/Detachments

2. MISSION:
Written in the directive form, using the third person voice.
    (Example: "2-274th Infantry attacks commencing 05 0625 JAN
    in zone seize Objective WOLF (LV 815200).)

3. EXECUTION:
Commander's intent *(Succinct definition of what must be done with respect to the enemy and the terrain, and the desired end state.)*
    a. Concept of the Operation *(Summarizes what is to be done to*
      achieve success.)
    b. Subunit Missions
    c. Coordinating Instructions

4. SERVICE AND SUPPORT:
    a. Rations and Water
    b. Equipment/Supplies/Fuel
    c. Maintenance Plan
    d. Casualty Procedures
    e. Evacuation of Captured Personnel and Equipment

5. COMMAND AND SIGNAL:
    a. Command
      (1) Chain of command
      (2) Location of key leaders and radiotelephone operators
    b. Signal

ment to describe actions during the operation.) Tasks should be definable, attainable, and measurable. Some tactical tasks are:

- Destroy
- Disrupt
- Suppress
- Fix
- Block
- Seize
- Secure
- Clear
- Isolate
- Breach

- Follow and support
- Follow and assume
- Support by fire
- Attack by fire
- Retain

(3) *Purpose.* A simple, clearly stated purpose tells the subordinates why the platoon is conducting the mission and how the platoon will operate with or provide support for other units.

Paragraph 3: Execution.

The commander's intent is always given at the company level and above. The platoon leader may give a general intention that defines the purpose of the operation and the relationship among the force, the enemy, and the terrain.

a. *Concept of the Operation.* Refer to the operation overlay, concept sketch, and/or terrain model. Explain in general terms how the platoon, as a whole, will accomplish the mission. Identify the most important task for the platoon (mission-essential task) and any other essential tasks. If applicable, designate the decisive point, form a maneuver of defensive techniques, and any other significant factors or principles. Attempt to limit this paragraph to about six sentences.

(1) *Maneuver.* Address all squads and attachments by name, giving each an essential task. Designate the platoon's main effort—that is, who will accomplish the most important task. All other tasks must relate to the main effort. Give mission statements to each subordinate element.

(2) *Fires.* Refer to the fire support overlay and target list. Describe the concept of fire support to synchronize and complement the scheme of maneuver. If applicable, address priority of fires (include changes), priority targets (who controls fires on them), and any restrictive control measures on the use of fires.

(3) *Additional combat support (CS) assets (engineer, air defense artillery [ADA]).* State the concept of employment of any CS attachments or who gets priority in their use, how they will be used, how they will be controlled, and by whom. (Do not include information that belongs in the coordinating instructions subparagraph.)

b. *Tasks to Maneuver Units.* Specify tasks other than those listed in paragraph 3a(1), and the purpose of each for squads and attachments. List each in separate numbered paragraphs. Address the reserve last. State any priority or sequence.

c. *Tasks to CS Elements.* A platoon may receive an attachment of CS units; for example, an engineer squad. List tasks to CS units in subparagraphs in the order they appear in the Task Organization section. List only those specific tasks that must be accomplished by these units not specified elsewhere.

d. *Coordinating Instructions.* List the details of coordination and control applicable to two or more units in the platoon or common to all units. Items that may be addressed include:

- Mission-oriented protective posture (MOPP) level
- Priority of intelligence requirements
- Troop safety and operational exposure guidance
- Engagement and disengagement criteria and instructions
- Fire distribution and control measures
- Consolidation and reorganization procedures other than those established in SOP
- Reporting requirements; for example, crossing phase lines or checkpoints
- Terrorism and counterterrorism instructions
- Mission timeline
- Rules of engagement
- Order of march and other movement instructions

Paragraph 4: Service and Support.

Include combat service support (CSS) instructions and arrangements supporting the operation that are of primary interest to the platoon, such as:

- Company trains, casualty and damaged equipment collection points, and routes to and from them
- Supply—ammunition, rations, POL
- Transportation
- Services
- Maintenance
- Medical evacuation
- Enemy prisoner of war (EPW) collection point and instructions on EPW handling
- Miscellaneous instructions for the destruction of supplies and equipment and any other information not covered elsewhere

Paragraph 5: Command and Signal.

a. *Command.*
- Location of the higher unit commander and command post (CP)
- Location of platoon leader and/or CP

- Location of platoon sergeant and/or alternate CP
- Succession of command (if different from SOP)

b. *Signal.*

- SOI (signal operation instructions) index in effect
- Listening silence, if applicable
- Methods of communication in priority
- Emergency signals and visual signals
- Code words

Annexes.

Annexes provide the instructions for conducting specific operations (such as air assaults, boat and truck movements, stream crossings, establishment of patrol bases, and airborne insertions) if they are so detailed that a platoon SOP is insufficient for a particular situation. The format is the same as the five-paragraph OPORD.

Overlays.

An operation overlay is a tracing of graphic control measures on a map. It shows boundaries, unit positions, routes, objectives, and other control measures. It helps to clarify the OPORD. Platoons normally trace their overlays from the company operations map. Squad leaders transfer control measures onto their maps as needed. The subordinate's need for higher-unit graphics must be balanced against the risk of the enemy obtaining this information.

When possible, the leader uses the actual terrain model to brief his OPORD. He may also use concept sketches—large, rough drawings of the objective areas—to show the flow of events and actions clearly.

Fragmentary Orders

The leader uses a FRAGO to change an existing order. He normally uses the OPORD format but addresses only those elements that have changed. The leader should make his instructions brief, simple, clear, and specific.

OPERATIONS SECURITY

All measures taken to maintain security and achieve tactical surprise constitute operations security (OPSEC). These measures include countersurveillance, physical security, signal security, and information security. OPSEC also involves the elimination or control of tactical indicators that can be exploited by the enemy. To provide the most effective OPSEC, you must see the enemy before it sees you. The following measures can be used to provide OPSEC:

- Use hide and defilade positions habitually.
- Position observation posts to observe enemy avenues of approach.
- Camouflage positions, vehicles, and equipment against both visual and infrared detection. Break up silhouettes, reduce glare, reduce vehicle signatures caused by dust, exhaust smoke, and tracks.
- Reduce infrared and thermal signatures by parking in shadows, turning off engines and heaters, and using terrain masking.
- Maintain noise and light discipline.
- Patrol aggressively to prevent enemy surveillance and to gather information about the enemy.
- Use smoke to screen movement.
- Enforce proper radio operating procedures: authentication, encoding, limiting transmission time, using low power, and tying down antennas.
- Use radio operators trained in antijam, interference, and deception procedures.
- Overwatch friendly barriers and obstacles.
- Maintain contact with adjacent units.

FRATRICIDE PREVENTION

The underlying principle of fratricide prevention is simple: Leaders who know where their soldiers are, and where they want them to fire, can keep those soldiers alive to kill the enemy. At the same time, leaders must avoid becoming tentative out of fear of fratricide; rather, they must strive to eliminate fratricide risk through tough, realistic combined arms training in which each soldier and unit achieves the set standard.

Some Causes

Leaders must identify any factors that may affect their units and then strive to eliminate or correct them. These can include:

- Failure in the direct fire control plan, especially designation of target engagement areas
- Land navigation failures
- Failures in combat identification
- Inadequate maneuver control measures
- Failures in reporting and communications
- Weapons errors
- Battlefield hazards, such as unexploded ordnance and unmarked or unrecorded minefields
- Reliance on instruments (failure to balance technology and basic soldier skills)

Prevention

Key to fratricide reduction and prevention are five key principles to be applied as appropriate:

- Identify and assess potential fratricide risks
- Maintain situational understanding
- Ensure positive target identification
- Maintain effective fire control
- Establish a command climate that emphasizes fratricide prevention

CONTINUOUS OPERATIONS

U.S. forces execute continuous operations to maintain constant pressure on the enemy without regard to visibility, terrain, or weather conditions. The ability to effectively sustain this pressure is often key to success on the battlefield. It is also the most difficult challenge that Army units face, placing enormous stress on soldiers, vehicles, and equipment. Continuous operations demand that units conduct planning, preparation, and execution activities around the clock while maintaining effective OPSEC at all times.

The leader must understand the demands of continuous operations under all possible conditions. During the planning and preparation phases of an operation, the commander dictates priorities of security, work, and rest. These priorities, in conjunction with readiness condition (REDCON) levels, enable the commander to develop his unit's timeline. He then uses TLPs to outline time requirements and disseminate them to the platoon leaders.

Readiness Conditions

Redcon levels allow quick responses to changing situations and ensure the completion of necessary work and rest plans. The commander uses the REDCON status as a standardized way to adjust the unit's readiness to move and fight.

REDCON-1: full alert; units ready to move and fight

- Nuclear, biological, and chemical (NBC) alarms and hot loop equipment stowed; OPs pulled in.
- All personnel alert and mounted on vehicles or are in final assembly areas; weapons manned and rucks packed.
- Unit is ready to move immediately.

REDCON-2: full alert; units ready to fight

- Equipment stowed (except hot loop and NBC alarms).
- All personnel alert and mounted in vehicles; weapons manned. (*Note*: Depending on the tactical situation and orders from the commander, dismounted OPs may remain in place.)

- All (100 percent) digital and FM communications links operational.
- Unit is ready to move within 15 minutes of notification.

REDCON-3: reduced alert
- Fifty percent of the unit executes work and rest plans; remainder of the unit executes security plan.
- Unit is ready to move within 30 minutes of notification.

REDCON-4: minimum alert
- OPs manned; one soldier per platoon designated to monitor radio and man turret or crew-served weapons.
- Digital and FM links with task force and other company teams maintained.
- Unit is ready to move within one hour of notification.

Stand-To

Stand-to encompasses all actions taken to bring the unit to a maximum state of preparedness. Times for stand-to are derived from the higher unit's OPORD. Unit SOP should specify stand-to requirements, which usually includes procedures for sending and receiving reports, use of accountability checks for personnel and equipment, and criteria for assuming REDCON levels 1 and 2. (*Note*: Stand-to procedures for digitized units include the updating of position navigation [POSNAV] systems, the intervehicular information system [IVIS] synchronization, and completion of log-on for SINC-GARS [single-channel ground and airborne] radio system.)

Work Plan

The work plan defines tasks and sets milestones for task completion. It enables subordinate leaders and soldiers to focus their efforts in preparing vehicles, equipment, and themselves for operations.

Rest Plan

The rest plan allows some soldiers to sleep while other crewmen conduct priorities of work and maintain security. To be effective in sustained combat, a soldier should get a minimum of 4 hours of uninterrupted sleep every 24 hours. The commander must ensure that subordinate leaders either have rest plans of their own or are following his rest plan as directed.

The unit SOP must provide for an adequate division of duties to allow leaders to sleep. This may require key leaders to share duties. When soldiers are tired, confirmation briefings become critical whenever orders are issued, even for the simplest task.

PRECOMBAT INSPECTIONS

Inspections allow leaders to check the unit's operational readiness. The key goal is to ensure that soldiers, equipment, weapons, and vehicles are fully prepared to execute the upcoming mission. Inspections also contribute to improved morale.

It is essential that all leaders know how to conduct precombat checks (PCCs) and precombat inspections (PCIs) in accordance with applicable unit SOPs and guidelines from appropriate battle doctrine. Leaders should focus

Soldier Precombat Inspection (PCI) Checklist
(No more than two minutes is spent inspecting each soldier.)

	GO	NO GO
LBE fits properly		
First-aid pouch w/dressing		
Full canteens w/M-1 drinking cap		
Ammo pouches w/3 loaded magazines each or full SAW drums		
Bayonet		
Helmet w/cover, band, chin strap, and rank		
Dog tags around neck soundproofed and ID card		
Weapon cleaned and zeroed		
Proper MOPP level		
Serviceable mask and hood		
Serviceable overgarments		
Serviceable overboots		
Personal decontamination kit available		
Completed witness statement and casualty feeder card on person		
Proper driver's license		
Understands current mission, commander's intent, situation		
Briefed and understands cold/hot weather injuries and safety		
Understands risk reductions methods for mission		
Flashlight w/colored lens (serviceable)		
Pistol secure w/lanyard		
Night vision serviceable and zeroed		
PAC-4s secure and serviceable/zeroed		
Weapon cleaning kit		
Appropriate inclement weather gear		
Combat lifesaver bag		

on the readiness of mission-essential equipment and ammunition and on the mission understanding of all subordinate leaders and individual soldiers.

Procedures for a comprehensive program of checks and inspections include the following:

- Perform before-operation maintenance checks; report or repair deficiencies.
- Perform prepare-to-fire checks for all weapons. Weapons should be bore sighted, and machine guns and individual weapons should be test fired, if possible.
- Perform communications checks of voice and digital systems.
- Ensure that soldiers in each subordinate element understand the plan, have posted current graphics, and are in the correct uniform and MOPP level.
- Upload vehicles in accordance with unit SOP. Quickly check accountability of equipment.
- Review the supply status of rations, water, fuel, oil, all types of ammunition, pyrotechnics, first-aid kits, combat lifesaver bags, MOPP suits, and batteries; and direct resupply operations as necessary.
- Ensure that vehicles are correctly camouflaged so they match the area of operations.

Each leader should observe his element throughout the process of preparation for combat. The platoon leader or commander should conduct the final inspection of each element once the leader reports that soldiers, vehicles, and equipment are prepared.

For years, leaders have used PCI checklists like the one shown above.

ASSEMBLY AREA PROCEDURES

An assembly area is a location where the unit prepares for future operations. Here the unit receives and issues orders; supplies and services; repairs vehicles and equipment; and feeds and rests soldiers. When an assembly area is used to prepare for an attack, it is usually well forward.

Before occupying an assembly area, the platoon leader designates a quartering party, which reconnoiters the assembly area to ensure that no enemy are present and to establish initial security. Each squad provides two men for the quartering party, with the platoon sergeant or selected NCO in charge. The quartering party determines initial positions for all elements, continues to secure the area, occupies covered and concealed positions, and as the main body approaches, moves out and guides elements from the release point to their initial positions. The unit occupies its positions in the assembly area and maintains local security. All elements are assigned a sector of the perimeter to ensure mutual support and to cover all gaps by observation and fire. OPs are designated and manned. A priority of work is established to complete the assembly area:

- Position crew-served weapons and chemical-agent alarms and designate principal directions of fire (PDF), final protective line (FPL), and final protective fires (FPF)
- Construct individual and crew-served fighting positions
- Set up wire communications between the elements (radio silence is observed)
- Prepare range cards
- Camouflage positions
- Clear fields of fire
- Distribute ammunition, rations, water, supplies, and special equipment
- Conduct preventive maintenance checks and services on weapons and equipment
- Prepare night sights
- Test fire small-arms weapons (if the tactical situation permits)
- Conduct personal hygiene and field sanitation
- Institute a rest plan

The platoon leader conducts adjacent unit coordination and assigns security patrols, if applicable. The platoon leader establishes responsibility for overlapping enemy avenues of approach between adjacent squads and platoons, and the leaders ensure that there are no gaps between elements. The platoon leader exchanges information on OP locations and signals and forwards a copy of the sector sketch to the company.

COMMUNICATIONS

Communications are necessary to control subordinate elements, to receive and disseminate information, and to coordinate CS and CSS. The commander is responsible for the discipline of the communications system within his unit and for its operation in the system of the next higher headquarters. Responsibilities for the establishment of communications are as follows:

- Senior unit to subordinate unit
- Supporting unit to supported unit
- Reinforcing unit to reinforced unit
- Left to right and rear to front

Both units take prompt action when communications cannot be established or when they are disrupted.

Five Basic Means of Communication

The commander has five basic means to communicate:

Radio

The company commander operates on the company net and monitors the battalion net; the XO operates on the battalion net and monitors the company net; the first sergeant operates on the battalion admin/log net and monitors the company net; platoon leaders operate on platoon nets and monitor the company net. Use of the radio is avoided until enemy contact is made. In some situations, special radios or satellite phones may be necessary for units to communicate long distances.

Wire

Wire hot loops are established within and between platoons and the company when the unit is stationary. OPs should be included within a hot loop.

Messenger

To reduce electronic signals, messengers are used whenever possible prior to battle. Normally, battalions send messengers to the company, and platoons send messengers to the company commander.

Visual Signals

Visual signals normally include hand and arm signals, flag signals, pyrotechnics, flashlights, and chemical lights. Visual signals should be planned together with, or as a backup to, voice communications. They are normally used either when other communications are lost or to overcome jamming.

Audible Signals

Audible signals are normally used to transmit prearranged messages, to attract attention, and to spread warning alarms. They should be simple to understand, and prearranged meanings should be covered in SOPs.

3

Movement

Infantry's key strength is its ability to cross almost any terrain during all weather conditions. When infantry can move undetected, it gains an advantage over the enemy. Movement fundamentals, formations, and techniques assist the leader in providing security during movement.

FUNDAMENTALS
- Ensure that movement supports a rapid transition to maneuver.
- Conduct reconnaissance of the terrain and the enemy to the extent possible.
- Move on covered and concealed routes and, if the situation permits, during limited visibility.
- Select routes that avoid natural lines of drift, likely ambush sites, and other danger areas.
- Establish security during movement and halts. Avoid moving directly forward from covered positions. All weapons should be prepared to engage targets. Enforce camouflage, noise, and light discipline.
- Designate air guards.
- Make enemy contact with the smallest element possible.

FORMATIONS
Formations are arrangements of elements and soldiers in relation to one another. Squads use formations for control flexibility and security. Leaders choose formations based on their analysis of the factors of METT-TC. Leaders are up front in formations. This allows the fire team leader to lead by example. All soldiers in the team must be able to see their leader.

PLATOON AND SQUAD FORMATION ABBREVIATIONS

PLT LDR	Platoon leader
PSG	Platoon sergeant
SL	Squad leader
TL	Team leader
RATELO	Radio-telephone operator
FO	Forward observer
R and RFLM	Rifleman
AR	Automatic rifleman/SAW gunner
GRN	Grenadier
MG	Machine gun
AIDMAN	Aidman/medic

Fire Team Formations

Wedge

The wedge is the basic formation for the fire team. The interval between soldiers in the wedge formation is normally 10 meters. The wedge expands and contracts, depending on the terrain. When rough terrain, poor visibility, or other factors make control of the wedge difficult, the normal interval is reduced so that all team members can still see their team leader and the team leaders can still see their squad leader. The sides of the wedge can contract to resemble a single file. When moving in less rugged terrain, where control is easier, soldiers expand the wedge or resume their original positions.

File

When the terrain precludes use of the wedge, fire teams use the file formation.

**Fire Team
Wedge**

**Fire Team
File**

MOVEMENT FORMATION	WHEN NORMALLY USED	CHARACTERISTICS			
		CONTROL	FLEXIBILITY	FIRE CAPABILITIES/ RESTRICTIONS	SECURITY
FIRE TEAM WEDGE	BASIC FIRE TEAM FORMATION	EASY	GOOD	ALLOWS IMMEDIATE FIRES IN ALL DIRECTIONS	ALL-ROUND
FIRE TEAM FILE	CLOSE TERRAIN, DENSE VEGETATION, LIMITED VISIBILITY CONDITIONS	EASIEST	LESS FLEXIBLE THAN WEDGE	ALLOWS IMMEDIATE FIRES TO THE FLANKS, MASKS MOST FIRES TO THE REAR	LEAST

Comparison of Fire Team Formations

Squad Formations
Squad formations describe the relationships between fire teams in the squad.

Squad Column
The squad column is the most common formation. It provides good lateral and deep dispersion without sacrificing control, and it facilitates maneuver. The lead fire team is the base fire team. When the squad moves independently or as the rear element of the platoon, the rifleman in the trail fire team provides rear security. Squads can move in normal or modified columns as terrain dictates.

Squad Column Wedge, Fire Teams in Wedge

Squad Line

The squad line provides maximum firepower to the front. When a squad is acting as the base squad, the fire team on the right is the base fire team.

Squad Line

Squad File

When not traveling in a column or line, squads travel in file. The squad file has the same characteristics as the fire team file. If the squad leader wants to increase his control over the formation, enhance morale by leading from the front, and be immediately available to make key decisions, he moves forward to the first or second position. Additional control over the rear of the formation can be provided by moving a team leader to the last position.

● TL

○ SL (optional)

● AR

● GRN

● R

● SL (normal)

● TL

● AR

● GRN

○ TL (optional)

● R

Squad File

MOVEMENT FORMATION	WHEN NORMALLY USED	CHARACTERISTICS			
		CONTROL	FLEXIBILITY	FIRE CAPABILITIES/ RESTRICTIONS	SECURITY
SQUAD COLUMN	SQUAD PRIMARY FORMATION	GOOD	FACILITATES MANEUVER, GOOD DISPERSION LATERALLY AND IN DEPTH	ALLOWS LARGE VOLUME OF FIRE TO THE FLANK— LIMITED VOLUME TO THE RIGHT	ALL-ROUND
SQUAD LINE	WHEN MAXIMUM FIREPOWER IS REQUIRED TO THE FRONT	NOT AS GOOD AS SQUAD COLUMN	LIMITED MANEUVER CAPABILITY (BOTH FIRE TEAMS COMMITTED)	ALLOWS MAXIMUM IMMEDIATE FIRE TO THE FRONT	GOOD TO THE FRONT, LITTLE TO THE FLANKS AND REAR
SQUAD FILE	CLOSE TERRAIN VEGETATION, LIMITED VISIBILITY CONDITIONS	EASIEST	MOST DIFFICULT FORMATION FROM WHICH TO MANEUVER	ALLOWS IMMEDIATE FIRE TO THE FLANK, MASKS MOST FIRE TO THE FRONT AND REAR	LEAST

Comparison of Squad Formations

Platoon Formations

Platoon Column

The platoon column is the primary movement formation. It provides good lateral and deep dispersion and simplifies control. The lead squad is the base squad. (*Note*: METT-TC will determine where crew-served weapons move in the formation. They normally move with the platoon leader so he can quickly establish a base of fire.)

Platoon Column

Platoon Line, Squads on Line

This formation allows the delivery of maximum fire to the front but little fire to the flanks. It is hard to control and does not lend itself well to rapid movement. When two or more platoons are attacking, the company commander chooses one as the base platoon. The base platoon's center squad is its base squad. When the platoon is not acting as the base platoon, its base squad is its flank squad nearest the base platoon. The machine guns can move with the platoon, or they can assume a support position. This is the basic platoon assault formation.

NOTE: The platoon leader (PLT LDR), forward observer (FO), radio-telephone operator (RATELO), platoon sergeant (PSG), and the squad leaders (SL) position themselves where they can best control the squad.

Platoon Line, Squads on Line

Platoon Line, Squads in Column

The platoon leader uses this formation when he does not want to deploy all personnel on line and when he wants the squads to react to unexpected contact. This formation is easier to control and it lends itself better to rapid

Platoon Line, Squads in Column

movement than the platoon line or squads on line formation; however, it is harder to control than a platoon column and does not facilitate rapid movement as well. When two or more platoons are moving, the company commander chooses one as the base platoon. The base platoon's center squad is its base squad. When the platoon is not the base platoon, its base squad is its flank squad nearest the base platoon.

Platoon Vee

This formation has two squads up front to provide a heavy volume of fire on contact. It also has one squad in the rear that can either overwatch or trail the other squads. This formation is hard to control, and movement is slow. The platoon leader designates one of the front squads as the platoon's base squad.

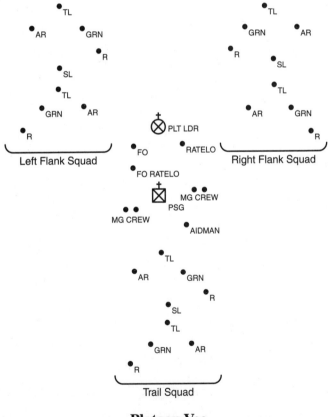

Platoon Vee

Platoon Wedge

This formation has two squads in the rear that can overwatch or trail the lead squad. It provides a large volume of fire to the front or flanks. It allows the platoon leader to make contact with a squad and still have one or two squads to maneuver. The lead squad is the base squad.

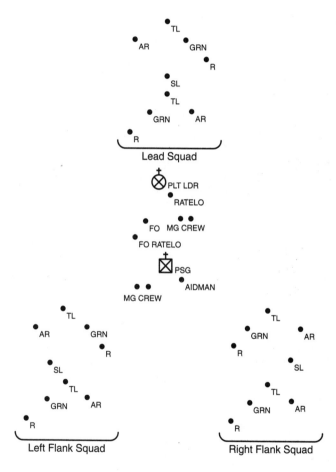

Platoon Wedge

Platoon File

This formation can be set up in several ways. One method is to have three-squad files follow one another using one of the movement techniques. Another method is to have a single platoon file with a front security element (point) and flank security elements. This formation is used when visibility is poor due to terrain, vegetation, or light conditions. The distance between soldiers is less than normal to allow communication by passing messages up and down the file. The platoon file has the same characteristics as the fire team and squad files.

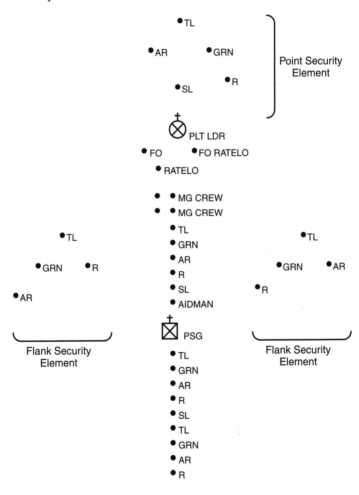

Platoon File

MOVEMENT TECHNIQUES

A movement technique is the manner used to traverse terrain. There are three movement techniques: *traveling*, *traveling overwatch*, and *bounding overwatch*. The selection of a movement technique is based on the likelihood of enemy contact and the need for speed. Factors to consider for each technique are control, dispersion, speed, and security. Movement techniques are not fixed formations. They refer to the distances between soldiers, teams, and squads, which vary based on mission, enemy, terrain, visibility, and other factors that affect control. Soldiers must be able to see their fire team leader. The squad leader must be able to see his fire team leaders. The platoon leader should be able to see his lead squad leader. Leaders control movement with arm and hand signals. They use radios only when needed. Any of the three movement techniques can be used with any formation.

MOVEMENT TECHNIQUES	WHEN NORMALLY USED	CHARACTERISTICS			
		CONTROL	DISPERSION	SPEED	SECURITY
TRAVELING	CONTACT NOT LIKELY	MORE	LESS	FASTEST	LEAST
TRAVELING OVERWATCH	CONTACT POSSIBLE	LESS	MORE	SLOWER	MORE
BOUNDING OVERWATCH	CONTACT EXPECTED	MOST	MOST	SLOWEST	MOST

Movement Techniques

Techniques of Squad Movement
The squad or platoon leader determines and directs which movement technique the squad will use.

Traveling
Traveling is used when contact with the enemy is not likely and speed is needed.

Squad Traveling

Traveling Overwatch
Traveling overwatch is used when contact is possible. Attached weapons move near the squad leader and are under his control so that he can employ them quickly.

Squad Traveling Overwatch

Bounding Overwatch

Bounding overwatch is used when contact is expected, when the squad leader believes that the enemy is near (based on movement, noise, reflection, trash, fresh tracks, or even a hunch), or when a large, open danger area must be crossed.

The lead fire team overwatches first. Soldiers scan for enemy positions. The squad leader usually stays with the overwatch team.

The trail fire team bounds and signals the squad leader when his team completes its bound and is prepared to overwatch the movement of the other team. Both team leaders must know whether successive or alternate bounds will be used and with which team the squad leader will be. The overwatching team leader must know the route and destination of the bounding team. The bounding team leader must know his team's destination and route, possible enemy locations, and actions to take when he arrives. He must also know where the overwatching team will be and how he will receive his instructions. The cover and concealment on the bounding team's route dictate how its soldiers move. Teams can bound successively or alternately. Successive bounds are easier to control; alternate bounds can be faster.

Alternate Bounds. Covered by the rear element, the lead element moves forward, halts, and assumes overwatch positions. The rear element advances past the lead element and takes up overwatch positions. The sequence continues as necessary, with only one element moving at a time.

Successive Bounds. The lead element, covered by the rear element, advances and takes up overwatch positions. The rear element advances to an overwatch position roughly abreast of the lead element and halts. This sequence continues as necessary. The rear element never advances forward of the lead element.

Techniques of Platoon Movement
The platoon leader determines and directs which movement technique the platoon will use.

Traveling
Traveling is used when enemy contact is not likely and speed is needed.

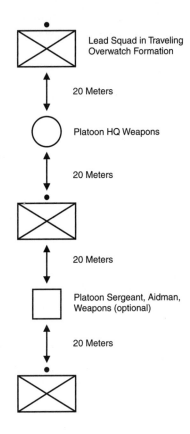

Lead Squad in Traveling Overwatch Formation

20 Meters

Platoon HQ Weapons

20 Meters

20 Meters

Platoon Sergeant, Aidman, Weapons (optional)

20 Meters

Platoon Traveling

Traveling Overwatch

Traveling overwatch is used when contact is possible but speed is needed. The platoon leader moves where he can best control the platoon. The platoon sergeant travels with the trailing squad, although he is free to move throughout the formation to enforce security, noise and light discipline, and distances between squads. The lead squad uses traveling overwatch, and the trailing squads use traveling.

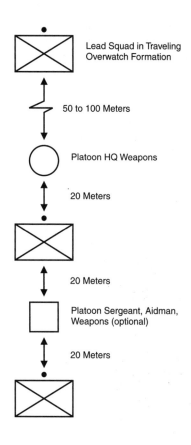

Platoon Traveling Overwatch

Bounding Overwatch

Bounding overwatch is used when contact is expected. Platoons conduct bounding overwatch using successive or alternate bounds. One squad bounds forward to a chosen position; then it becomes the overwatching element unless contact is made enroute. The bounding squad can use traveling overwatch, bounding overwatch, or individual movement techniques (low and high crawl, and short rushes by fire teams or pairs). One squad overwatches the bounding squad from covered positions where it can see and suppress likely enemy positions and view their assigned sector. The platoon leader remains with the overwatching squad. Normally, the platoon's machine guns are located with the overwatching squad. One squad is uncommitted and ready for employment as directed by the platoon leader. The platoon sergeant and the leader of the squad awaiting orders position themselves close to the platoon leader.

Platoon Bounding Overwatch

Considerations. When deciding where to have his bounding squad go, a platoon leader considers:
- The requirements of the mission
- Where the enemy is likely to be
- The routes to the next overwatch position
- The ability of an overwatching element's weapons to cover the bound
- The responsiveness of the rest of the platoon
- The fields of fire at the next overwatch position

Instructions. Before a bound, the platoon leader gives an order to his squad leaders from the overwatch position. He tells and shows them the following:

- The direction or location of the enemy (if known)
- The positions of the overwatching squad
- The next overwatch position
- The route of the bounding squad
- What to do after the bounding squad reaches the next position
- What signal the bounding squad will use to announce that it is prepared to overwatch
- How the squad will receive its next orders

DANGER AREAS

A danger area is any place on the movement route where the unit might be exposed to enemy observation, fire, or both. Units try to avoid danger areas. If a danger area must be crossed, it should be done with great caution and as quickly as possible. Do the following before crossing a danger area:

- Designate near- and far-side rally points.
- Secure the near side (both flanks and rear).
- Reconnoiter and secure the far side.

Lead team crosses danger area and clears for the platoon

Grenadier and rifleman remain on far side
Team leader and automatic rifleman return to signal platoon when all clear

Lead team continues to lead platoon after clearing danger area

Plt ldr moves up, waits for TL's all clear PSG assigns flank cover

Trail team moves up for flank cover

Trail team returns to position and crosses

Crossing a Danger Area

The unit halts when the lead elements signal "danger area." The leader confirms the danger area, then selects and informs subordinate leaders of near- and far-side rally points. Near-side security is posted to overwatch the crossing. The far-side security team crosses the danger area and clears the far side. Once the far side is cleared, the main body moves quickly and quietly across the danger area. A small unit may cross all at once, in pairs, or one soldier at a time. A large unit normally crosses its elements one at a time. As each element crosses, it moves to an overwatch position or to the far-side rally point. The near-side security element then crosses and resumes its place in the formation as the unit continues its mission.

Crossing Techniques

Open Areas
When crossing an open area, stay concealed and observe carefully from the near side. Post security to give early warning, and send an element across to clear the far side. When cleared, quickly cross the rest of the unit at the shortest exposed distance.

To cross large open areas, a combination of traveling overwatch and bounding overwatch is used. Bounding overwatch is used at any point in the open area where enemy contact may be expected or when the element comes within small-arms range (250 meters) of the far side.

Crossing a Large Open Area

Small open areas may be bypassed, by either using the detour bypass method or contouring around the open area. In the detour bypass method, the force moves around the open area using 90-degree turns to the right or left until the far side is reached. To contour around the open area, the unit uses the wood line and vegetation for cover and concealment as it moves around the open area until reaching the far-side rally point.

Crossing a Small Open Area

Roads and Trails
Cross a road or trail at or near a bend, at a narrow spot, or on low ground to reduce enemy observation and minimize the unit's exposure.

Villages
Pass on the downwind side and well away from a village. Avoid animals, especially dogs, which might reveal your presence.

Enemy Positions
Pass enemy positions on the downwind side (the enemy might have scout dogs). Be alert for trip wires or other warning devices.

Minefields

Bypass a minefield even if it means changing your route by a great distance. If you *must* pass through a minefield, the lead elements clear a lane for the rest of the unit. Soldiers use their hands to detect trip wires and use sharpened sticks to probe for mines.

Streams

When crossing a stream, select a narrow spot that offers concealment on both banks. Observe the far side carefully, and place security out for early warning. Clear the far side, then cross quickly but quietly.

Wire Obstacles

Avoid crossing wire obstacles if possible; they are normally under observation. If wire must be breached during daytime, use the method that exposes the unit for the shortest amount of time. Check the wire for mines, booby traps, and warning devices. To breach wire at night, either cross over or go under the wire using the following procedures:

To cross over the wire, grasp the first strand lightly, and cautiously lift one leg over. Lower your foot slowly to the ground, feeling carefully for sure footing, then lift the other foot over the wire. Quietly release this wire and feel for the next strand. Cross it in the same way.

To go under the wire, move headfirst. Lie on your back and slide under the bottom strands, pushing forward with your heels. Carry your weapon lengthwise on your body, steadying it with either hand. To prevent the wire from catching on clothing or equipment, let it slide along the weapon. Inch along, holding the wire up with one hand. Do not jerk or pull on the wire. Feel ahead with your free hand for low strands or trip wires.

If the wire must be cut, cut only the lower strands to minimize discovery of the gap. Soldiers should work in a team if possible. Wire should be wrapped with a cloth near a picket, cut partway through, and then bent back and forth until it breaks. The loose end is carefully rolled back to clear the lane. Concertina is hard to control after cutting and can snap back. If concertina must be cut, stake down two loops far enough apart so that a soldier can crawl between them. Then cut partway through and break as previously described.

Enemy Contact at Danger Areas

If the unit makes contact in or around a danger area, the leader determines whether to assault the enemy or break contact, depending on the situation and mission. If the unit becomes disorganized, the near-side and far-side rally points are used to link up and reorganize. Ideally, using movement fundamentals, the unit will see the enemy first, remain undetected, and ambush it.

(1) Recon element makes contact.
(2) Flank security fires on enemy.
(3) Main body takes overwatch position and fires on enemy.
(4) Security and recon return to main body.
(5) Smoke and indirect fire used to break contact.
(6) The platoon moves to different place to cross danger area; or
(7) Reorganizes and assaults enemy.

Crossing Danger Area—Enemy Contact on Far Side

Flank security warns the platoon, everyone freezes
and lets the enemy pass.
OR
(1) If spotted, security team blocks enemy with weapons
    fire and LAWs.
(2) The leader decides whether to cross road or stay on near side.
(3) Security team not in contact moves back to main body.
(4) The platoon crosses road, moves into overwatch position,
    and fires on enemy.
(5) Security team in contact breaks contact, crosses road where
    platoon crossed, and joins main body.
(6) Smoke or indirect fire is used to break contact and
    the platoon moves out of area; or
(7) Reorganizes and assaults enemy.

Crossing Danger Area—Enemy Contact on Road or Trail

(1) Flank security teams fire in the direction of the enemy.
(2) The platoon moves quickly across danger area.

(3) The platoon sets up overwatch position.
(4) Security teams cross danger area and rejoin platoon.
(5) Smoke or artillery used.
(6) The platoon moves out of area; or
(7) Platoon reorganizes and assaults enemy.

Crossing Danger Area—Enemy Contact on Near Side

SECURITY DURING MOVEMENT

Security during movement includes whatever the platoon or squads do to secure the unit or the larger force; such as:

Terrain

When planning movements, consider how terrain affects security.

Formations and Movement Techniques

When choosing a movement formation or technique, consider the most recent situation update and the level of C^2 needed for the mission. Choose the option that will provide the greatest security and is most likely to result in mission accomplishment. During individual platoon movement, place the smallest element forward. This gives the rest of the platoon freedom to maneuver.

Positioning of the Machine Gun Teams or Weapons Squad

The platoon leader positions his M240B machine guns and Javelins where they can best provide security to the platoon. METT-TC will determine the placement of the weapons. He may task-organize some of his weapons to the rifle squads or keep them together under the weapons squad leader (if he has a weapons squad) and close to his command post. Keeping the weapons squad close to the platoon leader allows him to quickly deploy the guns into an overwatch position or to provide a base of fire against a threat.

Light Discipline

If soldiers need more illumination than an image intensifier can provide in infrared mode during movement, they should use additional infrared light sources to provide the light needed with the least risk of enemy detection. When using infrared light, leaders must consider the enemy's night vision and infrared capabilities. For instance, an enemy with night vision capability can send infrared light signals, and he can concentrate direct and indirect fire on a platoon that is using infrared light.

SOLDIER'S LOAD

The soldier's load greatly affects movement and is of crucial concern to leaders. Research has shown that a soldier can carry up to 30 percent of his body weight and still retain a high percentage of his agility, stamina, alertness, and mobility. For the average soldier weighing 160 pounds, that would be a 48-pound load. The soldier loses a proportional amount of his functional ability for each pound over 30 percent.

Load Management

Use the following techniques for load management:
- Distribute loads evenly over body and load-bearing equipment (LBE), load-bearing vest (LBV), or Modular Lightweight Load-Carrying Equipment (MOLLE).
- Don't carry anything on the front of the body that would prevent the soldier from taking well-aimed shots.
- Distribute loads throughout the unit. If it is necessary to man-pack bulk ammunition, water, rations, or demolitions, divide them into small loads.
- Rotate heavy loads (radios, machine guns, mortars, and antitank weapons) among several soldiers.
- Always consider transportation assets to carry loads.
- Upon enemy contact, drop rucksacks or leave them in an objective rally point (ORP), an assault position, or the assembly area.
- Share or consolidate items. Carry only enough sleeping bags for those who will sleep at the same time. In the same manner, two or three soldiers can share a rucksack and take turns carrying it.
- Consider carrying fewer rations for short operations.
- While carrying rucksacks, use water and rations carried in it first. Then rucksacks can be dropped and soldiers will still have a full supply on their LBE, LBV, or MOLLE.

A recent combat load study was conducted on dismounted infantry serving in combat in Afghanistan and Iraq called "Soldier Loads in Combat." A cover letter summarized conditions as such: "Despite the best efforts made by military leaders, today's dismounted infantry soldier continues to carry excessive loads even during the conduct of short duration missions. This harsh reality is not due to these soldiers carrying unnecessary equipment, but due to the facts that the essential items that they must carry simply weigh too much and that we have few to no means today for offloading the dismounted soldier while keeping his gear near at hand." Leaders should always attempt to keep the combat load of the soldier as light as possible without sacrificing soldier protection and mission essential equipment. Until we can find better ways to lighten soldier loads and get him into battle, the following doctrine still applies:

Combat Load
The minimum mission-essential equipment, as determined by the commander responsible for carrying out the mission, required for soldiers to fight and survive immediate combat operations. The combat load is the essential load carried by soldiers in forward subunits or the load that accompanies soldiers other than fighting loads.

Fighting Load
The fighting load includes bayonet, weapon, clothing, helmet, and LBE, and a reduced amount of ammunition. Keep under 48 pounds when cross-loading small unit equipment.

Approach March Load
The approach march load includes clothing, weapon, basic load of ammunition, LBE, small assault pack, or lightly loaded rucksack or poncho roll. A limit of 72 pounds should be enforced.

Emergency Approach March Loads
Circumstances, such as approach marches through terrain impassable to vehicles or where ground/air transportation resources are not available, could require soldiers to carry loads heavier than 72 pounds. Therefore, larger rucksacks must be carried. These emergency approach march loads can be carried easily by well-conditioned soldiers. When the mission demands that soldiers be employed as porters, loads of up to 120 pounds can be carried for several days over distances of 20 km a day. Although loads of up to 150 pounds are feasible, the soldier could become fatigued or even injured. If possible, contact with the enemy should be avoided since march speeds will be slow.

FOOT MARCH

Foot marches are the movement of troops and equipment mainly by foot, with limited support by vehicles. They are characterized by combat readiness, ease of control, adaptability to terrain, slow rate of movement, and increased personnel fatigue. Foot marches do not depend on the existence of roads.

A dismounted company moves in a column of twos, a file on each side of the road. Distances: day, 2 to 5 meters between men, 50 meters between platoons; night, 1 to 3 meters between men, 25 meters between platoons. Rates: day, 4 kmph; night, 3.2 kmph. Cross country the rates are: day, 2.4 kmph; night, 1.6 kmph. Halts: 15 minutes after the first 45 minutes, 10 minutes out of every hour thereafter.

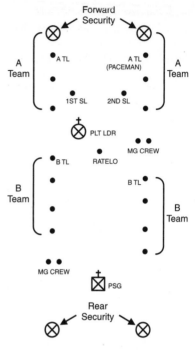

NOTE: 3rd squad can be on either side of the road.

Road March Formation

Road Space, Foot Column

The road space (RS) of a company foot column, used in determining time length of the column, consists of two parts: the space occupied by the men alone (including the distance between them), and the sum of distances between elements of the foot column. (Total RS = RS men + RS platoon distances.)

The RS of the men alone is determined by multiplying the number of men by the appropriate factor selected from the table below:

Formation	2 meters per man	5 meters per man
Single file	2.4	5.4
Column of twos	1.2	2.7

The total RS between platoons is obtained by multiplying the number of platoons (minus one) by the platoon distances.

Time Length (TL), Foot Column

Rate	Formula
4.0 kmph	TL (min.) = RS (meters) × .0150
3.2 kmph	TL (min.) = RS (meters) × .0187
2.4 kmph	TL (min.) = RS (meters) × .0250
1.6 kmph	TL (min.) = RS (meters) × .0375

Completion Time

The completion time of a foot march is determined by using this formula:
Completion time = SP (start point) time + TL + scheduled halts.

4

Offense

The four types of offensive operations are movement to contact (MTC), attack, exploitation, and pursuit. Companies can execute MTCs and attacks. Platoons generally conduct these forms of the offense as part of a company. Companies and platoons participate in an exploitation or pursuit as part of a larger force. The nature of these operations depends largely on the amount of time and enemy information available during the planning and preparation for the operational phases. This chapter will focus on the first two types of offense: attacks and movements to contact.

The MTC is a type of offensive operation designed to develop the situation and establish or regain contact. The platoon will likely conduct an MTC as part of a company when the enemy situation is vague or not specific enough to conduct an attack.

An attack is an offensive operation that destroys enemy forces or seizes or secures terrain. Movement supported by fires characterizes an attack. The platoon will likely participate in a synchronized company attack. However, the platoon may conduct a special purpose attack as part of or separate from a company offensive or defensive operation. Special purpose attacks consist of ambush, spoiling attack, counterattack, raid, feint, and demonstration.

FORMS OF MANEUVER

In typical offensive operations, the platoon maneuvers against the enemy in an area of operation (AO). Maneuver places the enemy at a disadvantage through the application of friendly fires and movement. The five forms of maneuver are envelopment, turning movement, infiltration, penetration, and frontal attack.

SEQUENCE OF OFFENSIVE OPERATION

As the platoon leader plans for an offensive mission, he generally considers the actions the unit must accomplish in the following phases of an offensive operation:

Assembly Area

To prepare the platoon for the upcoming battle, the platoon leader plans, directs, and supervises mission preparations in the assembly area (AA). This time allows the platoon to conduct precombat checks and inspections, rehearsals, and combat service support (CSS) activities. The platoon will typically conduct these preparations within a company AA.

Reconnaissance

Leaders should aggressively seek information about the terrain and the enemy. The enemy situation and available planning time may limit a unit's reconnaissance. In this circumstance, the platoon will likely conduct reconnaissance to answer the company commander's priority of intelligence requirement (PIR). An example may be to reconnoiter and time routes from the AA to the line of departure (LD).

Movement to the Line of Departure

The platoon will typically move from the AA to the LD as part of the company movement plan. This movement plan may direct the platoon to move to an attack position to await orders to cross the LD. If so, the platoon leader must reconnoiter, time, and rehearse the route to the attack position and reconnoiter the actual position. Section and squad leaders must know where they are to locate within the assigned attack position, which is the last position an attacking force occupies or passes through before crossing the LD.

Maneuver

The company commander will plan the approach of all platoons to the objective to ensure synchronization, security, speed, and flexibility. He will select the routes, movement techniques, formations, and methods of movement to best support his intended actions on the objective. The platoon leader must recognize this portion of the battle as a *fight*, not as a movement. He must be prepared to make contact with the enemy and plan accordingly to obtain the objective.

Deployment

The platoon deploys and moves toward the assault position with minimum delay and confusion and begins the final positioning of the squads as directed by the company commander. An assault position is the last covered and concealed position short of the objective from which final preparations are made to assault the objective. Movement should be as rapid as the terrain, unit mobility, and enemy situation permit. The probable line of deployment (PLD) may be located within the assault position. The PLD is a phase line where the company is completely deployed in assault formation before beginning the assault.

Assault
During an offensive operation, the platoon's objective may be terrain-oriented or force-oriented. Terrain-oriented objectives require the platoon to seize or retain a designated area and often require fighting through enemy forces. If the objective is force-oriented, the platoon's efforts are focused on the enemy's actual location. Actions on the objective begin when the company or platoon begins placing direct and indirect fires on the objective.

Consolidation and Reorganization
The platoon consolidates and reorganizes as required by the situation and mission. Consolidation is the process of organizing and strengthening a newly captured position so that it can be defended. Reorganization is the actions taken to shift internal resources within a degraded unit to increase its level of combat effectiveness.

BATTLEFIELD OPERATING SYSTEMS PLANNING CONSIDERATIONS
The BOS (Battlefield Operating Systems) are a listing of seven critical tactical activities that provides a means of reviewing preparation and execution. Synchronization and coordination among the BOS are critical for success.

1. **Maneuver**. The purpose of maneuver is to close with and destroy the defending enemy. Maneuver requires a base-of-fire element to suppress and or destroy enemy forces with accurate direct fires and bounding elements to gain positional advantage over the enemy.
2. **Fire Support**. The platoon may be able to employ indirect fires from field artillery or company and or battalion mortars to isolate part of the enemy defense or to suppress the enemy on the objective.
3. **Mobility, Countermobility, and Survivability**. The platoon will likely focus on mobility during offensive operations and may be required to breach obstacles as part of an offensive operation. These obstacles may be protective (employed to assist units in their close-in protection), which the platoon are expected to breach without additional assets. Tactical obstacles, however, which disrupt, turn, or fix unit formations, require engineer assets to breach.
4. **Air Defense**. The platoon leader should address how to react to enemy air attacks if no air defense assets are available or operating within his AO. Unit SOPs should stipulate internal air security measures and active air defense measures.

5. **Combat Service Support**. The primary purpose of CSS in the offense is to assist the platoon and company in maintaining momentum during the attack. Key CSS planning considerations for the platoon leader during the offense include a high expenditure of ammunition, an increase in casualties, and how to evacuate the casualties.

6. **Intelligence**. The generation of knowledge about the enemy. The platoon leader should be given as much information on the enemy as can be gotten in the time available.

7. **Command and Control**. Command and control refers to the process of directing, coordinating, and controlling a unit to accomplish a mission.

ATTACKS

Platoons and squads conduct an attack as part of the infantry rifle company. An attack requires detailed planning, synchronization, and rehearsals to be successful. The company commander designates and explains platoon objectives with tasks and milestones for his assault, support, and breach elements. To ensure synchronization, all leaders must know the location of their subordinates and adjacent units during the attack. Attacks are characterized as *hasty* or *deliberate*. The primary difference between the two is the extent of planning and preparation conducted by the attacking force. Attacks may take the forms of attacks against a stationary enemy force, attacks against a moving enemy force, or terrain-oriented attacks.

Organization for an Attack

In a company attack, the commander usually structures his force into assault, support, and breach elements. Platoon attacks may be similarly structured.

The assault element closes with and captures or destroys the enemy.

The support element provides a base of fire that supports the assault element and breach element when one is used.

The breach element's usual task is to breach the enemy's line or position or fortification, so as to facilitate the success of the assault element.

DELIBERATE ATTACK

Platoons and squads conduct deliberate attacks as part of a larger force. The commander may designate separate platoon objectives for his assault, support, and breach elements, resulting in decentralized execution at all levels. The four phases of the deliberate attack are reconnaissance, movement to the objective, isolate the objective, seize a foothold, and exploit.

Reconnaissance

Before a deliberate attack, the platoon and company should gain enemy and friendly information from the battalion reconnaissance platoon; however, this may not always occur. The platoon and company should be prepared to conduct a reconnaissance of the objective to confirm, modify, or deny their tentative plan. If possible, the company should determine the enemy's size, location, disposition, most vulnerable point, and most probable course of action (COA). The tentative plan may change as a result of the reconnaissance if the platoon or squad discovers that terrain or enemy dispositions are different than determined earlier in the troop-leading procedure, requiring a modification of the attack plan.

Movement to the Objective

The attacking force advances to within assault distance of the enemy position under supporting fires using a combination of traveling, traveling overwatch, and/or bounding overwatch. Platoons advance to successive positions using available cover and concealment. The company commander may designate support-by-fire (SBF) positions to protect friendly forces with suppressive direct fires. As the company maneuvers in zone, it employs fires to suppress, neutralize, and obscure the enemy positions.

Assembly Area to the Line of Departure

The LD is normally a phase line (or checkpoint) where elements of the attacking force transition to secure movement techniques in preparation for contact with the enemy. Platoons may maneuver from the LD to designated SBF positions, assault positions, or breach or bypass sites. Before leaving the AA, the platoon leader should receive an update of the location of forward and adjacent friendly elements. He should also receive updated enemy locations. The platoon moves forward from the AA to the LD, usually as part of a company formation, along a planned route. The platoon leader should have reconnoitered the route to the LD and specifically to the crossing point. The move from the AA is timed during the reconnaissance so the lead section crosses the LD at the time of attack without halting in the attack position. If the platoon must halt in the attack position, the squads establish security and take care of last minute coordination.

Line of Departure to Assault Position

The platoon's assault element moves from the LD to the assault position. The platoon leader plots waypoints to coincide with checkpoints along the route. During movement, he ensures the platoon navigates from checkpoint to checkpoint or phase line by using basic land navigation skills supplemented by precision navigation.

Assault Position to the Objective

The assault position is the last covered and concealed position before reaching the objective. Ideally, the platoon's assault element occupies the assault position without the enemy detecting any of the platoon's elements. Preparations in the assault position may include preparing bangalores, other breaching equipment, or demolitions; fixing bayonets; lifting or shifting fires; or preparing smoke pots. The platoon may halt in the assault position if necessary to ensure synchronization of friendly forces. Once the assault element moves forward of the assault position, *the assault must continue.*

Supporting fire from the heavy weapons must continue to suppress the enemy and must be closely controlled to prevent fratricide.

When the assault element moves to the breach point, the base-of-fire leader verifies the assault element is at the right location. The base-of-fire leader is responsible for tracking the assault element as it assaults the objective. The company commander shifts or lifts indirect fire when it endangers the advancing soldiers and coordinates this with the platoons' assaults. As the fire of the platoons' support is masked, the platoon leader shifts or lifts it or displaces the weapons squad to a position where continuous fire can be maintained.

Isolate the Objective

The goals of isolation are to prevent the enemy from reinforcing the objective and to prevent enemy forces on the objective from leaving. Infantry platoons will likely be an isolating force within a company.

Actions on the Objective:
Seize a Foothold and Exploit the Penetration

The platoon leader often designates assault, support, and breach elements within his platoon to conduct a deliberate attack. One technique is to designate the machine gun teams (or weapons squad) as the support element, an infantry squad as the breach element, and the remaining platoon as the assault element. The supporting elements support the breach element's initial breach with suppressive fires and as the breach is being established, the support element should shift fires to allow the breach element to penetrate the objective without committing fratricide. The support element positions itself to provide continual close-in suppressive fire to aid the actions of the assault squad or squads as they move across the objective. Once the breach element has seized the initial foothold on the objective, the assault element may then move through the breach lane to assault the objective. All communication from the support element to the breach, assault, and weapons squads is by FM radio or signals. Problems and status are continuously communicated or observed and changes are made as necessary.

Consolidation and Reorganization
Once enemy resistance on the objective has ceased, the platoon must quickly take steps to consolidate and prepare to defend against a counterattack. Consolidation techniques include:

- *Clock technique.* In this method, the platoon leader designates either a compass direction or the direction of attack as 12 o'clock. He then uses clock positions to identify the left and right boundaries for squads. The platoon leader positions key weapons along the most likely avenue of approach based on his assessment of the terrain.

Clock Technique of Consolidation

- *Terrain feature technique.* In a similar manner, the platoon leader identifies obvious terrain features as the left and right limits for squads.

In both techniques, the platoon leader ensures that squad sectors of fire overlap each other and provide mutual support for adjacent units.

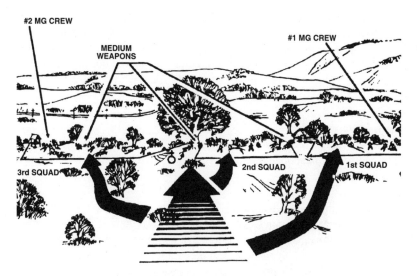

Terrain Technique of Consolidation

Once platoons have consolidated on the objective, they begin to reorganize to continue the attack. Reorganization involves:
- Reestablishing command and control
- Remanning key weapons and redistributing ammunition and equipment
- Clearing the objective of casualties and EPWs
- Assessing and reporting the platoon status of personnel, ammunition, supplies, and essential equipment

HASTY ATTACK
Platoons and squads normally participate in a hasty attack as part of a larger unit, during MTC, as part of a defense, or whenever the commander determines that the enemy is in a vulnerable position and can be quickly defeated by immediate offensive action. Hasty attacks are used to exploit a tactical opportunity, maintain the momentum, regain the initiative, prevent the enemy from regaining organization or balance, and gain a favorable position that may be lost with time. Because its primary purpose is to maintain momentum or take advantage of the enemy situation, the hasty attack is normally conducted with only the resources that are immediately available. Key to hasty attacks is to maintain unrelenting pressure on the enemy and to

attack before the enemy can act. Synchronization in the hasty attack can be degraded a bit, so commanders should minimize risk by maximizing the use of standard formations; well-rehearsed, thoroughly understood battle drills; and SOPs. The hasty attack is often the preferred option during continuous operations and it often results from an MTC, successful defense, or continuation of a previous attack.

Task Organization
The hasty attack is conducted using the principles of fire and movement. The controlling headquarters normally designates a base-of-fire force and a maneuver force.

Conduct of the Hasty Attack
The platoon must first conduct actions on contact, allowing the commander to gather the information he needs to make an informed decision. The term hasty refers to limits on planning and preparation time, not to any acceleration in the conduct of actions on contact. Because the intelligence picture is vague, the commander normally needs more time, rather than less, during this process to gain adequate information about the enemy force.

Execution begins with establishment of a base of fire, which then suppresses the enemy force. The maneuver force uses a combination of tactical techniques and combat multipliers (such as indirect fire) to maintain its security as it advances in contact to a position of advantage.

Once the maneuver force has gained the positional advantage, it can execute a tactical task such as assault to destroy the remaining enemy.

MOVEMENT TO CONTACT
Platoons and squads participate in an MTC as part of a company using movement formations and techniques explained in chapter 3. A company generally conducts an MTC when it must gain or maintain contact with the enemy or when it lacks sufficient time to gain intelligence or make extensive plans to defeat the enemy.

Planning an MTC
Firsthand enemy information provides the intelligence necessary to respond to the enemy, so reconnaissance is a critical aspect to planning. However, if the enemy situation remains vague, the platoon must be prepared to act in any situation. This is accomplished through proper planning, appropriate movement formations and techniques, fire control measures, platoon SOPs, engagement criteria, and studying the terrain before and during movement

to anticipate likely enemy locations. While moving, all leaders study the terrain and anticipate enemy contact. Based on these terrain studies, leaders should avoid likely areas of enemy ambush or exposing their platoon to long-range observation and fires.

Techniques

Infantry units will participate in two techniques for conducting an MTC—approach march or search and attack (discussed below). The approach march technique is used when the enemy is expected to deploy using relatively fixed offensive or defensive formations but the situation remains vague. The search and attack technique is used when the enemy is dispersed, when he is expected to avoid contact or quickly disengage and withdraw, or when the higher unit needs to deny him movement in an AO.

Command and Control

The company commander will dictate a number of C^2 techniques for the unit to employ and the platoon leader may modify these to better control his squads based on the commander's intent and guidance and METT-TC. Some examples of C^2 follow:

Line of Departure, Phase Lines, and Checkpoints

The company commander will normally assign LDs, phase lines, and checkpoints to control the forward movement of the platoons. The platoon does not stop at a phase line unless told to do so. If necessary, the platoon leader designates additional phase lines or checkpoints for use within the platoon to reduce the number and length of radio transmissions used to control movement.

Fire Control and Distribution

The platoon uses boundaries, direct fire plans, pyrotechnics, signals, and FRAGOs (fragmentary orders) for direct fire control and distribution. This takes on importance because of the scarcity of information about the enemy.

Indirect Fire Plan

The platoon leader must have a good indirect fire plan for his route to cover anticipated places of contact.

Developing the Situation

Once the platoon makes contact with the enemy, it maintains contact until the commander orders otherwise. The platoon leader develops the situation based on the effectiveness of enemy fire, friendly casualties, size of enemy force, and freedom to maneuver. He gathers and reports critical information about the enemy and recommends a COA (course of action). The platoon can bypass the enemy with permission from the commander, conduct an attack, fix the enemy so another platoon can conduct the assault, conduct a defense, establish an ambush, or break contact.

Defensive Considerations

In some situations, a platoon conducting an MTC makes contact with a much larger and more powerful enemy force. If the platoon encounters a larger enemy force where the terrain gives the platoon an advantage, it should attempt to fix the enemy force. This allows the rest of the company to maneuver against the force. If the platoon cannot fix the enemy, it may have to assume a defensive posture or break contact, but it should do so only if it is in danger of being overwhelmed.

Approach March Technique

The approach march technique may be used when the enemy is expected to deploy using relatively fixed offensive or defensive formations. The concept behind the approach march is to make contact with the smallest element, allowing the commander the flexibility of maneuvering or bypassing the enemy force. As part of a larger unit using the approach march technique, platoons may act as the advance, flank, or rear guard. They may also receive on-order missions as part of the main body.

Advance Guard

As the advance guard, the platoon finds the enemy and locates gaps, flanks, and weaknesses in its defense. The advance guard attempts to make contact on ground of its own choosing, to gain the advantage of surprise, and to develop the situation (either fight through or support the assault of all or part of the main body).

The advance guard operates within the range of the main body's indirect fire support weapons. One rifle squad leads the advance guard. The platoon uses appropriate formations and movement techniques, and the leader rotates the lead squad as necessary to keep soldiers fresh.

Flank or Rear Guard

The entire platoon may act as the flank or rear guard for a battalion conducting a movement to contact using this technique. The platoon moves using the appropriate formation and movement technique; provides early warning; destroys enemy reconnaissance units; and prevents direct fires or observation of the main body.

Main Body

When moving as part of the main body, platoons may be tasked to assault, bypass, or fix an enemy force or to seize, secure, or clear an assigned area. The platoon may also be detailed to provide squads as flank guards, stay-behind ambushes, rear security, or additional security to the front. These squads may come under the direct control of the company commander. Platoons and squads use appropriate formations and movement techniques, assault techniques, and ambush techniques.

Search and Attack Technique

Search and attack is used when the enemy is dispersed or is expected to avoid contact or quickly disengage and withdraw, or to deny the enemy movement in an area. The search and attack technique involves the use of multiple squads and fire teams in coordinated actions to make contact with the enemy. Platoons attempt to find the enemy and then fix and finish it. They combine patrolling techniques with the requirement to conduct hasty or deliberate attacks once the enemy has been found.

LIMITED VISIBILITY ATTACKS

Effective use of night vision devices (NVDs) during limited visibility attacks enhances squad and platoon ability to achieve surprise and cause panic in a lesser-equipped enemy. NVDs allow the soldier to see farther and with greater clarity, and provide a marked advantage over the enemy. Leaders have an increased ability to control fires during limited visibility.

The well-equipped platoon has three types of enhancements for use in fire control: target designators consisting of the GCP-1 and AIM-1; aiming lights consisting of the AIM-1 and AN/PAQ-4B/C; and target illuminators consisting of infrared parachute flares, infrared trip flares, infrared 40-mm rounds, infrared mortar rounds, infrared bike lights, and remote black lights. These assets greatly aid in target acquisition and fire control. The platoon leader and squad leaders follow tactical SOPs to synchronize the employment of infrared illumination devices, target designators, and aiming lights during their assault on the objective.

Leaders use luminous tape or chemical lights to mark assault personnel to prevent fratricide. The enemy must not be able to see the marking. Two techniques are to place tape on the back of the helmet or to use small infrared chemical lights (if the enemy has no night vision devices [NVDs]).

Search and Attack Technique

The supporting elements must know the location of the lead assault element. To reduce the risk to the assault element, the platoon leader may assign weapons control restrictions. For example, the squad on the right in the assault might be assigned weapons free to the right flank because no friendly soldiers are there. The squad on the left may be assigned weapons tight or weapons hold, which means that another friendly unit is located there.

The platoon leader may use the following techniques to increase control during the assault:

- Use no flares, grenades, or smoke on the objective.
- Allow only certain personnel with NVDs to engage targets on the objective.
- Use a magnetic azimuth for maintaining direction.
- Use mortar or artillery rounds to orient attacking units.
- Assign a base squad or fire team to pace and guide others.
- Reduce intervals between soldiers and squads.

Mortar, artillery, and antiarmor fires are planned as in a daylight attack. However, they are not fired unless the platoon is detected or is ready to assault. Some weapons may fire before the attack and maintain a pattern to deceive the enemy or to help cover noise made by the platoon's movement. This is not done if it will disclose the attack.

Indirect fire is hard to adjust when visibility is poor. If the exact location of friendly units is not clearly known, indirect fire is directed first at enemy positions beyond the objective and then moved onto the objective.

Illuminating rounds that are fired to burn on the ground can be used to mark objectives. This helps the platoon orient on the objective but may adversely affect NVDs.

Smoke is planned to further reduce the enemy's visibility, particularly if he has NVDs. The smoke is laid close to or on enemy positions so it does not restrict friendly movement or hinder the breaching of obstacles. Employing smoke on the objective during the assault may make it hard for assaulting soldiers to find enemy fighting positions. If enough thermal sights are available, smoke on the objective may provide a decisive advantage for a well-trained platoon.

Illumination is always planned for limited visibility attacks, giving the leader the option of calling for it. Battalion commanders normally control the use of conventional illumination but may authorize the company commander to do so. If the commander decides to use conventional illumination, he should not call for it until the assault is initiated or the attack is detected. It should be placed on several locations over a wide area to confuse the enemy as to the exact place of the attack. Also, it should be placed beyond the objective to help assaulting soldiers see and fire at withdrawing or counterattacking enemy soldiers.

Note: If the enemy is equipped with NVDs, leaders must evaluate the risk of using each technique and ensure the mission is not compromised because the enemy can detect infrared light sources.

SPECIAL PURPOSE ATTACKS

When the company commander directs it, the platoon conducts a special attack. The commander bases his decision on the METT-TC. Special purpose attacks are subordinate forms of an attack and they include the ambush, raid, counterattack, spoiling attack, feint, and demonstration. As forms of the attack, they share many of the same planning, preparation, and execution considerations of the offense. Feints and demonstrations are also associated with military deception operations. *Note:* To eliminate confusion, this guide will cover the ambush and raid in chapter 7 (Patrolling) until current doctrine agrees on category. They are actually a member of both offensive operations as much as they are a member of patrolling. See chapter 7 for their explanation.

Counterattack

The counterattack is a form of attack by part or all of a defending force against an enemy attacking force, with the general objective of denying the enemy his goal of attacking. This attack by defensive forces regains the initiative or denies the enemy success with his attack. The platoon may conduct a counterattack as a lightly committed force within a company or as the battalion reserve. The platoon counterattacks after the enemy begins his attack, reveals his main effort, or creates an assailable flank. As part of a higher headquarters, the platoon conducts the counterattack much like other attacks. However, the platoon leader must synchronize the execution of his counterattack within the overall defensive effort. Counterattacks afford the defender the opportunity to create favorable conditions for the commitment of combat power. The platoon should rehearse the counterattack battle drill and prepare the ground to be traversed. Counterattacks are more useful to the higher headquarters when the platoon anticipates employment; plans and prepares for employment; and executes with the other defending, delaying, or attacking forces in conjunction with the higher commander's plan.

Spoiling Attack

A spoiling attack is a form of attack that preempts or seriously impairs an enemy attack while the enemy is in the process of planning or preparing to attack. The purpose of a spoiling attack is to disrupt the enemy's offensive capabilities and timelines while destroying his personnel and equipment. The purpose is not to secure terrain or other physical objectives. A commander (company or battalion) may direct a platoon to conduct a spoiling attack during friendly defensive preparations to strike the enemy while he is in assembly areas or attack positions, preparing for his own offensive operation. The platoon leader plans for a spoiling attack as he does for other attacks.

Feint

A feint is a form of attack used to deceive the enemy as to the location and time of the actual operation. Feints attempt to induce the enemy to move reserves and shift his fire support to locations where they cannot immediately impact the actual operation. When directed to conduct a feint, the platoon seeks direct fire or physical contact with the enemy, but avoids decisive engagement. The commander (company or battalion) will assign the platoon an objective limited in size or scope. The planning, preparation, and execution considerations are the same as for the other forms of attack. The enemy must be convinced that the feint is the actual attack.

Demonstration

A demonstration is a form of attack designed to deceive the enemy as to the location or time of the actual operation by a display of force. Demonstrations attempt to deceive the enemy and induce him to move reserves and shift his fire support to locations where they cannot immediately impact the actual operation. When directed to conduct a demonstration, the platoon does not seek physical contact with the enemy. The planning, preparation, and execution considerations are the same as for the other forms of attack. It must appear to be an actual impending attack.

BATTLE DRILLS

Infantry battle drills describe how platoons and squads apply fire and maneuver to commonly encountered situations. The battle drill is not intended to replace the estimate of the situation but to reduce the estimate of the situation and the decision-making process to the essential elements. (Experience at the Army's combat training centers revealed a deficiency in the action and reaction of small units.) The emphasis on drills is intended to instill an immediate, aggressive response.

React to Contact Drill

The react to contact drill takes place when a squad or a platoon is receiving fire from enemy riflemen or an automatic weapon.

React to Contact Drill

Step 1. Soldiers take cover and return fire.

Step 2. Leaders locate known or suspected enemy positions and engage with well-aimed fire. Leaders control fire using the following standard fire commands: alert, direction, description of target, range, method of fire, and command to commence firing.

Step 3. Soldiers maintain contact to left and right, as well as with leaders, and report enemy locations.

Step 4. Leaders check the status of their men.

Step 5. The platoon leader moves to the squad in contact. He brings with him his radiotelephone operator (RATELO), forward observer (FO), the squad leader of the nearest squad, and a machine gun crew. The platoon sergeant moves forward with the second machine gun crew and links up with the platoon leader, ready to assume control of the base-of-fire element.

Step 6. The platoon leader determines whether he must move out of an enemy engagement area. If he is not in an engagement area, he determines whether he can gain and maintain suppressive fire with his element in contact, based on the volume and accuracy of the enemy fire.

Step 7. The platoon leader makes an assessment of the situation, identifying the following:

1. Location of the enemy position and obstacles
2. Size of the enemy force (the number of automatic weapons, the presence of vehicles, and the employment of indirect fires are indicators of enemy strength)
3. Vulnerable flanks
4. Covered and concealed flanking routes to the enemy position

Step 8. The platoon leader then determines his next course of action, such as fire and movement, assault, breach, knock-out bunker, or enter and clear a building or trench.

Step 9. The platoon leader reports the situation to the company commander and begins to maneuver, calling for an adjusting artillery or mortar fire.

Break Contact Drill

The break contact drill takes place when the squad or platoon is under enemy fire and must break contact.

Step 1. The platoon leader directs one squad in contact to support the disengagement of the remainder of the platoon.

Step 2. The platoon leader orders the first squad to move a certain distance and direction or to a terrain feature or the last objective rally point. Meanwhile, the base-of-fire (supporting) squad continues to suppress the enemy.

Step 3. The moving element uses smoke grenades to mask its movement until it takes up its designated position and engages the enemy position.

Step 4. The platoon leader then directs the base-of-fire squad to move to its next location.

Step 5. While continuing to suppress the enemy, the platoon bounds away from the enemy until it either breaks contact or passes through a high-level support-by-fire position.

Step 6. Once contact is broken, the platoon should change direction, if possible, to avoid indirect enemy fire.

Step 7. Leaders account for soldiers, report, reorganize as necessary, and continue the mission.

Break Contact Drills

React to Ambush Drill

In a near ambush (within hand-grenade range), use the following procedures:

Step 1. Immediately return fire.

Step 2. Take up covered positions.

Step 3. Throw fragmentation, concussion, and smoke grenades.

Step 4. Immediately after the grenades detonate, the soldiers in the kill zone assault through the ambush using fire and movement, while soldiers not in the kill zone identify enemy positions, initiate suppressive fire, take up covered positions, and shift fires as soldiers in the kill zone assault through the ambush.

In a far ambush (beyond hand-grenade range), use the following procedures:

React to Ambush Drills

Step 1. Soldiers receiving fire immediately return fire, take up covered positions, and suppress the enemy by destroying or suppressing enemy crew-served weapons first, obscuring the enemy position with smoke, and sustaining suppressive fires.

Step 2. Soldiers not receiving fires move by a covered and concealed route to a vulnerable flank of the enemy position and assault using fire and movement.

Step 3. Soldiers in the kill zone continue suppressive fires and shift fires as the assaulting element fights through the enemy position.

In both near and far ambushes, the platoon leader then calls for mortar or artillery fire to isolate the enemy or to attack as the enemy retreats. Leaders account for soldiers, report, reorganize as necessary, and continue the mission.

Knock-out Bunker Drill

The knock-out bunker drill is used when the platoon identifies enemy in bunkers.

Step 1. The platoon initiates contact.

1. The squad in contact establishes a base of fire.
2. The platoon leader, RATELO, FO, and one machine gun team move to the squad in contact.
3. The platoon sergeant moves the second machine gun team forward and takes charge of the base of fire.

Step 2. The base-of-fire element destroys or suppresses enemy crew-served weapons first and uses smoke to obscure the enemy position. The FO calls for and adjusts indirect fire.

Step 3. The platoon leader determines whether he can maneuver by identifying the following:

1. The enemy bunkers, other supporting positions, and any obstacles
2. The size of the enemy force engaging the platoon
3. A vulnerable flank of at least one bunker
4. A covered and concealed flanking route to the bunker

Step 4. The platoon leader determines which bunker to knock out and directs a squad not in contact to assault it.

Step 5. If necessary, the platoon sergeant repositions elements of the base of fire to isolate the enemy bunker.

Step 6. The assault squad, along with the platoon leader and FO, moves along the covered and concealed route.

1. The squad leader moves with the assaulting fire team.
2. The assaulting fire team approaches the bunker from its blind side.
3. Soldiers constantly watch for other bunkers or enemy positions in support of the known bunker.
4. Upon reaching the last covered and concealed position, the fire team leader and automatic rifleman remain in place and add their fires to suppressing the bunker, while the squad leader positions himself where he can best control his teams.

Knock Out a Bunker—Platoon

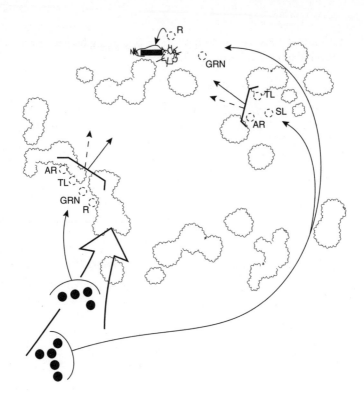

Knock Out a Bunker—Squad

5. On the squad leader's signal, the base-of-fire element lifts or shifts
   fires to the opposite side of the bunker from the assaulting team's
   approach.
6. A rifleman and grenadier continue forward to the blind side of the
   bunker. One soldier takes up a covered position near the exit while
   the other cooks off (two seconds maximum) a grenade, shouts "Frag
   out!" and throws it through an aperture.
7. After the grenade detonates, the soldier covering the exit enters the
   bunker, firing short bursts to destroy the enemy.
8. The squad leader inspects the bunker to ensure that it has been
   destroyed.
9. The squad leader then reports, reorganizes as needed, and continues
   the mission.

Step 7. The platoon leader repositions the base-of-fire element as necessary to continue to isolate and suppress the remaining bunkers as squads are maneuvered to knock them out.

Enter and Clear a Trench Drill

The enter and clear a trench drill is used when the platoon is moving and identifies enemy in a trench line, and the platoon leader determines that he can maneuver and assault the trench line.

Step 1. The platoon leader directs one squad to enter the trench and secure a foothold.

Step 2. The platoon leader designates the entry point of the trench line and the direction of movement once the platoon begins clearing.

Step 3. The platoon sergeant positions soldiers and machine guns to suppress the trench and isolate the entry point.

Step 4. The platoon leader directs the platoon forward observer (FO) to initiate a fire mission, if necessary, in support of the assault. The platoon FO maintains accurate battle tracking of all friendly elements to facilitate quick clearance of fires. He lifts or shifts fires to isolate the objective as the assault team advances.

Step 5. The assaulting squad executes actions to enter the trench and establish a foothold. The squad leader signals to the platoon leader that the foothold is secure, and the follow on elements can move into the trench. The

Clearing a Trench—Platoon

Entering a Trench—Squad

squad leader remains at the entry point and marks it. The platoon follows the success of the seizure of the foothold with the remainder of the platoon as part of the platoon actions to clear a trench line.

Step 6. The platoon leader moves into the trench with the assaulting squad.

Step 7. The platoon leader directs one of the base-of-fire squads to move into the trench and begin clearing it in the direction of movement from the foothold.

Step 8. The base-of-fire element repositions as necessary to continue suppressive fires.

Step 9. The assaulting squad passes the squad that has secured the foothold and executes actions to take the lead and clear the trench.

- The squad leader designates a lead fire team and a trail fire team.
- The lead fire team and the squad leader move to the forward most secure corner or intersection. The squad leader tells the team securing that corner or intersection that his squad is ready to continue clearing the trench. The trail fire team follows, maintaining visual contact with the last soldier of the lead team.
- *Note:* The fire support element must be able to identify the location of the lead fire team in the trench at all times.
- *Note:* Throughout this battle drill, the team leader positions himself at the rear of the fire team to have direct control (physically, if necessary) of his soldiers. Other soldiers in the fire team rotate the lead to change magazines and prepare grenades. Rotating the lead provides constant suppressive fires down the trench and maintains the momentum of the attack as the squad clears the trench.
- The lead fire team passes the element securing the foothold. The following then occurs:
  — The lead soldier of the fire team moves abreast of the soldier securing the corner or intersection, taps him, and announces, "Taking the lead."
  — The soldier securing the corner or intersection acknowledges that he is handing over the lead by shouting, "Okay!" He allows the fire team to pass him.
- The lead fire team starts clearing in the direction of movement. They arrive at a corner or intersection. The following then occurs:
  — Allowing for cook-off (2 seconds maximum) and shouting, "Frag out," the second soldier prepares and throws a grenade around the corner.
  — Upon detonation of the grenade, the lead soldier moves around the corner firing three-round bursts and advancing as he fires. The entire fire team follows him to the next corner or intersection.
- The squad leader:
  — Follows behind the team.
  — Ensures that the trailing fire team moves up and is ready to pass the lead at his direction.
  — Rotates fire teams as necessary to keep his soldiers fresh and to maintain the momentum of the attack.
  — Requests indirect fires, if required, through the platoon leader. The squad leader also directs the employment of the M203 to provide immediate suppression against positions along the trench line.

— Ensures fire teams maintain sufficient interval to prevent them from being engaged by the same enemy fires.

- At each corner or intersection, the lead fire team performs the same actions previously described.
- If the lead soldier finds that he is nearly out of ammunition before reaching a corner or intersection, he announces, "Ammo!" The following then occurs:
  — The lead soldier stops and moves against one side of the trench, ready to let the rest of the team pass. He continues to aim his weapon down the trench in the direction of movement.
  — The next soldier ensures that he has a full magazine, moves abreast of the lead soldier, taps him, and announces, "Taking the lead."
  — The lead soldier acknowledges that he is handing over the lead by shouting, "Okay." Positions rotate and the squad continues forward.
- The trailing fire team secures intersections and marks the route within the trench as the squad moves forward. The trailing fire team leader ensures that follow-on squads relieve his buddy teams to maintain security.
- The squad leader reports the progress of the clearing operation. The base-of-fire element must be able to identify the location of the lead fire team in the trench at all times.

Step 10. The platoon leader rotates squads to keep the soldiers fresh and to maintain the momentum of the assault.

Step 11. The platoon sergeant (PSG) calls forward ammunition resupply and organizes teams to move it forward into the trench.

Step 12. The base-of-fire element ensures that all friendly forces move into the trench only through the designated entry point to avoid fratricide.

Step 13. The platoon leader reports to the company commander that the trench line is secured, or he is no longer able to continue clearing. If trench line is secured, then the platoon leader directs the platoon FO to develop a fire plan to support the defense of the platoon position.

Enter Building and Clear Room Drill

This drill is used in urban combat. See also chapter 8.

Step 1. The fire team initiating contact establishes a base of fire and suppresses the enemy in and around the building.

Step 2. The squad leader determines whether he can maneuver by identifying the building and any obstacles, the size of the enemy force engaging the squad, an entry point, and a covered and concealed route to the entry point.

Step 3. The squad leader directs the fire team in contact to support the entry of the other fire team. He designates the entry point. The platoon and squad shift direct fires and continue to suppress the enemy in adjacent positions and to isolate the building. Indirect fires are lifted or shifted, as necessary.

Step 4. The squad leader and assaulting fire team approach the building and position themselves at either side of the entry point. (Doors and windows should be avoided because they will normally be covered by enemy soldiers inside the building.)

Entering a Building—Squad

Step 5. The lead soldier of the assaulting fire team cooks-off the grenade(s) (two seconds maximum), shouts, "Frag out" if element of surprise is lost, then throws the grenade(s) into the building/room rules of engagement (ROE) dependent.

- Three types of hand grenades can be used when assaulting in an urban objective: *stun, concussion*, and *fragmentation*. METT-TC factors and types of construction materials used in the objective building influence the type of grenades that can be used.
- Soldiers should engage upper-level openings with grenades (by hand or launcher) before entering to eliminate enemy who might be near the entrance.

Step 6. After the grenade detonates, the next soldier enters the building and positions himself to the left or right of the entrance, up against the wall; engages all identified or likely enemy positions with rapid, short bursts of automatic fire; and scans the room. The rest of the team provides immediate security outside the building. The size and shape of the room causes the soldier entering the room to move to the left or right.

1. The first man then decides where the next soldier should position himself. (In the rest of this battle drill, for examples only, one set of directions is given.) The first soldier in the room gives the command, "Next man in, left." *Note:* Depending on the enemy's situation, the size of the entry, and the training of the squad, four soldiers can enter the room simultaneously after the grenade detonates. The soldier from the right side of the entry enters, fires from left to right, and moves to the right with his back to the wall. At the same time, the soldier on the left enters from the left, fires from right to left, and moves to the left with his back to the wall. One soldier goes high, the other low, to prevent firing at one another. This method puts more firepower in the room quickly but is more difficult and requires more practice.

2. The soldier inside the room shouts, "Next man in, left." The next man shouts, "Coming in, left," enters the building/room, positions himself to the left of the entrance up against the wall, and scans the room from the left to right. Once in position, he shouts, "Next man in right."

Step 7. The assaulting fire team leader shouts, "Coming in, right," and positions himself where he can control the actions of his team. He ensures he does not block the entrance, makes a quick assessment of the size and shape of the room and begins to clear the room, and he determines if the remaining man in his team is required to assist in clearing the room.

Note: If the team leader decides to bring the last man in, he shouts, "Next man in, left." The last man in the fire team shouts, "Coming in, left," enters the building, and begins to clear through the room. If the team leader decides not to bring the last man in, he shouts, "Next man, stand fast." The last man remains outside the building and provides security from there. The team leader then directs the soldier on the right of the entrance to begin clearing. The team leader reports to the squad leader and then assumes the duties of the soldier on the right of the entrance to provide support.

Step 8. Once the room is cleared, the team leader of the assaulting fire team signals to the squad leader that the building/room has been entered and the footholds gained. The squad leader enters the building and marks the entry point in accordance with the unit tactical SOP (TSOP). He determines whether or not his squad can continue to clear rooms and maintain superiority outside with the base-of-fire team. (Normally, it takes a platoon to clear a building.) The squad leader then:

- Reports to the platoon leader that the squad has entered the building and seized a foothold.
- Determines which room to clear next, selects an entry point, then designates a lead fire team.
- Moves, along with the lead fire team, to the entrance of the next room to be cleared. They position themselves at either side of the entrance.
- Directs the team to continue and clear the next room. The lead fire team performs the same actions previously described.

Clearing a Room—Squad

Step 9. The squad leader directs the team to continue and clear the next room. The squad leader rotates fire teams as necessary to keep the soldiers fresh and to continue the momentum of the attack. The squad leader follows the fire team that is clearing to ensure that cleared rooms are properly marked IAW the unit TSOP. Once the room is cleared, the team leader of the assaulting fire team signals to the squad leader that the building/room has been entered and the footholds gained.

Step 10. The squad consolidates its position in the building and then reorganizes as necessary.

Note: Normally the squad or platoons will use large-caliber weapons (if available) to suppress enemy in buildings.

Breach an Obstacle Drill

The breach an obstacle drill is used when the lead squad identifies a wire obstacle, reinforced with mines, that cannot be bypassed and there are enemy positions on the far side of the obstacle.

Step 1. The platoon leader moves forward with his FO and one machine gun team.

Step 2. The platoon leader determines whether he can maneuver.

Step 3. The platoon leader directs one squad to be the base-of-fire element, another to be the breach squad, and a third to be the assault squad once the breach has been made.

Step 4. The base-of-fire squad is joined by the platoon sergeant and the second machine gun team, and together they begin to suppress the enemy and obscure the enemy positions with smoke.

Step 5. The platoon leader leads the breach and assault squads to the breach point.

1. The breach squad leader designates a breach fire team and a support fire team.
2. The breaching fire team moves to the breach point using the covered and concealed route. The squad and fire team leader obscure the breach point, using smoke grenades.
3. The breaching fire team leader and an automatic rifleman are positioned on one flank of the breach point to provide security.
4. The grenadier and rifleman of the breaching fire team probe for and mark mines and cut the wire obstacle, marking their path as they proceed. (If available, bangalore torpedoes are preferred for clearing a lane through a minefield.)

Step 6. Once the obstacle has been breached, the fire team leader and the automatic rifleman move to the far side of the obstacle and take up covered and concealed positions with the rifleman and the grenadier.

Step 7. The squad leader signals the supporting fire team to move up and through the breach to the far side, where it takes up covered and concealed positions. The squad leader then moves through the breach and joins the breaching fire team.

Step 8. The squad leader reports to the platoon leader and consolidates as needed.

Step 9. The platoon leader leads the assault squad through the breach and positions it to support the movement of the remainder of the platoon, or assaults the enemy position covering the obstacle.

Step 10. The platoon leader reports to the company commander.

Initial Breach of a Mined Wire Obstacle—Platoon

5

Defense

Platoons and squads normally defend as part of a larger force to disrupt, disorganize, delay, or defeat an attacking enemy, deny an area to an enemy, or protect a flank. They may also defend as part of a larger unit in a retrograde operation. The challenge to the defender is to retain the initiative, that is, to keep the enemy reacting and unable to execute its own plan. The characteristics of the defense are preparation, security, disruption, mass and concentration, and flexibility. These are also the planning fundamentals for the combat leader.

CHARACTERISTICS OF DEFENSE

Preparation. The defender arrives in the battle area before the attacker. The platoon must take advantage of this by making all possible preparations for combat in the time available.

Security. The goals of the platoon's security efforts are normally tied to the company's efforts. Security efforts include providing early warning, destroying enemy reconnaissance units, and impeding and harassing elements of the enemy's main body.

Disruption. Defensive plans vary with the circumstances, but all defensive concepts of the operation aim at disrupting the attacker's synchronization. Counterattacks, indirect fires, obstacles, and the retention of key terrain prevent the enemy from concentrating his strength against selected portions of the platoon's defense.

Mass and Concentration. The platoon masses to concentrate combat power at the decisive place and time if it is to succeed. Offensive action may also be necessary. For concentration, all available combat power should be requested and employed, not just numbers of soldiers and weapons systems.

Flexibility. Flexibility is derived from sound preparation and effective command and control (C^2). The platoon must be agile enough to counter an attack, withstand the attacker's blows, and then strike back effectively.

SEQUENCE OF THE DEFENSE

As part of a larger element, the platoon conducts defensive operations in a sequence of integrated and overlapping actions:

1. Reconnaissance, security operations, and enemy preparatory fires
2. Occupation of a defensive position
3. Approach of the enemy main attack
4. Enemy assault
5. Counterattack or withdrawal
6. Consolidation and reorganization.

Reconnaissance, Security Operations, and Enemy Preparatory Fires

Security forces forward of the battle area must protect friendly forces in the main battle area (MBA) and allow them to prepare for the defense. The goals of a forward security force are to provide early warning, destroy enemy reconnaissance elements (within its capability), and disrupt enemy forward detachments or advance guard elements. During this step, the platoon may be attached to a larger element or remain with the parent company. Additionally, the platoon conducts counter-reconnaissance and security operations by conducting patrols or manning observation points (OPs) to observe named areas of interest (NAIs).

Occupation of a Defensive Position

The platoon plans, reconnoiters, and occupies the defensive position. This involves moving from one location to the defensive location. A quartering party that will clear the defensive position and prepare it for occupation normally leads this movement. The battalion establishes security forces, and the remaining forces prepare the defense.

Occupation and preparation of the defense site is conducted in accordance with the company commander's plan and the results of the reconnaissance. The quartering party reconnaissance element marks the friendly positions, and these are entered onto the operational graphics. Each squad moves in or is led in by a guide to its marker. Once in position, each squad leader checks his position location. As the platoon occupies its positions, the platoon leader manages the positioning of each squad to ensure they locate in accordance with the initial plan. The unit leader should personally walk the positions to ensure that everyone understands the plan in terms of:

- Weapons orientation
- Machine gun or weapons squads' positions
- Rifle squads' positions
- The location of the platoon leader and the platoon sergeant

Once the position is occupied, subordinate leaders begin to develop their sector sketches based on the basic fire plan developed during the leader's reconnaissance. Positions are improved continuously. In addition to establishing the platoon's primary positions, the platoon leader and subordinate leaders normally plan for alternate, supplementary, and subsequent positions in accordance with the company order. The following are tactical considerations for these positions:

Alternate Position. Covers the same avenue of approach or sector of fire as the primary position. It is located slightly to the front, flank, or rear of the primary position, positioned forward of the primary defensive positions during limited visibility operations, and is normally employed to supplement or support positions with weapons of limited range, such as infantry squad positions.

Supplementary Position. Covers an avenue of approach or sector of fire different from those covered by the primary position, and is occupied based on specific enemy actions.

Subsequent Position. Covers the same avenue of approach and or sector of fire as the primary position, is located in depth through the defensive sector, and it is occupied based on specific enemy actions or conducted as part of the higher headquarters' scheme of maneuver.

Approach of the Enemy Main Attack

Higher-level units engage the enemy at long range using combat multipliers in an effort to disrupt his synchronization, and degrade his combat power. Platoons cease security patrolling and usually bring OPs back into the defense position. Positions may be shifted in response to enemy actions or other tactical factors.

Enemy Assault

During this step, enemy forces attempt to fix friendly forces and complete their assault. During execution of the defense, friendly forces attempt to mass effects of fires to destroy the assaulting enemy. The platoon leader determines if the platoon can destroy the enemy from its assigned positions and if it can, the platoon continues to fight the defense:

The platoon leader continues to call for indirect fires as the enemy approaches. The platoon begins to engage the enemy at maximum effective range and attempts to mass fires and initiate them simultaneously to achieve maximum weapons effects. Indirect fires and obstacles integrated with direct fires should disrupt the enemy's formations, channel him toward engagement areas (EAs), prevent or severely limit his ability to observe the location of friendly positions, and destroy him as he attempts to breach tactical obstacles.

Leaders control fires using standard commands, pyrotechnics, and other prearranged signals. The platoon increases the intensity of fires as the enemy closes within range of additional weapons. Squad leaders work to achieve a sustained rate of fire from their positions by having buddy teams engage the enemy so that both soldiers are not reloading their weapons at the same time.

The enemy closes on the platoon's protective wire. Machine guns and squad automatic weapons (SAWs) fire along interlocking principal directions of fire (PDFs) or final protective lines (FPLs) as previously planned and designated. These include the platoon's M240Bs. Other weapons fire at their designated PDFs. Grenadiers engage the enemy with M203 grenade launchers in dead space or as the enemy attempts to breach protective wire. The platoon leader requests final protective fire (if assigned in support of his positions).

The platoon continues to defend until it repels the enemy or is ordered to disengage. If the platoon cannot destroy the enemy from its assigned positions, the platoon leader reports the situation to the company commander and continues to engage the enemy. He repositions the platoon (or squads of the platoon) when directed by the commander to continue fires into the platoon sector, occupy supplementary positions, reinforce other parts of the company, counterattack locally to retake lost fighting positions, and/or withdraw from an indefensible position using fire and movement to break contact.

Counterattack

As the enemy's momentum is slowed or stopped, friendly forces may counterattack. Counterattack may be launched purely for offensive purposes to seize the initiative from the enemy, or, it may be mainly defensive, for example to reestablish the forward edge of the battle area (FEBA) or to restore control of the sector. The company or platoon may participate in the counterattack as a base-of-fire element or as the counterattack force.

Consolidation and Reorganization

The platoon secures its sector and reestablishes the defense by repositioning forces, destroying enemy elements, processing EPWs, and reestablishing obstacles. The platoon conducts all necessary CSS functions as it prepares to continue defending. Consolidation includes organizing and strengthening a position so that it can continue to hold against the enemy using such means as: adjusting other positions to maintain mutual support; reoccupying and repairing prior positions; relocating selected weapons to alternate positions if leaders believe that the enemy may have pinpointed them during the attack; repairing damaged obstacles; replacing mines (Claymore) and booby traps; and reestablishing security and communications. Reorganization includes shifting internal resources within a degraded unit to increase its level of combat effectiveness using such means as: manning key weapons, providing first aid and preparing injured soldiers for casualty evacuation (CASEVAC), redistributing ammunition and supplies, and processing and evacuating EPWs.

BATTLEFIELD OPERATING SYSTEMS PLANNING CONSIDERATIONS

The Battlefield Operating Systems (BOS) are the seven critical tactical activities whose synchronization and coordination are critical for success. The following BOS pertain to defense operations.

Maneuver. Effective weapons positioning enables the platoon to mass fires at critical points on the battlefield and to enhance survivability. The combat leader must maximize the strengths of the platoon's weapons systems while minimizing its exposure to enemy observation and fires.

Fire Support. For the indirect fire plan to be effective in the defense, the unit must plan and execute indirect fires in a manner that achieves the intended task and purpose of each target. Indirect fires slow and disrupt the enemy, prevent enemy breaching operations, destroy or delay enemy forces at obstacles, defeat attacks along dismounted avenues of approach using FPF, obscure enemy observation, among other effects.

Mobility, Countermobility, and Survivability. Mobility in defense means the ability to reposition forces, including unit displacement and the commitment of reserve forces. The company commander's priorities may specify that some routes be improved to support such operations. Countermobility (obstacles) limits the maneuver of enemy forces and enhances the effectiveness of the defender's direct and indirect fires. Survivability focuses on protecting friendly forces from the effect of enemy weapons systems.

Air Defense. The focus of an air defense plan is on likely air avenues of approach for enemy fixed-wing, helicopters, and unmanned aerial vehicles, which may not correspond with the enemy's ground avenues of approach. A platoon leader is not likely to emplace air defense assets; however, he must be aware that higher headquarters may employ air defense assets near his defensive position.

Combat Service Support. In addition to the CSS functions required for all, the platoon leader's mission analysis (or guidance) may reveal that the unit's ammunition needs during an operation may exceed its basic load. This requires the platoon to establish ammunition caches. The caches, which may be positioned at alternate or subsequent positions, should be dug in and security provided by active or passive means (such as guarded or observed) or passive measures employed to indicate when and if the cache is tampered with.

Intelligence. Gaining information about the enemy is critical in defense.

Command and Control. Command and control refers to the process of directing, coordinating, and controlling a unit to accomplish a mission. Having effective communication to higher and supporting units is an essential BOS.

ENGAGEMENT AREA (EA) DEVELOPMENT

The EA is the place where the unit leader intends to destroy an enemy force using the massed fires of all available weapons. The success of any engagement depends on how effectively the leader can integrate the obstacle and indirect fire plans with his direct fire plan in the EA to achieve the unit's purpose. Despite its complexity, EA development resembles a drill. The leader and his subordinate leaders use a standardized set of procedures. Beginning with an evaluation of the factors of METT-TC, the development process covers these steps:

1. Identify likely enemy avenues of approach
2. Identify the enemy scheme of maneuver
3. Determine where to kill the enemy
4. Emplace weapons systems
5. Plan and integrate obstacles
6. Plan and integrate indirect fires
7. Conduct an EA rehearsal

Identify Likely Enemy Avenues of Approach

The infantry leader conducts an initial reconnaissance of the enemy's probable avenue of approach into the sector or EA. He confirms key terrain identified by the company commander, including locations that afford positional advantage over the enemy and natural obstacles and choke points that restrict forward movement. The platoon leader determines which avenues will afford cover and concealment for the enemy while allowing him to maintain his tempo. The leader also evaluates lateral mobility corridors (routes) that adjoin each avenue of approach.

Identify the Enemy Scheme of Maneuver

The leader greatly enhances his planning by gaining information early. He attempts to receive answers (from higher headquarters) about the enemy's purpose, direction, terrain orientation, mission, objectives, attack structure, recon assets, expected rate of movement, and response to friendly actions.

Determine Where to Kill the Enemy
As part of his troop-leading procedures, the infantry leader must determine where he will mass combat power on the enemy to accomplish his purpose. This decision is tied to his assessment of how the enemy will fight into the platoon's EA. Normally this entry point is marked by a prominent target reference point (TRP) that all platoon elements can engage with their direct fire weapons. This allows the commander to identify where the platoon will engage enemy forces through the depth of the company EA. In addition, the leader:
- Identifies TRPs that match the enemy's scheme of maneuver, allowing the platoon (or company) to identify where it will engage the enemy through the depth of the EA
- Identifies and records the exact location of each TRP
- Determines how many weapons systems can focus fires on each TRP to achieve the desired purpose
- Determines which squad(s) can mass fires on each TRP
- Begins development of a direct fire plan that focuses at each TRP

Note: In marking TRPs, use thermal sights to ensure visibility at the appropriate range under varying conditions, including daylight and limited visibility.

Emplace Weapons Systems
To position weapons effectively, leaders must know the characteristics, capabilities, and limitations of the weapons as well as the effects of terrain and the tactics used by the enemy. Platoon leaders should position weapons where they have protection, where they can avoid detection, and where they can surprise the enemy with accurate, lethal fires. In order to position the weapons, the platoon leader must know where he wants to destroy the enemy and what effect he wants the weapon to achieve. He should also consider:
- Selecting tentative squad defensive positions
- Conducting a leader's reconnaissance of the tentative defensive positions
- Walking the EA to confirm that the selected positions are tactically advantageous
- Confirming and marking the selected defensive positions
- Developing a direct fire plan that accomplishes the platoon's purpose

- Ensuring the defensive positions do not conflict with those of adjacent units and are effectively tied in with adjacent positions
- Selecting primary, alternate, and supplementary fighting positions to achieve the desired effect for each TRP
- Ensuring the squad leaders position weapons systems so the required numbers of weapons or squads effectively cover each TRP
- Inspecting all positions

Note: When possible, select fighting and crew-served weapon positions while moving in the EA. Using the enemy's perspective enables the platoon leader to assess survivability of the positions.

Plan and Integrate Obstacles

To be successful in the defense, the platoon leader will integrate tactical obstacles with the direct fire plan, taking into account the intent of each obstacle. Obstacles disrupt, turn, or fix the enemy. A combat platoon must have a clear task and purpose in order to properly emplace a tactical obstacle. Once the tactical obstacle has been emplaced, the platoon leader must report its location and any gaps in the obstacle to the company commander.

There are two types of obstacles: existing and reinforcing. *Existing obstacles* are those natural or cultural restrictions to movement that are part of the terrain when battle planning begins, such as slopes, gullies, rivers, swamps, trees, or built-up areas. *Reinforcing obstacles* are those specifically constructed, emplaced, or detonated to tie together, strengthen, and extend existing obstacles. Reinforcing obstacles include road craters, abatis, ditches, log hurdles, cribs, rubble, or wire entanglements.

Wire Obstacles. Wire is classified by its use and location.

- *Tactical wire* is sited parallel to and along the friendly side of the final protective line (FPL). It breaks up the enemy attack and holds the enemy where its troops can be killed or wounded by automatic rifle fire, Claymores, hand grenades, and machine gun fire.
- *Protective wire* is located to prevent surprise assaults from points close to the defense area. It is close enough for day and night observation but far enough away (40 to 100 meters) to keep the enemy from using hand grenades. Protective wire of adjacent platoons is connected by supplementary wire; this encloses the entire defensive position. Gaps must be provided, however, to allow patrols to exit and enter the position.
- *Supplementary wire* is used to disguise the exact lines of the tactical wire. It prevents the enemy from locating the unit's perimeter and machine guns by following the wire.

Ditch

TREES FELLED TOWARD
ENEMY AT 45° ANGLE

ENEMY

75 METERS

TREES NOT DETACHED
FROM TRUNKS

Abatis

Log Crib

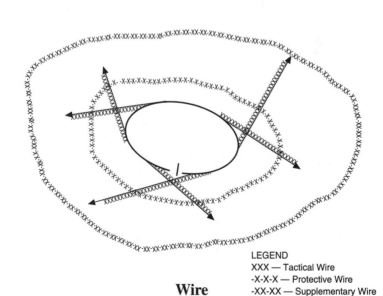

LEGEND
XXX — Tactical Wire
-X-X-X — Protective Wire
-XX-XX — Supplementary Wire

Wire

Minefields. Mines are one of the most effective tank destroyers and personnel killers on the battlefield. Minefields the infantry platoon most commonly emplaces are the hasty protective, point, and phony. (See Appendix C.)

Plan and Integrate Indirect Fires

In planning and integrating indirect fires, the platoon leader must accomplish the following:

- Determine the purpose of fires if the company commander has not already done so.
- Determine where that purpose will best be achieved if the company commander has not done so.
- Establish the observation plan with redundancy for each target. Observers will include the platoon leader as well as members of subordinate elements (such as team leaders) with fire support responsibilities.
- Establish triggers based on enemy movement rates.
- Obtain accurate target locations using survey and navigational equipment.

Integrated Engagement Area Plan—Platoon

- Refine target locations to ensure coverage of obstacles.
- Register artillery and mortars and plan final protective fires (FPF).

Conduct an Engagement Area Rehearsal

The purpose of rehearsal is to ensure that every leader and every soldier understands the plan and is prepared to cover his assigned areas with direct and indirect fires. The platoon will likely participate in a company level EA rehearsal. The company commander has several options for conducting a rehearsal, but the combined arms rehearsal produces the most detailed understanding of the plan. One rehearsal technique is to have the platoon sergeant and squads conduct a movement through the EA to depict the attacking enemy force, while the platoon leader and squad leaders rehearse the battle from the platoon defensive positions. The rehearsal should cover:

- Rearward passage of security forces (as required)
- Closure of lanes (as required)
- Use of fire commands, triggers, and/or maximum engagement lines (MELs) to initiate direct and indirect fires
- Shifting of fires to refocus and redistribute fire effects
- Disengagement criteria
- Identification of displacement routes and times
- Preparation and transmission of critical reports
- Assessment of the effects of enemy weapons systems
- Displacement to alternate, supplementary, or subsequent defensive positions
- Cross-leveling or resupply of Class V items
- Evacuation of casualties

Note: When conducting his rehearsal, the platoon leader should coordinate the platoon rehearsal with the company to ensure other units' rehearsals are not planned for the same time and location, and to eliminate the danger of misidentification of friendly forces in the rehearsal area.

Fire Commands and Engagement Priorities

Leaders use fire commands to direct the fires of the unit. A fire command has six parts:

1. *Alert.* The leader alerts the soldiers by name or unit designation, by some type of visual or sound signal, by personal contact, or in any other practical way.
2. *Direction.* The leader tells the soldiers the general direction or pinpoint location of the target.
3. *Description.* The leader describes the target briefly but accurately. The formation of enemy soldiers is always given.

4. *Range*. The leader tells the range to the target in meters.
5. *Method of fire*. The leader designates the weapons to fire. He can also tell the type and amount of ammunition to fire and the rate of fire.
6. *Command to fire*. The leader tells soldiers when to fire. He can use an oral command, a sound, or a visual signal. When he wants to control the exact moment, he says, "At my command." When he wants firing to start at the completion of the command, he just says, "Fire."

Targets appear in random order at different times and locations throughout the battlefield. *Engagement priorities* allow the leader to designate which target he wants destroyed first. Engagement priorities are usually done by weapons systems. For example, Dragon gunners would fire first at the most threatening armored vehicle and then at any armored vehicle in the kill zone or primary sector. Machine guns would fire at groups of five or more in the primary sector and then at automatic weapons. Riflemen would fire in their primary and secondary sectors from nearest to farthest, starting on the flank and working toward the center. Any number of priorities can be assigned to any weapon system.

OCCUPATION AND PREPARATION OF DEFENSIVE POSITIONS
Occupying and preparing a defensive position is not sequential. One potential problem is the lack of adequate preparation time if the platoon has also several other defensive positions (alternate, supplementary, and subsequent) and EAs to develop.

Occupation of Defensive Positions
The platoon occupies defensive positions in accordance with the leader's plan which has been based on prior reconnaissance.

To ensure an effective and efficient occupation, rifle squads move to the locations marked previously by the reconnaissance element. Once in position, each squad leader checks his location on the map to ensure he is complying with the platoon leader's graphics. As the platoon occupies its positions, the platoon leader verifies squad locations and corrects discrepancies.

Once each rifle squad has occupied its position, the platoon leader must walk the positions to verify weapons orientation, positioning of the rifle squads, and understanding of the plan are in accordance with the preestablished plan. For C^2 purposes, each squad leader must know the location of the platoon leader and the platoon sergeant.

Night vision equipment enhances the occupation process under limited visibility conditions. For instance, the platoon leader can mark his position with an infrared light source and the squad leaders can move to premarked positions with infrared light sources showing them where to locate.

The platoon may conduct a hasty occupation in the defense during a counterattack or after disengagement and movement to alternate, supplementary, or subsequent defensive positions.

The platoon conducts deliberate occupation of defensive positions when time is available, when enemy contact is not expected, and when friendly elements are positioned forward in the sector to provide security for forces in the main battle area. Actually establishing defensive positions is accomplished concurrently with the development of the EA. The platoon leader directs the initial reconnaissance from the EA and then tentatively emplaces crew-served weapon systems.

Once the defensive positions are established, subordinate leaders can begin to develop their sector sketches and fire plans based on the basic fire plan developed during the leader's reconnaissance. Fighting positions are improved while the direct fire plan is finalized and proofed. The platoon leader, with guidance from the company commander, designates the level of preparation for each defensive position based on the time available and other tactical considerations for the mission.

In addition to establishing the platoon's primary defensive positions, the platoon leader and subordinate leaders normally plan for preparation and occupation of alternate, supplementary, and subsequent defensive positions in accordance with the company order.

Priority of Work

Leaders must ensure that soldiers prepare for the defense quickly and efficiently. Work must be done in order of priority to accomplish the most in the least amount of time while maintaining security and the ability to respond to enemy action. Below are basic considerations for priorities of work:

- Emplace local security
- Position and assign sectors of fire for each squad (platoon leader)
- Position and assign sectors of fire for the Javelins and M240B machine gun teams (platoon leader)
- Position and assign sectors of fire for SAW, grenadiers, and then riflemen (squad leader)
- Clear fields of fire and prepare range cards
- Prepare sector sketches (leaders)
- Dig fighting positions (stage 1; see chapter 13)
- Establish communication/coordination with the company and adjacent units

- Coordinate with adjacent units. Review sector sketches
- Emplace AT and Claymore mines, then wire and other obstacles
- Improve primary fighting positions and add overhead cover (stage 2; see chapter 13)
- Prepare supplementary and then alternate positions (same procedure as the primary position)
- Distribute and stockpile ammunition, food, and water

Priorities of work are dictated by unit SOPs and commander's guidance based on METT-TC. Many actions are completed at the same time; thus it is important that leaders are constantly supervising activities.

Security in the Defense

Security in the defense includes all active and passive measures taken to avoid detection by the enemy, deceive the enemy, and deny enemy reconnaissance elements accurate information on friendly positions. The two primary tools available to the platoon leader are observation posts (OPs) and patrols. In planning for the security in the defense, the platoon leader considers the terrain and intelligence updates to plan his courses of action.

Observation Posts. An OP gives the platoon its first echelon of security in the defense. The OP provides early warning of impending enemy contact by reporting direction, distance, and size. It detects the enemy early and sends accurate reports to the platoon. The platoon leader establishes OPs along the most likely enemy avenues of approach into the position or into the EA. Leaders ensure that OPs have communication with the platoon.

Patrols. Platoons actively patrol in the defense. Patrols enhance the platoon's ability to fill gaps in security between OPs. The platoon leader forwards his tentative patrol route to the commander to ensure that it does not conflict with other elements within the company. The commander forwards the entire company's patrol routes to the battalion. This allows the battalion S3 and S2 to ensure all routes are coordinated for fratricide prevention and to ensure the company and platoons are conforming to the battalion intelligence, surveillance, and reconnaissance (ISR) plan.

Establishment of Defensive Positions

Platoons establish defensive positions in accordance with the platoon leader and commander's plan. They mark EAs using marking techniques prescribed by unit SOP. The platoon physically marks obstacles, TRPs, targets, and trigger lines in the EA. During limited visibility, the platoon can use infrared light sources to mark TRPs for the rifle squads. When possible, platoons should mark TRPs with both a thermal and an infrared source so the rifle squads can use the TRP.

Range Cards

A range card is a sketch of a sector that a direct fire weapons system is assigned to cover. A range card aids in planning and controlling fires and aids the crew in acquiring targets during limited visibility. It also is an aid for replacement personnel, platoons, or squads to move into the position and to orient on their sector. During good visibility, the gunner should have no problems maintaining orientation in his sector. During poor visibility, he may not be able to detect lateral limits. If the gunner becomes disoriented and cannot find or locate reference points or sector limit markers, he can use the range card to locate the limits. The gunner should make the range card so that he becomes more familiar with the terrain in his sector. Range cards are prepared immediately during stage 1 of defensive fighting positions (see chapter 13) and are updated as necessary. Two copies of the range card are prepared, one for the position and one for the squad leader to prepare his sketch.

The range card has two sections—a sector sketch section, and a data section. The marginal information at the top of the card is listed as follows:

- SQD, PLT, CO. The squad, platoon, and company designations are listed. Units higher than company are not listed.
- MAGNETIC NORTH. The range card is oriented with the terrain, and the direction of magnetic north arrow is drawn.

The gunner's sector of fire is drawn in the sector sketch section. It is not drawn to scale, but the data referring to the targets must be accurate.

- The weapon symbol is drawn in the center of the small circle.
- Left and right limits are drawn from the position. A circled "L" and "R" are placed at the end of the left and right limit lines.
- The value of each circle is determined by using a terrain feature farthest from the position that is within the weapon's capability. The distance to the terrain is determined and rounded off to the next even hundredth, if necessary. The maximum number of circles that will divide evenly into the distance is determined and divided. The result is the value for each circle. The terrain feature is then drawn on the appropriate circle.
- All target reference points (TRPs) and reference points are drawn in the sector. They are numbered consecutively and circled.
- Dead space is drawn in the sector.
- A maximum engagement line is drawn on range cards for antiarmor weapons.
- The weapon reference point is numbered last. The location is given a six-digit grid coordinate. When there is no terrain feature to be designated, the location is shown as an eight-digit grid coordinate.

Primary sector with FPL

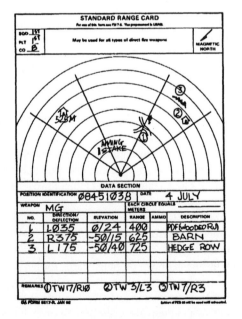

Primary sector with PDF

Completed Range Card—Machine Gun

Completed Range Card—Javelin

The data section is filled in as follows:
- Position Identification: The position is identified as primary, alternate, or supplementary.
- Date: The date and time the range card was completed are entered.
- Weapon: The weapon block indicates the weapons used.
- Each circle equals meters. Write in the distance in meters between circles.
- No.: Starting with left and right limits, TRPs and reference points are listed in numerical order.
- Direction/deflection: The direction is listed in degrees. The deflection is listed in mils.
- Elevation: The elevation is listed in mils.
- Range: The distance in meters from the position to the left and right limits and TRPs and reference points.
- Ammo: The type of ammunition used is listed.
- Description: The name of the object is listed, for example, farm house, wood line, hilltop.
- Remarks: The weapon reference point data and any additional information are listed.

Sector Sketches

Leaders prepare sector sketches based on their defensive plan. They use the range card for each fighting position (prepared by the soldiers in each position). Detailed sketches aid in the planning, distribution, and control of the platoon fires. Gunners prepare the range cards. Squad leaders prepare squad sector sketches, section leaders prepare section sketches, and the platoon leader prepares the platoon sketch.

    Squad Sector Sketch. Each squad leader prepares a sector sketch to help him plan his defense and help him control fire. The squad leader prepares two copies of the sector sketch. He gives one copy to the platoon leader and keeps the second copy at his position. The SOP should state how soon after occupying the position the leader must forward the sketch. The sketch shows the following:

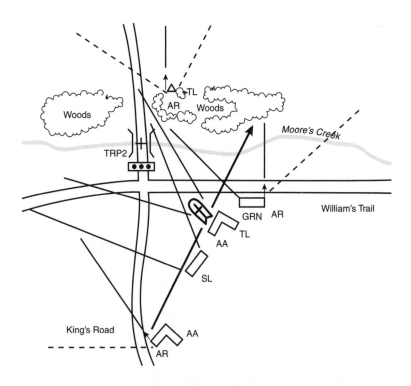

Squad Sector Sketch

- Squad and platoon identification
- Date/time group
- Magnetic north
- The main terrain features in his sector of fire and the ranges to them
- Each primary fighting position
- Alternate and supplementary positions
- The primary and secondary sectors of fire of each position
- Maximum engagement line
- Machine gun FPLs or PDF
- Dragon positions with sectors of fire
- The type of weapon in each position
- Observation posts and the squad leader's position
- Dead space to include coverage by grenade launchers
- Location of night vision devices (NVDs)
- Obstacles, mines, and booby traps

Platoon Sector Sketch. The platoon leader checks range cards and squad sector sketches. If he finds gaps or other flaws in his fire plan, he adjusts the weapons or sectors as needed. If he finds any dead space, he takes steps to cover it with mines, grenade launcher fire, or indirect fire. He then makes two copies of his platoon sector sketch—one for his use, and the other for the company commander. His sketch shows the following:

Platoon Sector Sketch

- Squad sectors of fire
- Machine gun and antiarmor weapon positions and their sectors of fires, including FPLs and PDFs of the automatic rifles and machine guns and TRPs for the antiarmor weapons
- Maximum engagement lines for antiarmor weapons
- Mines (Claymores) and obstacles
- Indirect fire planned in the platoon's sector of fire (targets and FPF)
- OPs and patrol routes, if any
- Platoon CP
- Platoon/company identification
- Date/time group
- Magnetic north
- Location of casualty collection point
- Location of NVDs/thermal sights that are part of the limited-visibility security plan
- Adjustments during limited visibility to maintain coverage of assigned TRPs

Establishment of Command Post and Wire Communications
The platoon command post (CP) is set up where the platoon leader can best see and control his platoon. If he cannot see all of the platoon sector from one place, he sets up where he can see and control the main effort. He then sets up an alternate CP where the platoon sergeant can see and control the rest of the platoon.

In the defense, the platoon CP ties in to the company wire net with a field telephone. Wire is the primary means of communications between the platoon leader and squad leaders. The platoon has its own radio net, and the platoon leader also uses messengers, visual signals, personal contact, or whistles to communicate.

Weapons and Soldier Placement
To position weapons effectively, leaders must know the characteristics, capabilities, and limitations of the weapons; the effects of terrain; and the tactics used by the enemy. Additionally, the platoon leader must consider whether his primary threat will be vehicles or infantry. His plan should address both mounted and dismounted threats.

Javelin (Antiarmor) Employment. The Javelin's (or antiarmor weapon such as the older M-47 Dragon) primary role is to destroy enemy armored vehicles. When there is no armored vehicle enemy, the Javelin can be

1st SQUAD · 2d SQUAD · 3d SQUAD
CP-OP PLT LDR RATELO · FO RATELO · PSG · AIDMAN

1st SQUAD · 2d SQUAD · 3d SQUAD · Alternate CP-OP
PLT LDR · FO RATELO · PSG · AIDMAN
Primary CP-OP · RATELO

Command Post, Observation Post

employed in a secondary role of providing fire support against point targets such as crew-served weapons positions. In addition, the Javelin's CLU (command launch unit) can be used alone as an aided vision device for reconnaissance, security operations, and surveillance. Reduced or limited visibility will not degrade the effectiveness of the Javelin. This fact allows the antiarmor specialist to continue to cover his sector without having to reposition closer to the avenue of approach.

M240B and M249 Machine Gun Employment. These are the platoon's primary crew-served weapons and are positioned first if the enemy is a dismounted force. Once these guns are sited, the leader positions riflemen to protect them. The guns are positioned to place direct fire on locations where the platoon leader wants to concentrate combat power to destroy the enemy. Each gun is usually given a primary and secondary sector of fire. These sectors should overlap each other and those of adjacent platoons (if possible). Additionally, the platoon leader will designate final protective lines (FPL)

Grazing Fire

and/or final protective fires (FPF). Each machine gun's primary sector includes an FPL or a principal direction of fire (PDF). The gun is laid on the FPL or the PDF unless engaging other targets. When FPFs are called for, the gunner shifts to and engages on the FPL or PDF. Where terrain allows, the platoon leader assigns a machine gun an FPL. The FPL is a line along which *grazing fire* is placed to stop an assault. Grazing fire is no more than 1 meter above the ground. The FPL is fixed in elevation and direction. A soldier walks the FPL to find dead space. The gunner watches the soldier walking the line and marks spaces that cannot be grazed. The dead space is covered with obstacles, grenade launcher fire, or mines.

When the terrain does not lend itself to an FPL, the platoon leader assigns the machine gun a PDF to cover an area that provides good fields of fire or has a likely avenue of approach. FPFs are prearranged barriers of indirect fires used to defeat the assaulting enemy unit as soon as possible after it moves into its assault formation. The FPF can be anywhere between the forward position of the friendly unit and the enemy's assault position, which is normally just out of range of the platoon's organic weapons. The FPF should be fired only to stop an enemy assault. On signal, the FPF is fired continuously until the order is given to stop or the mortar or artillery unit runs out of ammunition. All other platoon weapons fire while the FPF is being fired.

M203 Grenade Launcher Employment. The M203 grenade launcher is the squad leader's indirect fire weapon. He positions it to cover dead space in the squad's sector, especially the dead space for the M240Bs and M249s. The grenadier is also assigned a sector of fire overlapping the riflemen's sectors of fire. The HEDP round is effective against lightly armored enemy vehicles.

Employment of Riflemen

The platoon and squad leaders assign positions and sectors of fire to each rifleman in the platoon. Normally, they position the riflemen to support and protect the machine guns, SAWs, and antiarmor weapons. Riflemen also are positioned to cover obstacles, provide security, cover gaps between platoons and companies, or provide observation.

Coordination

Coordination is important in every operation. In the defense, coordination ensures that units provide mutual support and interlocking fires. In most circumstances, the platoon leader conducts face-to-face coordination to facilitate understanding and to resolve issues. The platoon leader should send and receive the following information prior to conducting face-to-face coordination:

- Location of leaders
- Location of primary, alternate, and supplementary positions and sectors of fire of machine guns, antiarmor weapons, and subunits
- Route to alternate and supplementary positions
- Location of dead space between platoons and squads and how to cover it
- Location of OPs and withdrawal routes back to the platoon's or squad's position
- Location and types of obstacles and how to cover them
- Patrols to be conducted, including their size, type, times of departure and return, and routes
- Location, activities, and passage plans for scouts and other units forward of the platoon's position
- Signals for fire, cease-fire, and any others that may be observed
- Engagement and disengagement criteria

Fire team leaders should also coordinate to ensure that each position knows who and what weapons are to the left and right. This ensures that all positions and all units are mutually supportive and that any gaps between units are covered by fire, observation, patrols, or sensors.

Preparation of Fighting Positions. As mentioned earlier, defensive positions are classified as *primary*, *alternate*, *supplementary*, or *subsequent*. All positions should provide observation and fields of fire within the weapon's or platoon's assigned sector of fire. They should take advantage of natural cover and concealment even before soldiers camouflage them. Soldiers prepare their positions in four stages (see chapter 13).

As a guideline, a squad can physically occupy a front of about 100 meters. From this position, it can defend 200 to 250 meters of frontage. The frontage distance between two-man fighting positions should be about 20 meters (allowing for a "lazy W" configuration on the ground, which would put fighting positions about 25 meters apart physically). Every position should be observed and supported by the fires of at least two other positions. One-man fighting positions may be located closer together to occupy the same platoon frontage. The distance between fighting positions depends on the leader's analysis of the factors of METT-TC. In determining the best distance between fighting positions, the squad leader must consider:

- The requirement to cover the squad's assigned sector by fire
- The need for security—that is, to prevent infiltrations of the squad position
- The requirement to prevent the enemy from using hand grenades effectively to assault adjacent positions, should it gain a fighting position

FIGHTING THE DEFENSE

Forces defend aggressively, continually seeking opportunities to take advantage of the enemy's errors or failures. Defense includes maneuver and counterattack, as well as keeping key positions secure. The battle begins when the planned signal or event for beginning fire occurs. The platoon leader determines whether the platoon can destroy the enemy from its assigned positions. If the answer is *yes*, the platoon continues to fight the defense. The platoon leader or FO continues to call for indirect fires as the enemy approaches. The platoon normally begins engaging the enemy at maximum effective range. It attempts to mass fires and initiate them simultaneously to achieve surprise. Long-range fires tied in with obstacles should disrupt enemy formations, channelize the enemy toward engagement areas, prevent or severely limit its ability to observe the location of friendly positions, and destroy the enemy as it attempts to breach tactical obstacles.

Leaders control fires using standard commands, pyrotechnics, and other prearranged signals. The platoon increases the intensity of fires as the enemy closes within range of additional weapons. Squad leaders work to achieve a sustained rate of fire from their positions by having buddy teams fire their weapons so that both are not reloading at the same time. In controlling and distributing fires, the platoon and squad leaders consider:

- Range to the enemy
- Priority targets (what to fire at, when to fire, and why)
- Nearest or most dangerous targets
- Shifting to concentrate fires on their own initiative or as directed by higher headquarters
- Ability of the platoon to engage dismounted enemy with enfilading, grazing fires
- Ability of the platoon's antiarmor weapon to achieve flank shots against enemy vehicles

As the enemy closes on the platoon's protective wire, the platoon leader initiates FPFs.

- Machine guns and automatic weapons fire along interlocking PDFs or FPLs as previously designated and planned. Other weapons fire at designated PDFs. M203 grenade launchers engage the enemy in dead space or against enemy attempts to breach protective wire.
- The platoon continues to fight with Claymores and hand grenades.
- If applicable, the platoon leader requests indirect FPFs if they have been assigned in support of his positions.

The platoon continues to defend until the enemy is repelled or the platoon is ordered to disengage.

If the platoon cannot stop or destroy the enemy from its current position, the platoon leader reports the situation to the company commander and continues to engage the enemy or repositions the platoon (or squads of the platoon). In this situation—and when directed by the company commander—the platoon leader may:

- Continue fires into the platoon sector (engagement area).
- Occupy supplementary positions.
- Reinforce other parts of the company.
- Counterattack locally to retake lost fighting positions.
- Withdraw from an untenable position using fire and movement to break contact (the platoon leader will not be ordered to move his platoon out of position if it will destroy the integrity of the company defense). In any movement out of a defensive position, the platoon must employ all direct and indirect fire means available to suppress the enemy long enough for the unit to move.

DEFENSIVE TECHNIQUES
The company commander's analysis will determine the most effective manner in which to defend. He will direct the platoons in what defensive techniques to employ. The platoon normally will defend using one of these basic techniques.

1. Defend in sector or Area of Operations (AO)
2. Defend a battle position (BP)
3. Defend a strongpoint
4. Defend a perimeter
5. Defend a reverse slope

Defend in Sector/AO.
Defending an area allows a unit to maintain flank contact and security, affords depth in the platoon defense, and facilitates clearance of supporting fires. Area/sector defense is used when flexibility is desired, when retention of specific terrain features is not necessary, or when the unit cannot concentrate fires because of extended frontages, intervening terrain features, and/or multiple avenues of approach. The platoon is assigned an AO defense mis-

Concept of the Operation for a Defend in Sector (AO)

sion to prevent a specific amount of enemy forces from penetrating the rear boundary of the AO. To maintain the integrity of the AO defense, the platoon must remain tied to adjacent units on the flanks. The company commander may direct the platoon to conduct the defense in one of two ways:

1. He may specify a series of subsequent defensive positions within the AO from which the platoon will defend to ensure that the fires of two platoons can be massed.

2. He may assign an AO to the platoon. The platoon leader assumes responsibility for most tactical decisions and controlling maneuvers of his subordinate squads by assigning them a series of subsequent defensive positions in accordance with guidance from the company commander in the form of intent, specified tasks, and the concept of the operation. The company commander normally assigns an AO to a platoon only when it is fighting in isolation.

Defend a Battle Position

The company commander assigns this defensive technique to his platoons when he wants to mass the fires of two or more platoons in a company engagement area (EA) or to position a platoon to execute a counterattack. A unit defends from a battle position (BP) to destroy an enemy force in the EA, block an enemy avenue of approach, control key or decisive terrain, and/or fix the enemy force to allow another unit to maneuver. The company commander designates EAs to allow each platoon to concentrate its fires or to place it in an advantageous position for the counterattack. BPs are developed in such a manner to provide the platoon the ability to place direct fire throughout the EA. The size of the platoon BP can vary, but it should provide enough depth and maneuver space for subordinate squads to maneuver into alternate or supplementary positions and to counterattack. The BP is a general position on the ground. The platoon leader places his squads on the most favorable terrain in the BP based on the higher unit mission and commander's intent. The platoon then fights to retain the position unless ordered by the company commander to counterattack or displace. The basic methods of employing a platoon in a BP are:

- Same BP, same avenue of approach
- Same BP, different avenues of approach
- Different BPs, same avenue of approach
- Different BPs, different avenues of approach

Same Battle Position, Same Avenue of Approach

Rifle squads are on the same BP covering the same avenue of approach. The platoon can defend against mounted and dismounted attacks and move rapidly to another position. All squads are in the same BP when the terrain provides good observation, fields of fire, and cover and concealment. Employing all the squads of the platoon on the same BP covering the same avenue of approach is the most conservative use of the platoon. Its primary advantages are that it facilitates C^2 functions because of the proximity of squad elements on the same approach and it provides increased security.

Same Battle Position, Same Avenue of Approach

Same Battle Position, Different Avenues of Approach
Rifle squads occupy the same BP but cover different enemy avenues of approach.

Same Battle Position, Different Avenues of Approach

Different Battle Positions, Same Avenue of Approach

Rifle squads are on different BPs covering the same avenue of approach. If positioned on separate BPs, rifle squads must fight in relation to each other when covering the same avenues of approach. A weapons squad can provide supporting fires for the rifle squads from their primary, alternate, or supplementary positions. All squads are positioned to engage enemy forces on the same avenue of approach, but at different ranges.

Different Battle Positions, Same Avenue of Approach

Different Battle Positions, Different Avenues of Approach

Squads may be employed on different BPs and different avenues of approach. Caution should be taken in planning to ensure that the squad BPs cannot be either fixed or isolated and defeated by the enemy.

Different Battle Positions, Different Avenues of Approach

Defend a Strongpoint

Defending a strongpoint is not a common mission for an infantry platoon. A strongpoint defense requires extensive engineer support (in terms of expertise, materials, and equipment) and takes a long time to complete. When the

Defend a Strongpoint

platoon is directed to defend a strongpoint, it must retain the position until ordered to withdraw. The success of the strongpoint defense depends on how well the position is tied into the existing terrain. This defense is most effective when it is employed in terrain that provides cover and concealment to both the strongpoint and its supporting obstacles. Mountainous, forested, or urban terrain can be adapted easily to a strong-point defense. Strongpoints placed in more open terrain require the use of reverse slopes or of extensive camouflage and deception efforts. This defensive mission may require the platoon to:

- Hold key or decisive terrain critical to the company or battalion scheme of maneuver
- Provide a pivot to maneuver friendly forces
- Block an avenue of approach
- Canalize the enemy into one or more EAs.

The prime characteristic of an effective strongpoint is that it cannot be easily overrun or bypassed. It must be positioned and constructed so that the enemy knows he can reduce it only at the risk of heavy casualties and significant loss of materiel. Techniques and considerations involved in establishing and executing the strongpoint defense include the projected size of the strongpoint versus available troops and equipment, routes in and out, placement of antiarmor weapons in and outside the defense, availability of 360-degree observation, number of needed EAs, placement and use of platoon reserve, and best use of internal squad battle positions. Engineers support a strongpoint defense by reinforcing the existing obstacles. Priorities of work will vary depending on the factors of METT-TC, especially the enemy situation and time available. For example, the first 12 hours of the strongpoint construction effort may be critical for emplacing countermobility and survivability positions and C^2 bunkers. On the other hand, if the focus of engineer support is to make the terrain approaching the strongpoint impassable, the battalion engineer effort must be adjusted accordingly.

Defend a Perimeter

A perimeter defense allows the defending force to orient in all directions. In terms of weapons emplacement, direct and indirect fire integration, and reserve employment, a platoon leader conducting a perimeter defense should consider the same factors as a strongpoint operation.

1. The perimeter defense allows only limited maneuver and limited depth. Nonetheless, the platoon may be called on to execute a perimeter defense under a variety of conditions that include:
   - Holding critical terrain in areas where the defense is not tied in with adjacent units

Defend a Perimeter

- Defending in place when it has been bypassed and isolated by the enemy
- Conducting occupation of an independent avenue of approach (AA) or reserve position
- Preparing a strongpoint
- Concentrating fires in two or more adjacent avenues of approach
- Defending CS or CSS assets
- Occupying a patrol base

2. The major advantage of the perimeter defense is the platoon's ability to defend against an enemy avenue of approach. A perimeter defense differs from other defenses in that:
    - The trace of the platoon is circular or triangular rather than linear
    - Unoccupied areas between squads are smaller
    - Flanks of squads are bent back to conform to the plan
    - The bulk of combat power is on the perimeter
    - The reserve is centrally located

Note: A variant of the perimeter defense is the use of the shaped defense, which allows two of the platoon's squads to orient at any particular time on any of three EAs.

Reverse Slope Defense

The platoon leader's analysis of the factors of METT-TC often leads him to employ his forces on the reverse slope. If the rifle squads are on a mounted avenue of approach, they must be concealed from enemy direct-fire systems. This means rifle squads should be protected from enemy tanks and observed artillery fire. Some reverse slope defense considerations are:

  1. The majority of a rifle squad's weapons are not effective beyond 600 meters. To reduce or preclude destruction from enemy direct and

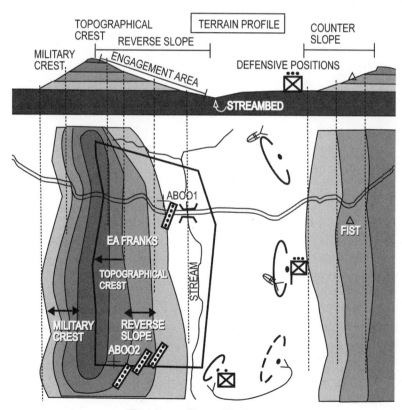

Reverse Slope Defense

indirect fires beyond that range, a reverse-slope defense should be considered. In some cases it may be necessary for these weapons systems to be deployed forward while the rifle squads remain on the reverse slope (to take advantage of their long ranges). The Javelins withdraw from their forward positions as the battle closes. Their new positions should be selected to take advantage of their long-range fires and to get enfilade shots from the depth and the flanks of the reverse slope.

2. The nature of the enemy may change at night, and the rifle squads may occupy the forward slope or crest to deny it to the enemy. In those circumstances, it is feasible for a rifle squad to have an alternate night position forward. The area forward of the topographical crest must be controlled by friendly forces through aggressive patrolling and both active and passive reconnaissance measures.

3. The company commander normally makes the decision to position platoons on a reverse slope when:
   - He wishes to surprise or deceive the enemy about the location of his defensive position.
   - A forward slope might be made untenable by direct enemy fire.
   - Occupation of the forward slope is not essential to achieve depth and mutual support.
   - Fields of fire on the reverse slope are better or at least sufficient to accomplish the mission.
   - Forward slope positions are likely to be the target of concentrated enemy artillery fires.

Obstacles are necessary in a reverse-slope defense. Since the enemy will be engaged at close range, obstacles should prevent the enemy from closing too quickly and overrunning the positions. Obstacles on the reverse slope can halt, disrupt, and expose enemy vehicles to flank AT fires. Obstacles should also facilitate the platoon's disengagement.

Reorganization in Combat
Reorganization begins automatically at team and squad levels during the battle to prepare for the next battle. To prepare for the next attack, the platoon should accomplish the following:

Man Key Weapons
Replace key soldiers lost during battle; for example, ensure that crew-served weapons are manned and new team leaders are designated.

Reestablish Security
If soldiers withdrew from the OPs to their fighting positions, return them to their OPs. If some did not get back to their positions, check their status and replace casualties. As soon as possible, reestablish the sleep-alert system.

Treat and/or Evacuate Casualties
Treat casualties as far forward as possible. Return those who can continue to fight to their positions; evacuate the others.

Redistribute Ammunition and Supplies
Distribute remaining ammunition and supplies equally among the soldiers, including ammunition from the casualties.

Relocate Fighting Positions and Weapons Positions
During the assault, the enemy may have pinpointed some of the fighting and weapons positions. If certain positions are in danger, move soldiers and weapons (especially crew-served weapons) to their alternate positions.

Reestablish Communications
If a phone line was cut during the attack, soldiers on each end of the line try to find and repair the break or lay new wire. If a signal, such as a green star cluster, was used to cease fire, consider changing the signal, since its meaning may now be known by the enemy.

Repair Fighting Positions
Each soldier checks and replaces the camouflage, overhead cover, and sandbags on existing positions and camouflages new positions.

Repair and/or Replace Obstacles
Repair and/or replace damaged or breached obstacles, mines, and booby traps only if enemy soldiers are far enough away that it can be done safely. Otherwise, wait for poor visibility to do so, or use smoke to hinder observation.

6

Tactical Enabling Operations

The infantry platoon may conduct other tasks to complement or support its primary mission. Enabling operations include reconnaissance, retrograde (withdrawal, delay, and retirement), special purpose operations (linkup, stay-behind, relief in place, and passage of lines), air assaults, and security operations (convoy security, checkpoints, roadblocks, and observation posts (OPs). Squads and platoons conduct these operations on their own or as part of a larger force.

RECONNAISSANCE
Reconnaissance is any mission undertaken, using visual observation or other methods, to seek out and obtain information regarding the activities and resources of enemy forces or the physical characteristics of a particular area.

Reconnaissance Planning
Before an operation, the company commander determines what he must know about the enemy and terrain.

Types of Reconnaissance
The platoon may be called upon or required to conduct reconnaissance before or after an operation in the following situations:
- Reconnaissance by a quartering party of an assembly area (AA) and the associated route to it
- Leader's reconnaissance from the AA to and in the vicinity of the line of departure (LD) before an offensive operation
- Reconnaissance by rifle squads to probe enemy positions for gaps open to attack or infiltration
- Reconnaissance by rifle squads to observe forward positions and to guide elements to key positions such as support or assault on the battlefield

- Reconnaissance by rifle squads to locate bypasses around obstacle belts or to determine the best locations and methods for breaching operations
- Reconnaissance by rifle squads of choke points or other danger areas in advance of the remainder of the company
- Leader's reconnaissance of defensive positions or engagement areas (EAs) for conducting the defense
- Reconnaissance rifle squads as part of security operations to secure friendly obstacles, to clear possible enemy OPs, or to cover areas not observable by stationary operations

See chapter 7 for more information on reconnaissance patrolling.

LINKUP OPERATIONS

Linkup entails the meeting of friendly ground forces (or their leaders or designated representatives). Linkups depend on control, detailed planning, and stealth. Night vision devices (NVDs) enhance the execution of linkup operations and reduce the likelihood of fratricide.

The platoon conducts linkup activities independently or as part of a larger force. The platoon may lead the linkup force. The linkup consists of three steps:

1. **Far Recognition Signal.** The units or elements involved in the linkup establish communication before they reach direct fire range utilizing a far recognition signal.
2. **Coordination.** Before initiating movement to the linkup point, the forces coordinate necessary tactical information including the enemy situation, type and number of friendly elements and vehicles, disposition of stationary forces, routes to the linkup point and rally point, fire control measures, near recognition signal(s), communications information, combat support (CS) and combat service support (CSS) coverage, finalized location of the linkup and rally points, special coordination such as covering maneuver instructions or requests for medical support, and visual linkup signals or alternate linkup locations (in case of contact).
3. **Movement to the Linkup Point and Linkup.** All units or elements involved in the linkup must enforce strict fire control measures to prevent fratricide. Linkup points and restrictive fire lines (RFLs) must be recognizable by moving or converging forces. Linkup elements ensure they conduct long-range (far) recognition by FM radio, conduct short-range (near) recognition using the designated signal,

complete movement to the linkup point, establish local security at the linkup point, and conduct additional coordination and linkup activities as necessary.

PASSAGE OF LINES

A passage of lines entails movement of one or more units through another unit. This operation is necessary when the moving unit(s) cannot bypass the stationary unit and must pass through it. The primary purpose of the passage is to maintain the momentum of the moving elements. A passage of lines may be either forward or rearward. The controlling unit is responsible for planning and coordinating a passage of lines involving the platoon. In some situations, the platoon leader must take responsibility for planning and coordinating each phase of the operation. Also, platoons may conduct passages of lines when conducting patrols, ambushes, raids, or other operations requiring them to pass through friendly units.

Planning Considerations

In planning passage of lines, the platoon leader must consider the following tactical factors and procedures:

1. The passage should be large enough to support doctrinal formations for the passing units.
2. Deception techniques such as the use of smoke may be employed to enhance security during the passage.
3. The controlling commander must clearly define the battle handover criteria and procedures to be used during the passage. His order should cover the roles of both the passing unit and the stationary unit and the use of direct and indirect fires in both a forward or rearward passage.
4. The passing and stationary units coordinate obstacle information including the location of enemy and friendly obstacles, existing lanes and bypasses, and guides for the passage.
5. Air defense coverage is imperative during the high-risk passage operation; normally, the stationary unit will be responsible for providing air defense.
6. Responsibility for CSS actions such as vehicle recovery or casualty evacuation in the passage lane must be clearly defined for both passing and stationary units.
7. To enhance C^2 during the passage, the platoon will co-locate a C^2 element, normally the platoon leader or platoon sergeant, with a similar element from the stationary or moving unit.

Reconnaissance and Coordination

Detailed reconnaissance and coordination are critical in a passage of lines. The platoon leader or a designated representative coordinates the following items:

- Unit designation and composition including type and number of passing vehicles (if any) and soldiers
- Passing unit arrival time(s)
- Location of attack positions or AAs (should be confirmed by reconnaissance)
- Current enemy situation
- Obstacles
- Stationary unit's mission and plan (to include OP, patrol, and obstacle locations)
- Location of movement routes, contact points, passage points, and passage lanes (*Note:* The use of global positioning system [GPS] waypoints will simplify this process and speed the passage.)
- Guide requirements
- Order of march
- Anticipated actions on enemy contact
- Requirements for supporting direct and indirect fires, including the location
- NBC conditions
- Available CS and CSS assets and their locations
- Radio frequencies and near and far recognition signals
- Criteria for battle handover and location of the battle handover

In a forward passage, the passing unit first moves to an AA or an attack position behind the stationary unit. Designated liaison personnel move forward to link up with guides and confirm coordination information with the stationary unit. Guides from the stationary unit lead the passing elements through the passage lane. In a rearward passage of lines, the risk of fratricide is increased, so coordination of recognition signals and fire restrictions is critical.

RELIEF IN PLACE

A relief in place may be needed to maintain combat effectiveness during prolonged combat operations. A relief in place is an operation in which a platoon is replaced in combat by another platoon. The incoming platoon assumes responsibility for the combat mission and assigned sector or zone of action of the outgoing platoon.

Coordination

Platoon responsibility is usually limited to the detailed coordination between key personnel and their counterparts.

Leaders must reconnoiter different routes into and out of the position; assembly area; logistics points; primary, alternate, and supplementary positions; obstacles; immediate terrain; and, when possible, patrol routes and OP locations. The outgoing leader must provide copies of the platoon sector sketch, fire plan, range cards for all weapons, barrier plan, minefield records, counterattack plans, and plans for any other tasks the platoon may have been ordered to perform.

Both leaders must know which method and sequence of relief has been prescribed in the higher unit order and how they will execute the plan. They are responsible for the following:

- Knowing whether their platoons will execute the relief by squads or as a complete platoon (method). Platoons may also execute the relief by occupying adjacent terrain or terrain in depth (to the rear) rather than by relieving soldiers in position.
- Knowing the order of relief (sequence) for platoons within the company.
- Coordinating the use of guides (outgoing unit provides guides to move incoming unit to positions), signals, challenge and password, and passage of responsibility for the mission and control of the platoon (normally when the majority of the incoming platoon is in place).
- Coordinating the exchange of tripods for crew-served weapons, phones or switchboards, and emplaced munitions. Platoons do not exchange radios.
- Identifying numbers, types, and location of supplies to be left behind, including sensors, construction materiel, wire, and any supplies that might slow down the movement of the outgoing platoon.

Execution

During the execution, both leaders should co-locate at the outgoing platoon leader's command post (CP). The leader of the outgoing platoon remains responsible for the defense of the area until the majority of the incoming platoon is in position. If the enemy attacks during the relief, the leader who has responsibility at the time is in control. The other leader assists with assets under his control as directed.

Squad leaders physically walk soldiers to positions and trade them out on a one-for-one basis. They allow time for outgoing soldiers to brief their reliefs on their position, range cards, and other pertinent information. Both the relieved and relieving platoons must maintain security to deny the enemy knowledge of the relief. The relieved platoon keeps local security elements in place. These elements are the last soldiers to be relieved. Both platoons observe strict communications security and maintain normal movement and activity. All leaders report completion of their portion of the relief as soon as possible.

WITHDRAWAL

In a withdrawal, all or part of a deployed force voluntarily disengages from the enemy to free itself for a new mission. The mission might be to defend another position or to attack someplace else. Units withdraw either under pressure or not under pressure. Platoons have three basic methods of disengaging from the enemy: They can thin their lines or move out either by fire team or by squad.

- To *disengage by thinning the lines*, squad and team leaders direct soldiers to move rearward in buddy teams, with each soldier covering the other as they move back in turn. Smoke must be used for concealment if the soldiers are moving across open areas.

Disengagement by Individuals (Thinning the Lines)

- To *disengage by fire teams*, one team fires while the other one moves, alternating roles. This method can be used if thinning the lines is not needed because enemy fire is light or teams have already moved back far enough.
- To *disengage by squads*, the platoon leader has each squad move back in turn, covered by the fire of the others. The platoon moves back by squads if thinning the lines or maneuver by fire teams is not needed because enemy fire is light or squads have already moved back sufficiently.

Disengagement by Fire Teams

Withdrawal Not Under Pressure

Withdrawal not under pressure is conducted with speed, secrecy, and deception and is best performed at night or during periods of reduced visibility. The company disengages and moves to the rear while the enemy is not attacking. The company leaves a detachment left in contact (DLIC) as a security force to cover the withdrawal by deception, fire, or maneuver. A platoon or one squad from each platoon serves as the DLIC. The composite platoon is normally the best method because there is less repositioning involved. As the DLIC, platoons perform the following:

- Reposition squads and weapons to cover the company's withdrawal.
- Reposition a squad in each of the other platoon positions to cover the most dangerous avenue of approach into the area.
- Continue the normal operating pattern of the company.
- Cover the company withdrawal by fire if the company is attacked during withdrawal.
- Withdraw once the company is at its next position. If under contact, the DLIC might have to maneuver to the rear until contact is broken, then assemble to move to the company.

Withdrawal Under Pressure

The amount of enemy pressure determines how the withdrawal is conducted. If it is not possible to prepare and position the security force, the platoon conducts a fighting withdrawal. The platoon disengages from the enemy by maneuvering to the rear. Soldiers, fire teams, and squads not in contact are withdrawn first so they can provide suppressive fires to allow the soldiers, team, or squad in contact to withdraw. If enemy pressure is light enough to permit a security force, a platoon (or a composite platoon) repositions itself to fight the enemy as the rest of the company withdraws.

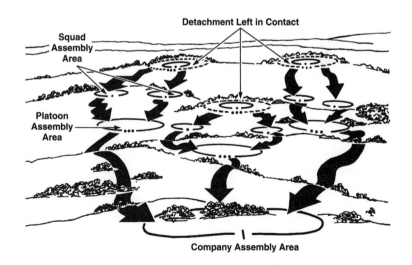

Company Withdrawl / Not Under Pressure

DELAY

In a delay, the enemy slows its movement when the platoon forces him to repeatedly deploy for the attack. After causing the enemy to deploy, the delaying force withdraws to new positions. The squads or sections and platoons disengage from the enemy as described in a withdrawal under pressure and move directly to their next position and defend again. The squads and platoons slow the advance of the enemy by causing casualties and equipment losses by employing ambushes, snipers, obstacles, minefields (including phony minefields), and artillery and mortar fire.

STAY-BEHIND OPERATIONS

Stay-behind operations can be used as part of defensive or delay missions. In the defense, once the enemy's combat units have passed, his weakest point (CS and CSS units) can be attacked. The two types of stay-behind operations are unplanned and deliberate.

Unplanned. An unplanned stay-behind operation is one in which a unit finds itself cut off from other friendly elements for an indefinite time without specific planning or targets and must rely on its organic assets.

Deliberate. A deliberate stay-behind operation is one in which a unit plans to operate in an enemy-controlled area as a separate yet cohesive element for a certain amount of time or until a specified event occurs. A deliberate stay-behind operation requires extensive planning. Squads, sections, and platoons conduct this type of operation as part of larger units.

Planning

The most important troop-leading procedures (TLP) that apply to stay-behind operations are task organization, reconnaissance, and combat service support.

Task Organization. The stay-behind unit includes only the soldiers and equipment needed for the mission. It needs minimal logistics support and can provide its own security. It must be able to hide easily and move through restrictive terrain.

Reconnaissance. This is most important in a stay-behind operation. Reporting tasks and information requirements can include suitable sites for patrol bases, hide positions, OPs, caches, water sources, dismounted and mounted avenues of approach, kill zones, EAs, and covered and concealed approach routes.

Combat Service Support. Because the stay-behind unit will not be in physical contact with its supporting unit, supplies of rations, ammunition, radio batteries, water, and medical supplies are cached. Provisions for casualty and enemy prisoner of war (EPW) evacuation depend on the company and battalion plans.

AIR ASSAULT OPERATIONS

Infantry platoons may be required to participate in air assault operations as part of the tactical plan. The platoon has the ability to be airlifted as part of a larger operation. The battalion is the lowest level with sufficient personnel to plan, coordinate, and control an air assault. When company-size or smaller unit operations are conducted, the planning takes place at battalion or higher headquarters.

Ground Tactical Plan

The foundation of a successful air assault operation is the commander's ground tactical plan, around which subsequent planning is based. The ground tactical plan specifies actions that must be performed in the objective area and addresses subsequent operations. The ground tactical plan contains essentially the same elements as any other infantry attack plan but capitalizes on speed and mobility to achieve surprise.

Landing Plan

The landing plan must support the ground tactical plan. This plan sequences elements into the areas of operations (AOs) to ensure that platoons arrive at designated locations and times prepared to execute the ground tactical plan. The following should be taken into account in the landing plan:

- The availability, location, and size of potential landing zones (LZs) are overriding factors.
- The company is most vulnerable during landing.
- Elements must land with tactical integrity.
- Troops are easily disoriented if the landing direction changes and they are not kept informed.
- The company must be prepared to fight in any direction after landing, since there may be no other friendly troops in the area.
- The landing plan should offer flexibility so that a variety of options is available in developing a scheme of maneuver.
- Supporting fires (artillery, attack helicopters, close air support, naval gunfire) must be planned in and around each LZ.
- Although the objective may be beyond the range of supporting artillery fire, artillery or mortars can be brought into the LZs early to provide fire support for maneuver troops.
- Resupply and medical evacuation by air must be provided for.

Selection of Landing Zones
Each LZ is selected using the following criteria:
- *Location.* It can be located on, near, or away from the objective, depending on METT-TC.
- *Capacity.* The size determines how much combat power can be landed at one time. Size also determines the need for additional LZs or separation between serials.
- *Alternates.* An alternate LZ should be planned for each primary LZ to ensure flexibility.
- *Enemy disposition and capabilities.* Enemy troop concentrations, air defenses, and their capability to react are considered when selecting an LZ.
- *Cover and concealment.* LZs are selected that deny enemy observation and acquisition of friendly ground and air elements while they are en route to or from (and in) the LZ. Depending on METT-TC, the LZ and approaches should be masked from the enemy by terrain features.
- *Obstacles.* If possible, the company should land on the enemy side of obstacles when attacking, and at other times use the obstacles to protect LZs from the enemy. LZs must be free of obstacles. Engineers must be part of the task organization for contingency breaching of obstacles.
- *Identification from the air.* LZs should be easily identifiable from the air. If pathfinder support or friendly reconnaissance units are present, they should mark the LZ with chemical lights, preferably of the infrared type, if the assault troops wear night vision goggles.
- *Approach and departure routes.* Approach and departure routes should avoid continued flank exposure of aircraft to the enemy.
- *Weather.* Reduced visibility or strong winds may preclude or limit the use of marginal LZs.

Single Versus Multiple Landing Zones
In addition to deciding where to land in relation to the objective, consideration is given to the use of a single LZ or multiple LZs. The following are the advantages of using a single LZ:
- Allows concentration of combat power
- Facilitates control of the operation
- Concentrates supporting fire
- Provides better ground security for subsequent lifts
- Requires fewer attack helicopters for security

- Makes it more difficult for the enemy to detect the operation by the reduced number of flight routes in the operation area
- Centralizes any required resupply efforts
- Concentrates efforts of limited LZ control personnel and engineers on one LZ
- Requires less planning and rehearsal time

The following are the advantages of using multiple LZs:

- Avoids grouping assets in one location and creating a lucrative target for enemy fire
- Allows rapid dispersal of ground elements to accomplish tasks in separate areas
- Reduces the enemy's ability to detect and react to the initial lift
- Forces the enemy to fight in more than one direction
- Reduces the troop and aircraft congestion that can occur on one LZ
- Makes it difficult for the enemy to determine the size of the air assault force and the location of supporting weapons

Air Movement Plan

The air movement plan is based on the ground tactical and landing plans. It specifies the schedule and provides the instructions for air movement of soldiers, equipment, and supplies from pickup zones (PZs) and landing zones (LZs).

Loading Plan

The loading plan is based on the movement plan. It ensures soldiers, equipment, and supplies are loaded on the correct aircraft and that platoon integrity is maintained. Cross-loading of essential personnel and equipment is imperative to ensure survivability of C^2 assets and to ensure that the mix of personnel and weapons arriving at the LZ is ready to fight. The platoon leader or squad leader should always ensure the aircraft is loaded so that dismounting soldiers react promptly. The platoon leader must have a bump plan. A bump plan

UH-60 Loading Diagram

UH-60 Unloading Diagram

ensures essential soldiers and equipment are loaded ahead of less critical loads in case of aircraft breakdown or other problems.

Planning must cover the organization and operation of the pickup zone (PZ), including load positions, day and night markings, and communications. The loading plan is most important when mixing aircraft types. Ground and aviation unit movement to the PZ is scheduled so that only the troops to load and the helicopter to be loaded arrive at the PZ at the same time. To coordinate movement of units to the PZ, assembly areas, holding areas, and routes of movement are selected.

At company and lower levels, each man and major items of equipment or supplies are assigned to specific aircraft by an airloading table. The airloading table is an accountability tool, a loading manifest for each aircraft. When time is limited, the table can be a sheet of paper from the squad leader's notebook. These lists are left with a specified person in the PZ. This procedure ensures that if an aircraft is lost, a list of personnel and equipment on board is available.

During load planning, unit leaders attempt to maintain the following:

• *Tactical integrity of units.* Fire teams and squads are loaded intact on the same aircraft, and platoons in the same serial. This ensures integrity as a fighting unit upon landing.

• *Self-sufficiency of loads.* Each load should be functional by itself whenever possible. Every towed item is accompanied by its prime mover. Crews are loaded with their vehicle or weapon. Ammunition is carried with the weapon. Component parts accompany the major items of equipment. Sufficient personnel are on board to unload the cargo.

- *Tactical cross-loading*. Loads should be planned so that all leaders, or all crew-served weapons, are not loaded on the same aircraft. Thus if an aircraft is lost, the mission is not seriously hampered.

Aircraft Bump Plan

Each aircraft load has a bump sequence designated on its airloading table. Bump priority ensures that the most essential personnel and equipment arrive at the objective area first. It specifies personnel and equipment that may be bumped and delivered later. If all personnel within the load cannot be lifted, individuals must know who is to off-load and in what sequence. This ensures that key personnel are not bumped arbitrarily.

Also, bump sequence is designated for aircraft within each serial or flight. This ensures that key aircraft loads are not left in the PZ. When an aircraft within a serial or flight cannot lift off and key personnel are on board, they off-load and reboard another aircraft that has priority. A PZ bump and straggler collection point is established to account for, regroup, and reschedule these personnel and/or loads for later delivery.

Lifts, Serials, and Loads

To maximize operational control, aviation assets are designated as lifts, serials, or loads.

A *lift* is one sortie of all utility and cargo aircraft assigned to a mission. Each time all assigned aircraft pick up troops and/or equipment and set them down on the LZ, one lift is completed. The second lift is completed when all lift aircraft place their second loads on the LZ.

When a lift is too large to fly in one formation, it is organized into a number of *serials*. A serial is a tactical grouping of two or more aircraft under the control of a serial commander and separated from other tactical groupings within the lift by time or space. Serials also may be organized when the capacity of available PZs or LZs is limited or to take advantage of available flight routes.

A *load* is personnel or equipment designated to be moved by a specific aircraft. Each aircraft within the lift is termed a load. For example, within a lift of ten, there are aircraft loads one through ten.

Staging Plan

The staging plan is based on the loading plan and prescribes the arrival time of ground units (soldiers, equipment, and supplies) at the PZ in the order of movement.

Helicopters

Several types of helicopters may be used in air assault operations: observation, utility, cargo, and attack.

Observation Helicopters (OHs). OHs are used to provide command and control, aerial observation and reconnaissance, and aerial target acquisition.

Utility Helicopters (UHs). UHs are the most versatile of all helicopters, performing a variety of tasks. As such, they are available in almost every unit possessing helicopters. UHs are used to conduct combat assaults and provide transportation, command and control, and resupply. When rigged with special equipment, they also may be used to provide aeromedical evacuations, conduct radiological surveys, and dispense scatterable mines.

Cargo Helicopters (CHs). These aircraft are organic to corps aviation units. They normally provide transportation, resupply, and recovery of downed aircraft.

Attack Helicopters (AHs). AHs are organized in groups varying in size from company to battalion and can also be task organized to meet mission needs. They are used to provide overwatch, destroy point targets, provide security, and suppress air defense weapons.

Capabilities

Under normal conditions, helicopters can ascend and descend at relatively steep angles; this enables them to operate from confined and unimproved areas. Troops and their combat equipment can be unloaded from a helicopter hovering a short distance above the ground with troop ladders and rappelling means, or if the helicopter can hover low enough, the troops may jump to the ground. The troop ladder can also be used to load personnel when the helicopter cannot land. Cargo can be transported as an external load and delivered to areas inaccessible to other types of aircraft or to ground transportation.

Because of a wide speed range and high maneuverability at slow speeds, helicopters can fly safely and efficiently at low altitudes, using terrain and trees for cover and concealment. Because of their ability to fly at high or low altitudes, decelerate rapidly, maintain slow forward speed, and land nearly vertically, helicopters can operate under marginal weather conditions. Helicopters can land on the objective area in a tactical formation, LZs permitting. Night and/or limited-visibility landings and liftoffs can be made with a minimum of light. Helicopters flying at low levels are capable of achieving surprise, deceiving the enemy at the LZs, and employing shock effect through the use of suppressive fires. Engine and rotor noise may deceive the enemy as to the direction of approach and intended flight path.

Limitations

The high fuel consumption of helicopters imposes limitations on range and allowable cargo load (ACL). Helicopters may reduce fuel loads to permit an increased ACL, but reducing the fuel load also reduces the range and flexibility. The load-carrying capability of helicopters decreases with increases in altitude, humidity, and temperature. This limitation may be compensated for through reduction of fuel load. Weight and balance affect flight control. Loads must be properly distributed to keep the center of gravity within allowable limits.

Hail, sleet, icing, heavy rains, and gusty winds (30 knots or more) limit or preclude the use of helicopters. Crosswind velocities above 15 knots for utility helicopters and 10 knots for cargo helicopters, and downwind velocities above 5 knots for either type of helicopter, affect the selection of the direction of landing and liftoff.

Engine and rotor noise may compromise secrecy. Aviator fatigue requires greater consideration in the operation of rotary-wing aircraft than in the operation of fixed-wing aircraft.

Loads

The *type-load method* is the most efficient method used in the conduct of air assault operations and in operational planning. Army aviation units are frequently required to support numerous major units operating over expansive tactical zones. Standardization of type loads within the theater of operations ensures responsive and effective air mobility with a minimum of time required for planning.

The use of type loads does not limit the flexibility of a ground tactical unit to be airlifted. The type-load method is very useful at battalion and company levels to plan and conduct air assault operations. Your supporting aviation unit will supply you with necessary load and type-load planning information.

Seats-Out Operation

With the UH-60, if the troop seats are removed, 22 combat-loaded soldiers and their rucksacks can be loaded. Conducting combat operations with seats out reduces the number of aircraft needed for each mission. The aircraft can be loaded from either or both sides. Loading is quicker if both sides are used. Before the soldiers enter the aircraft, each soldier's rucksack is placed on the floor of the aircraft where the soldier will sit. Once all rucksacks are loaded, the soldiers are loaded from rear to front. Soldiers in the aircraft help by pulling the others in tightly until they are all loaded and the doors are closed. The aircraft doors should be opened as the helicopter approaches the

UH-60 Seats-out Loading Diagram

LZ. Soldiers hold on to each other until time to unload. They should unload from both sides if the ground slope permits. (*Caution:* The seats-out technique is used in combat only—never in training.)

Air Assault Lessons Learned in Operations Enduring Freedom and Iraqi Freedom

From a unit First Sergeant. Many lessons were learned on air assault. It was always seats-out due to the limited number of aircraft and the number of personnel we had to get in. Some problems were encountered with offloading a fully-packed CH-47 on a hot LZ, which became an extremely slow process. Landing was the most dangerous part because of the mountainous conditions, terrain, and altitude caused the helicopter to land hard. The lack of seats and seatbelts resulted in many broken bones. If possible, you should send in the first few lifts with seats-in. That will get the helicopter off the LZ much quicker. You can then secure the area and follow the first lifts with the seats-out sorties.

AREA SECURITY OPERATIONS

Area security operations protect specific critical and vulnerable assets or terrain from enemy observation and direct fire. These operations can consist of escorting friendly convoys (with an augmentation of vehicles); protecting critical points such as bridges, C^2 installations, or other key and vulnerable sites; or participating in protection of large areas such as airfields. During stability or support operations, the platoon may be required to establish OPs, roadblocks, or checkpoints. The platoon normally performs an area security operation when conventional security or combat operations would not work, and it does so independently or as part of a larger force. Infantry platoons normally conduct area security missions to protect high-value points, areas, or assets. Whether these need protection, how much protection they require, and the defensive technique chosen to protect them depends on the factors of METT-TC. The platoon leader must integrate his elements into the overall security plan for the area he must protect. Area security operations rely on various techniques, which may include reconnaissance, security, defensive tasks, and offensive tasks.

CONVOY AND ROUTE SECURITY

Company and larger organizations usually perform convoy or route security missions. Convoy security provides protection for a specific convoy. Route security aims at securing a specific route for a designated period of time, during which multiple convoys may use the route. These missions include tasks such as escorting, reconnaissance, and establishing a combat reaction force. These tasks become missions for subordinate units. The size of the unit performing a convoy or route security operation depends on many factors, including the size of the convoy, the terrain, and the length of the route.

Vehicles

In order for an infantry platoon to conduct convoy or route security, it must be augmented with vehicles. Vehicles may include up-armored high mobility multipurpose wheeled vehicles (HUMVEES), light medium tactical vehicles (LMTVs), 5-ton trucks, and even civilian trucks. Driver training and licensing requirements must be considered if the platoon's infantrymen are to be used as drivers. Vehicles should be hardened and protected as much as possible before operations are conducted, by use of sandbags, Kevlar blankets, metal plates, and other materials.

Route Reconnaissance

In this mission, the platoon leader focuses on the route's trafficability and on enemy forces that might influence the route. The platoon must plan to call for engineer assets to aid in breaching point-type obstacles. Command-detonated devices pose a major threat during route reconnaissance.

Convoy Escort

The platoon may perform a convoy escort mission either independently or as part of a larger unit's convoy security mission. The convoy escort mission requires that the platoon provide the convoy with limited close-in protection from direct small arms fire. Vehicles include military CSS and C^2 vehicles and civilian trucks and buses. Leaders must carefully evaluate the enemy before assigning a convoy escort mission to platoon-sized elements.

Command and Control

Because of the task organization of the convoy escort mission, C^2 is especially critical. The relationship between the platoon and the convoy commander must provide unity of command and effort if combat operations are required during the course of the mission. In most cases, the platoon will execute the escort mission under the control of the security force commander, who is usually under the operational control (OPCON) of, or attached to, the convoy commander. It is vital that the convoy commander issues a complete operation order (OPORD) to all convoy vehicle commanders before executing the mission because the convoy may itself be task-organized from a variety of units and some vehicles may not have tactical radios. Ensure all immediate action drills are covered and rehearsed.

Convoy Security Operations

Tactical Disposition. During all escort missions, the convoy security commander and platoon leader must establish and maintain security in all directions. Several factors, including convoy size, affect this disposition. The key consideration is whether the platoon is operating as part of a larger escort force or is executing the escort mission independently. Additional METT-TC considerations include the employment of rifle squads during the mission, and whether fire teams ride in escorted vehicles.

Actions on Contact. As the convoy moves to its new location, the enemy may attempt to harass or destroy it. This contact usually will occur in the form of an ambush, often with the use of a hastily prepared obstacle. The safety of the convoy rests on the speed and effectiveness with which escort elements can execute appropriate actions on contact. Based on the factors of METT-TC, portions of the convoy security force such as the platoon may be designated as a reaction force. The reaction force performs its escort duties, conducts tactical movement, or occupies an AA (as required) until enemy contact occurs and the convoy commander gives it a reaction mission.

Actions at an Ambush. An ambush is one of the more effective ways to interdict a convoy. Reaction to an ambush must be immediate, overwhelming, and decisive. Actions on contact must be planned for and rehearsed so they can be executed quickly.

Actions at an Obstacle. Obstacles are a major impediment to convoys. The purpose of reconnaissance ahead of a convoy is to identify obstacles and either breach them or find bypasses. In some cases the enemy or its obstacles may avoid detection by the reconnaissance element.

Actions during Halts. During a short halt, the convoy escort remains alert for possible enemy activity. If the halt is for any reason other than an obstacle, the convoy will be halted for an extended period of time. If this is the case, the element must move into a security formation such as a herringbone (be aware of mines on the edges of the road) and tactical support and security vehicles will move into a security and ready posture. This activity needs to be rehearsed prior to the convoy departure.

CHECKPOINTS, ROADBLOCKS, AND OBSERVATION POSTS
Construction and manning of checkpoints, roadblocks, and observation posts (OPs) are high-frequency tasks for an infantry company and subordinate elements when they must establish area security during stability operations.

A **checkpoint** is a predetermined point used as a means of controlling movement, such as a place where military police check vehicular or pedestrian traffic to enforce circulation control measures and other laws, orders, and regulations.

A **roadblock** is used to limit the movement of vehicles along a route or to close access to certain areas or roads. Checkpoints and roadblocks can be either deliberate or hasty, the primary difference being the extent of planning and preparation conducted by the establishing force.

An **observation post** is a position from which military observations are made or fire directed and adjusted and which has appropriate communications. They are both overt (conspicuously visible, unlike their tactical counterparts) and deliberately constructed. OPs are similar in construction to bunkers and are supported by fighting positions, barriers, and patrols.

The platoon may be directed to establish a checkpoint, roadblock, or OP for the following reasons:
- Show a military presence to all parties and to the population in the area.
- Survey all activity in the terrain, along roads, and in inhabited areas.
- Check and/or inspect and register all personnel and vehicles in and out of the controlled area.
- Survey airspace, coastal areas, airfields, cease-fire lines, and borders.
- Deter illegal movement.
- Create an instant roadblock.
- Control movement into the AOs or on a specific route.
- Prevent smuggling of contraband.
- Enforce the terms of peace agreements.
- Ensure proper use of routes by both civilian and military vehicles.

Planning and Establishing
The layout, construction, and manning of checkpoints, roadblocks, and OPs should reflect the factors of METT-TC, especially the time available for

emplacing them. The layout of deliberate checkpoints can be found in various battle books. The following procedures and considerations may apply:

1. Position the checkpoint or roadblock where it is visible and where traffic cannot turn back, get off the road, or bypass without being observed.

2. Position a combat vehicle (up-armored HUMVEE with a mounted machine gun or MK19) off the road, but within sight, to deter resistance to soldiers manning the checkpoint. The vehicle should be in a defensive position and protected by local security. It must be able to engage vehicles attempting to break through or bypass the checkpoint.

3. If combat vehicles are not available, place M240B machine gun defensive positions in locations to cover and engage vehicles attempting to break through or bypass the checkpoint.

4. Place obstacles in the road to slow or canalize traffic into the search area.

5. Establish a reserve.

6. Establish wire communications in the checkpoint area to connect the checkpoint bunker, the combat vehicle, the search area, security forces, the rest area, and any other elements involved in the operation.

7. Designate the search area. If possible, it should be below ground to provide protection against such incidents as the explosion of a booby-trapped vehicle. Establish a parking area adjacent to the search area.

8. If applicable, checkpoint personnel should include linguists and women soldiers in case indigenous women need to be searched.

9. Establish an early warning system around the perimeter of the OP (trip flares, empty cans, dry branches, and so on).

10. Prepare shelters and defensive positions.

Manning Observation Posts and Checkpoints

When manning OPs and checkpoints, proper order and a systematic approach must be emphasized. Personnel must behave so that no misunderstanding occurs. The personnel manning the checkpoint must be in complete control of the surrounding terrain.

1. Although the OP is usually manned on a 24-hour basis, it may be manned only by day or night. During darkness, at least two persons must be in the OP; one observes while the other is resting. In remote areas, or if the situation in the area is tense, more personnel man the OP for security and observation.

2. A minimum of two soldiers should man the checkpoint, depending on traffic and the general situation. One soldier examines people and vehicles; the other soldier covers the area where people and vehicles are checked. The soldier covering the other area is armed and has easy access to radio and telephone. If more soldiers are manning the checkpoint, one of them should be ready to set up obstacles to stop vehicles trying to force their way through the checkpoint.

Communication

All OPs and checkpoints are connected to their unit or directly to the battalion operations center by radio and telephone. A spare radio and batteries should be supplied to the OP and checkpoint, especially to remote OPs located in dangerous areas. Radio and telephone checks are carried out at least twice every 24 hours; three times is recommended. Special code words are prepared for use in certain situations. Conversation must be coded. Reserve frequencies must be available. OPs and checkpoints of great operational value may be connected by direct landline to ensure rapid coordination in urgent situations.

Equipment

Many items are used to reinforce a roadblock, checkpoint, or OP. Recommended equipment includes:

- Barrels filled with sand, water, or heavy concrete blocks (emplaced to slow and canalize vehicles)
- Concertina wire (emplaced to control movement around the checkpoint)
- Secure facilities for radio and wire communications with the controlling headquarters
- First aid kit or a medic if available
- Sandbags for defensive positions
- Bunker construction material
- Binoculars, NVDs, and flashlights
- Long-handled mirrors (used to inspect vehicle undercarriages)
- Signs stating the speed limit into and out of the checkpoint. The text of these signs must be written in English and the local language
- Floodlights
- Duty log
- Flag and unit sign
- Barrier pole that can be raised and lowered
- Generators with electric wire

Control

During periods in which the civilian administration is not functioning, refugees will be traveling routinely throughout the area. All soldiers participating in these operations must fully understand the procedures for identifying and controlling personnel and vehicles moving through their AO.

Personnel Identification. People who have permission to enter a sector are regulated by special instructions to the patrol conducting the operation. Often local and civilian employees, mayors, and chiefs of tribes in villages in the AO are given special identification (ID) cards and may pass without being checked. These ID cards must be registered. Other personnel must identify themselves with an ID card, passport, and so on. Such ID cards are written in the local language. Examples of different ID cards must be kept in the checkpoint. A U.S. translator on site is helpful, if available.

Personnel Control. Personnel control is conducted in different ways. Soldiers manning the checkpoint should watch for people acting strangely or with bulging clothing. If there is a danger of car bombs, special attention should be paid to cars containing only one person. When conducting body searches, soldiers should feel along clothes and not just pat them. Special attention must be paid to the lower parts of the back and from the shoes up to the knees. Armpits also must be checked. The wide trousers used by some cultures should be carefully examined. Soldiers also should check boots and hats. Extreme caution should be taken when suicide vehicle or human bombers are a threat.

Checking Women and Clerical Personnel. Making a body search of women and clerical personnel is often difficult in Moslem countries and may lead to strong reactions. The commander must thoroughly discuss this with mayors and other leaders, and the procedure used must be consistent with agreements and treaties. Women usually are only checked with a metal detector. One technique used in Afghanistan to search women was for the husband to be searched with the metal detector wand and then have him wand his wife and any other female family members. Elderly women often remain in the vehicle during inspection of a car. If there is a suspicion that the "rules" are being misused, then other and better checks must be made. The battalion commander makes these decisions.

Detailed information on OPs, checkpoints, control of civilian movement, prisoner exchanges, and convoy security may be had at Bonn and Baker, *Guide to Military Operations Other Than War: Tactics, Techniques, and Procedures* (Stackpole: 2000).

7

Patrolling

Patrols are missions to gather information, to conduct combat operations, or to establish a presence in an area of operations (AO) as part of a stability operation. Infantry platoons and squads conduct four types of patrols: reconnaissance, combat, presence, and tracking. This chapter describes the planning considerations used in preparation for patrols, conduct of patrols, and establishment of and actions taken in a patrol base.

ORGANIZATION AND PLANNING

To accomplish its mission, a patrol must perform specific tasks—for example, secure itself, cross danger areas; establish rally points; reconnoiter the patrol objective; and breach, support, or assault. When possible, in assigning tasks, the leader should maintain squad and fire team integrity. The chain of command continues to lead its elements during a patrol. Some squads and fire teams may perform more than one task in an assigned sequence; others may perform only one task. The leader must plan carefully to ensure that he has identified and assigned all required tasks in the most efficient way. Elements and teams for platoons conducting patrols include the common and specific elements for each type of patrol. The following elements are common to all patrols.

Headquarters Element. The headquarters consists of the platoon leader, radiotelephone operator (RATELO), platoon sergeant, forward observer (FO), and FO RATELO. It may consist of other attachments that the platoon leader or the platoon sergeant must control directly.

Surveillance Team. A surveillance team keeps watch on the objective from the time the leader's reconnaissance ends until the unit deploys for actions on the objective. It then joins its element.

En route Recorder. The en route recorder records all information collected during the mission.

Compass Man. The compass man assists in navigation by ensuring that the lead fire team leader remains on course at all times. Instructions to the compass man must include an initial azimuth, with subsequent azimuths provided as necessary. The compass man should preset his compass on the initial azimuth before moving out, especially if the move will be during limited-visibility conditions. The platoon or squad leader should designate an alternate compass man.

Pace Man. The pace man maintains an accurate pace at all times and reports the pace at intervals designated by the platoon or squad leader and at the end of each leg. The leader should designate an alternate pace man.

Aid and Litter Team. Aid and litter teams are responsible for treating and evacuating casualties.

Enemy Prisoner of War Team. EPW teams are responsible for controlling enemy prisoners in accordance with the five S's (search, silence, segregate, safeguard, and speed to the rear) and the leader's guidance.

Initial Planning and Coordination

Leaders plan and prepare for patrols using troop-leading procedures (TLPs) and the estimate of the situation. Leaders identify required actions on the objective, then plan backward to the departure from friendly lines and forward to the reentry of friendly lines. They normally receive the operation order (OPORD) in the battalion or company command post (CP), where communications are good and key personnel are available. Because patrols act independently, move beyond the direct-fire support of the parent unit, and operate forward of friendly units, coordination must be thorough and detailed. Leaders normally coordinate directly with three different elements: higher headquarters (usually battalion staff or the company commander); the unit through which the platoon or squad will conduct its forward and rearward passage of lines; and the leaders of other units that will be patrolling in adjacent areas at the same time. Patrol leaders use checklists to preclude the omission of any items vital to the accomplishment of the mission.

Higher Headquarters Coordination

Items coordinated between the leader and the battalion staff or company commander include:

- Changes or updates in the enemy situation
- Best use of terrain for routes, rally points, and patrol bases
- Light and weather data
- Changes in the friendly situation
- The attachment of soldiers with special skills or equipment; for example, engineers, sniper teams, scout dog teams, FOs, or interpreters
- Use and location of landing zones
- Departure and reentry of friendly lines

- Fire support on the objective and along the planned routes, including alternate routes
- Rehearsal areas and times
- Special equipment requirements
- Transportation support, including transportation to and from the rehearsal site
- Signal plan—call sign frequencies, code words, pyrotechnics, and challenge and password.

Forward Unit Coordination

The departure from friendly lines must be thoroughly planned and coordinated. The leader should consider the following sequence of actions:

- Make contact with friendly guides at the contact point.
- Move to the coordinated initial rally point.
- Complete final coordination.
- Move to and through the passage point.
- Establish a security-listening halt beyond the friendly unit's final protective fires.

The coordination includes signal operation instructions (SOI) information, signal plan, fire plan, running password, procedures for departure and reentry lines, dismount points, initial rally points, departure and reentry points, and information about the enemy. The platoon leader provides the forward unit leader with the unit identification, size of the patrol, departure and return times, and area of operation. The forward unit leader provides the patrol leader with the following:

- Additional information on terrain
- Known or suspected enemy positions
- Likely enemy ambush sites
- Latest enemy activity
- Detailed information on friendly positions and obstacle locations, including the location of observation posts (OPs)
- Friendly unit fire plan
- Support that the unit can provide; for example, fire support, litter teams, guides, communications, and reaction force

Completion of the Plan

As the platoon leader completes his plan, he considers the following.

Essential and Supporting Tasks. The leader ensures that he has assigned all essential tasks to be performed on the objective, at rally points, at danger areas, at security or surveillance locations, along the route(s), and at passage lanes.

Key Travel and Execution Times. The leader estimates time requirements for movement to the objective, the leader's reconnaissance of the objective, the establishment of security and surveillance, the completion of all assigned tasks on the objective, the movement to an objective rally point to debrief the platoon, and the return to and through friendly lines.

Primary and Alternate Routes. The leader selects primary and alternate routes to and from the objective. The return routes should differ from the routes to the objective.

Signals. The leader should consider the use of special signals, such as arm and hand signals, flares, voice, whistles, radios, and infrared equipment. All signals must be rehearsed so that all soldiers know what they mean.

Challenge and Password Forward of Friendly Lines. The challenge and password from the SOI must not be used beyond the forward edge of the battle area (FEBA). In the odd-number system, the leader specifies an odd number. The challenge can be any number less than the specified number. The password is the number that must be added to it to equal the specified number.

The platoon leader can also designate a running password. This code word alerts a unit that friendly soldiers are approaching in a less than organized manner and possibly under pressure. This may be used to get soldiers quickly through a compromised passage of friendly lines. The running password is followed by the number of soldiers approaching (for example, "Moosebreath five"). This prevents the enemy from joining a group in an attempt to penetrate a friendly unit.

Location of Leaders. The leader considers where he and the platoon sergeant and other key leaders should be located for each phase of the patrol mission. The platoon sergeant is normally with the following elements for each type of patrol:

- On a raid or ambush, he normally controls the support element.
- On an area reconnaissance, he normally stays in the objective rally point (ORP).
- On a zone reconnaissance, he normally moves with the reconnaissance element that sets up the linkup point.

Actions on Enemy Contact. Unless required by the mission, the platoon avoids enemy contact. The leader's plan must address actions on chance contact at each phase of the patrol mission. The platoon's ability to continue the mission will depend on how early contact is made, whether the platoon is able to break contact successfully (so that its subsequent direction of movement is undetected), and whether the platoon receives any casualties as a result of the contact.

The plan must also address the handling of seriously wounded soldiers and those killed in action (KIAs), as well as the handling of prisoners who are captured as a result of chance contact and are not part of the planned mission.

Contingency Plans. The leader leaves for many reasons throughout the planning, coordination, preparation, and execution of his patrol mission. Each time the leader departs without radio or wire communications, he must issue a five-point contingency plan that covers:

1. Where the leader is going.
2. Who he is taking with him.
3. The amount of time he plans to be gone.
4. The actions taken if the leader does not return.
5. The unit's and the leader's actions on chance contact while the leader is gone.

RALLY POINTS

The leader considers the use and locations of rally points. A rally point is a place designated by the leader where the platoon moves to reassemble and reorganize if it becomes dispersed.

Selection of Rally Points

The leader physically reconnoiters routes to select rally points whenever possible. He selects tentative points if he can conduct only a map reconnaissance. He confirms them by actual inspection as the platoon moves through them. Rally points must:

- Be easy to find
- Have cover and concealment
- Be away from natural lines of drift
- Be defendable for short periods

Types of Rally Points

The most common types of rally points are initial, en route, objective, reentry, and near- and far-side rally points. Soldiers must know which rally point to move to at each phase of the patrol mission. They should know what actions are required there and how long they are to wait at each rally point before moving to another.

Initial Rally Point (IRP)

An IRP is a place inside friendly lines where a unit may assemble and reorganize if it makes enemy contact during the departure of friendly lines or before reaching the first en route rally point.

Enroute Rally Point (ERP)

The leader designates ERPs every 100 to 400 meters (based on the terrain, vegetation, and visibility). When the leader designates a new ERP, the previously designated one goes into effect. This precludes uncertainty over which one soldiers should move to if contact is made immediately after the leader designates a new rally point. There are three ways to designate a rally point:

1. Physically occupy it for a short period. This is the preferred method.
2. Pass by at a distance and designate using arm and hand signals.
3. Walk through and designate using arm and hand signals.

Objective Rally Point (ORP)

The ORP is a point out of sight, sound, and small-arms range of the objective area. It is normally located in the direction that the platoon plans to move after completing its actions on the objective. The ORP is tentative until the objective is pinpointed. Actions at or from the ORP include:

- Reconnoitering the objective
- Issuing a fragmentary order (FRAGO)
- Disseminating information from reconnaissance if contact was not made
- Making final preparations before continuing operations; for example, recamouflaging; preparing demolitions; lining up rucksacks for quick recovery; preparing enemy prisoner of war (EPW) bindings, first-aid kits, and litters; and inspecting weapons
- Accounting for soldiers and equipment after actions at the objective are complete
- Reestablishing the chain of command after actions at the objective are complete

Occupation of an ORP by a Squad. In planning the occupation of an ORP, the squad leader follows this sequence:

- Halt beyond sight, sound, and small-arms weapons range of the tentative ORP (200 to 400 meters in good visibility; 100 to 200 meters in limited visibility).
- Position security.
- Move forward with a compass man and one member of each fire team to confirm the location of the ORP and determine its suitability. Issue a five-point contingency plan before departure.
- Position the Team A soldier at 12 o'clock and the Team B soldier at 6 o'clock in the ORP. Issue them a contingency plan and return with the compass man.

- Lead the squad into the ORP; position Team A from 9 to 3 o'clock and Team B from 3 to 9 o'clock.

The squad may also occupy the ORP by force. This requires more precise navigation but eliminates separating the squad.

Occupation of an ORP by a Platoon. The platoon leader should consider the same sequence in planning the occupation of an ORP. He brings a soldier from each squad on his reconnaissance of the ORP and positions them at the 10, 2, and 6 o'clock positions. The first squad in the order of march establishes the base leg (10 to 2 o'clock). The trailing squads occupy from 2 to 6 o'clock and 6 to 10 o'clock positions, respectively.

Reentry Rally Point (RRP)

The RRP is located out of sight, sound, and small-arms weapons range of the friendly unit through which the platoon will return. This also means that the RRP should be outside the final protective fires of the friendly unit. The platoon occupies the RRP as a security perimeter.

Near- and Far-Side Rally Points

These rally points are on the near and far sides of danger areas. If the platoon makes contact while crossing the danger area and control is lost, soldiers on either side move to the rally point nearest them. They establish security; reestablish the chain of command; determine their personnel and equipment status; and continue the patrol mission, link up at the ORP, or complete their last instructions.

LEADER'S RECONNAISSANCE OF THE OBJECTIVE

The plan must include the leader's reconnaissance of the objective once the platoon or squad establishes the ORP. During his reconnaissance, the leader pinpoints the objective; selects security, support, and assault positions for his squads and fire teams; and adjusts his plan based on his observation of the objective. Each type of patrol requires different tasks during the leader's reconnaissance. The platoon leader takes different elements with him. The leader must plan time to return to the ORP, complete his plan, disseminate information, issue orders and instructions, and allow his squads to make any additional preparations.

REENTRY OF FRIENDLY LINES

The platoon leader's initial planning and coordination must include the reentry of friendly lines and should follow this sequence:

- The platoon halts in the RRP and establishes security.
- The platoon leader radios the code word advising the friendly unit of its location and that it is ready to return. The friendly unit must acknowledge the message and confirm that guides are waiting before the platoon moves from the RRP.
- If radio communications are not possible, the platoon leader, RATELO, and a two-man (buddy team) security element move forward and attempt to contact an OP using the challenge and password. The OP notifies the friendly unit that the platoon is ready to return and requests a guide.
- If the platoon leader cannot find an OP, he moves with the RATELO and security element to locate the coordinated reentry point. He must move straight toward (and away from) friendly lines, never parallel to them. All lateral movement should be outside of small-arms weapons range. (*Note*: The platoon leader should attempt this procedure only during daylight. At night, he should use other backup signals to make contact with friendly units. The preferred method is to wait until daylight if contact with the friendly unit cannot be made as planned.)
- Once the friendly unit acknowledges the return of the platoon, the platoon leader issues a five-point contingency plan and moves with his RATELO and a two-man (buddy team) security element on a determined azimuth and pace to the reentry point.
- The platoon leader uses far and near recognition signals to establish contact with the guide.
- The platoon leader signals the platoon forward (radio) or returns and leads it to the reentry point. He may post the security element with the guide at the enemy side of the reentry point.
- The platoon sergeant counts and identifies each soldier as he passes through the reentry point.
- The guide leads the platoon to the assembly area.
- The platoon leader reports to the command post of the friendly unit. He tells the commander everything of tactical value concerning the friendly unit's area of responsibility.

RECONNAISSANCE PATROLS

The three types of reconnaissance patrols are area, zone, and route. Reconnaissance patrols provide timely and accurate information on the enemy and terrain. The commander must inform the patrol leader of the specific information requirements for each mission.

Organization

Besides the common elements, reconnaissance patrols use a reconnaissance team and/or a reconnaissance and security (R&S) team. Reconnaissance teams reconnoiter the objective area once the security teams are in position. Normally these are two-man (buddy) teams to reduce the possibility of detection. R&S teams are normally used in a zone reconnaissance but may be useful in any situation when it is impractical to separate the responsibilities for reconnaissance and security.

Area Reconnaissance

An area reconnaissance is conducted to obtain information about a specified location and the area around it. The location may be given as a grid coordinate or an objective on an overlay. In an area reconnaissance, the platoon or squad uses surveillance or vantage points around the objective from which to observe it and the surrounding area. After observing the objective for a specified time, all elements return to the ORP and report their observations to the leader or the recorder. Once all information is collected, it is disseminated to every soldier.

Zone Reconnaissance

A zone reconnaissance is conducted to obtain information on enemy, terrain, and routes within a specified zone. Zone reconnaissance techniques include the use of moving elements, stationary teams, or a series of area reconnaissance actions.

Moving Elements

The leader plans the use of squads or fire teams moving along multiple routes to cover the entire zone. Methods for planning the movement of multiple elements through a zone include the fan, the box, converging routes, and successive sectors.

Fan Method. The leader first selects a series of ORPs throughout the zone. The platoon establishes security at the first ORP. Each R&S team moves from the ORP along a different fan-shaped route that overlaps with others to ensure reconnaissance of the entire area. The leader maintains a reserve at the ORP. When all R&S teams have returned to the ORP, the platoon collects the information and disseminates it to every soldier before moving on to the next ORP.

Fan Method

Box Method. The leader sends his R&S teams from the ORP along routes that form a boxed-in area. He sends other teams along routes through the area within the box. All teams meet at a linkup point at the far side of the box from the ORP.

Box Method

Converging Routes Method. The leader selects routes from the ORP through the zone to a linkup point at the far side of the zone from the ORP. Each R&S team moves along a specified route and uses the fan method to reconnoiter the area between routes. The leader designates a time for all teams to linkup.

Converging Routes Method
Using Fans Enroute

Successive Sector Method. The leader divides the zone into a series of sectors. Within each sector, the platoon uses the converging routes method to reconnoiter to an intermediate linkup point, where it collects and disseminates the information gathered so far before reconnoitering the next sector.

Successive Sector Method

Stationary Teams
Using this technique, the leader positions surveillance teams in locations where they can collectively observe the entire zone for long-term, continuous information gathering. He must consider sustainment requirements when developing his soldiers' load plan.

Multiple Area Reconnaissance
The leader tasks each of his squads to conduct a series of area reconnaissance actions along a specified route.

Route Reconnaissance
A route reconnaissance is conducted to obtain detailed information about one route and all the adjacent terrain or to locate sites for emplacing obstacles. A route reconnaissance is oriented on a road; a narrow axis, such as an infiltration lane; or a general direction of attack. Normally, engineers are attached to the infantry unit for a complete route reconnaissance. Infantry can conduct a hasty route reconnaissance without engineer support. A route reconnaissance results in detailed information about trafficability, enemy activity, NBC contamination, and aspects of adjacent terrain from both the enemy and the friendly viewpoint. In planning a route reconnaissance the leader considers the following:
- The preferred method for conducting a route reconnaissance is the fan method described above. The leader must ensure that the fans are extensive enough to reconnoiter intersecting routes beyond direct-fire range of the main route.
- If all or part of the proposed route is a road, the leader must treat the road as a danger area. The platoon moves parallel to the road using a covered and concealed route. When required, R&S teams move close to the road to reconnoiter key areas.

Route Reconnaissance Using Fans

COMBAT PATROL

Combat patrols are conducted to destroy or capture enemy soldiers or equipment; destroy installations, facilities, or key points; or harass enemy forces. They also provide security for larger units. The two types of combat patrol missions are *ambush* and *raid*.

Organization

Besides the common elements, combat patrols also have the following elements and teams.

Assault Element

The assault element seizes and secures the objective and protects special teams as they complete their assigned actions on the objective.

Security Element

The security element provides security at danger areas, secures the ORP, isolates the objective, and supports the withdrawal of the rest of the platoon once it completes its assigned actions on the objective.

Support Element

The support element provides direct fire support and may control indirect fires for the platoon.

Breach Element

The breach element breaches the enemy's obstacles when required.

Demolition Team

Demolition teams are responsible for preparing and exploding the charges to destroy equipment, vehicles, or facilities on the objective.

Search Team

The assault element may comprise two-man (buddy) teams or four-man (fire team) search teams to search bunkers, buildings, or tunnels on the objective. These teams may search the objective or kill zone for casualties, documents, or equipment.

Leader's Reconnaissance of the Objective

In a combat patrol, the leader has additional considerations when conducting his reconnaissance of the objective from the ORP. He is normally the assault element leader, and should also take the support element leader, the security element leader, and a surveillance team (a two-man team from the assault element) with him. The leader designates a release point halfway between the ORP and the objective. Squads and fire teams separate at the release point and move to their assigned positions. The platoon leader confirms the location of the objective and determines that it is suitable for the assault or ambush. He notes the terrain and identifies where he can place mines or Claymores to cover dead space. He notes any other features of the objective that may cause him to alter his plan. If the objective is the kill zone for an ambush, the leader's reconnaissance party should not cross the objective—doing so would leave tracks that might compromise the mission. The platoon leader confirms the suitability of the assault and support positions and routes from them back to the ORP. The platoon leader posts the surveillance team and issues a five-point contingency plan before returning to the ORP.

AMBUSH

An ambush is a surprise attack from a concealed position on a moving or temporarily halted target. Antiarmor ambushes are established when the mission is to destroy enemy armored or mechanized forces. Ambushes are classified by category—hasty or deliberate; type—point or area; and formation—linear or L-shaped. The leader uses a combination of category, type, and formation in developing his ambush plan. The key planning considerations include:

- Covering the entire kill zone by fire
- Using existing or reinforcing obstacles (Claymores and other mines) to keep the enemy in the kill zone
- Protecting the assault and support elements with mines, Claymores, or explosives
- Using security elements or teams to isolate the kill zone
- Assaulting into the kill zone to search dead and wounded, assemble prisoners, and collect equipment (the assault element must be able to move quickly through its own protective obstacles)
- Timing the actions of all elements of the platoon to preclude loss of surprise
- Using only one squad to conduct the entire ambush and rotating squads over time from the ORP (this technique is useful when the ambush must be manned for a long time)

Linear Ambush

In an ambush using a linear formation, the assault and support elements deploy parallel to the enemy's route. This positions both elements on the long axis of the kill zone and subjects the enemy to flanking fire. This formation can be used in close terrain that restricts the enemy's ability to maneuver against the platoon or in open terrain, provided a means of keeping the enemy in the kill zone can be effected.

Linear Ambush Formation

L-Shaped Ambush

In an L-shaped ambush, the assault element forms the long leg parallel to the enemy's direction of movement along the kill zone. The support element forms the short leg at one end of and at right angles to the assault element.

L-shaped Ambush Formation

This provides both flanking (long leg) and enfilading (short leg) fires against the enemy. The L-shaped ambush can be used at a sharp bend in a trail, road, or stream. It should not be used where the short leg would have to cross a straight road or trail.

Hasty Ambush

A platoon or squad conducts a hasty ambush when it makes visual contact with an enemy force and has time to establish an ambush without being detected. The actions for a hasty ambush must be well rehearsed so that soldiers know what to do on the leader's signal. They must also know what action to take if detected before they are ready to initiate the ambush.

Deliberate Ambush

A deliberate ambush is conducted against a specific target at a predetermined location. The leader requires detailed information in planning a deliberate ambush, including:

- Size and composition of the targeted enemy unit
- Weapons and equipment available to the enemy
- The enemy's route and direction of movement
- Times that the targeted unit will reach or pass specified points along the route

Point Ambush

In a point ambush, soldiers deploy to attack an enemy in a single kill zone. The security or surveillance teams should be positioned first, and the support element should be in position before the assault element moves forward of the release point. The support element must overwatch the movement of the assault element into position.

The platoon leader is the leader of the assault element. He must check each soldier once the assault position has been established. He signals the surveillance team to rejoin the assault element.

Actions of the *assault element* include:

- Identify individual sectors of fire as assigned by the platoon leader. Emplace aiming stakes.
- Emplace Claymores and other protective devices.
- Emplace Claymores, mines, or other explosives in dead space within the kill zone.
- Camouflage positions.
- Take weapons off "SAFE." Moving the selection lever on the weapon causes a metallic click that could compromise the ambush if soldiers

wait until the enemy is in the kill zone. This must be the last action performed by all soldiers before waiting to initiate the ambush.

Actions of the *support element* include:

- Identify sectors of fire for all weapons, especially machine guns. Emplace limiting stakes to prevent friendly fires from hitting the assault element in an L-shaped ambush.
- Emplace Claymores and other protective devices.

Instructions to security teams must include how to notify the platoon leader of the enemy's approach into the kill zone (SALUTE [size, activity, location, unit, time, equipment] report). The security element must also keep the platoon leader informed if any enemy forces are following the lead force.

The platoon leader must determine how large an element his ambush can engage successfully. He must be prepared to let units pass that are too large and report to higher headquarters any units that pass his ambush unengaged.

The platoon leader initiates the ambush. He may use a command-detonated Claymore and should also plan a backup method for initiating the ambush should the primary means fail. This should also be a casualty-producing device such as a machine gun. This information must be passed out to all soldiers and practiced during rehearsals.

Soldiers must have a means of engaging the enemy in the kill zone during periods of limited visibility if it becomes necessary to initiate the ambush then. Use of tracers must be weighed against how it might help the enemy identify friendly positions. The platoon leader may use handheld or indirect illumination flares.

The platoon leader should include indirect fire support as part of his plan. Indirect fires can cover the flanks of the kill zone to help isolate it. They can also help the platoon disengage if the ambush is compromised or the platoon must depart the ambush site under pressure.

The platoon leader must have a good plan to signal the advance of the assault element into the kill zone to begin its search and collection activities. Smoke may not be visible to the support element. All soldiers must know and practice relaying this signal during rehearsals.

The assault element must be prepared to move across the kill zone using individual movement techniques if there is any return fire once they begin to search. Otherwise, the assault element moves across by bounding fire teams. Other actions in the kill zone include the following.

- Collect and secure all EPWs and move them out of the kill zone before searching bodies. Establish a location for EPWs and enemy wounded who will not be taken back that provides them cover yet allows them to be found easily by their units.

- Search from one side to the other and mark bodies that have been searched to ensure that the area is thoroughly covered.
- Use the two-man search technique. As the search team approaches a dead enemy soldier, one man guards while the other man searches.
- Identify and collect equipment to be carried back and prepare it for transport. (Clear all weapons and place them on "safe.")
- Identify and collect remaining equipment for destruction. The demolition team prepares dual-primed explosives (C4 with two M60 fuse lighters and time fuse) and awaits the signal to initiate. This is normally the last action performed before departing the objective and may signal the security elements to return to the ORP.

The platoon leader must plan the withdrawal from the ambush site:

- Elements normally withdraw in the reverse order that they established their positions.
- The elements may return first to the release point, then to the ORP, depending on the distance between elements.
- The security element at the ORP must be alert to assist the platoon's return to the ORP. It maintains security for the ORP while the rest of the platoon prepares to leave.

Area Ambush

In an area ambush, soldiers deploy in two or more related point ambushes. A platoon is the smallest unit to conduct an area ambush. Platoons conduct area ambushes where enemy movement is largely restricted to trails or streams.

The platoon leader selects one principal ambush site around which he organizes outlying ambushes. These secondary sites are located along the enemy's most likely approach to and escape from the principal ambush site. Squad-sized elements are normally responsible for each ambush site. They establish an area ambush as described above.

The platoon leader must determine the best employment of his machine guns. He normally positions them both with the support element of the principal site.

Squads responsible for outlying ambushes do not initiate their ambushes until after the principal one is initiated. They then engage to prevent enemy forces from escaping or reinforcing.

Antiarmor Ambush

The purpose of an antiarmor ambush is to destroy armored vehicles. A squad can conduct a dismounted antiarmor ambush, organizing into an armor-killer team and a support-and-security team. The armor-killer team fires into the kill zone. Normally, the Dragon is the main weapon of this team. Where fields of fire are less than 100 meters, light antitank weapons (LAWs) may be the main antiarmor weapon. In that case, the armor-killer team must mass LAW fires into the kill zone to make sure the enemy vehicle is destroyed. The support-and-security team provides security and should be positioned where it can cover the withdrawal of the armor-killer team.

ARMOR-KILLER TEAM

LAW
SAW

DRAGON
M16

SQUAD LEADER
LAW
M16

SUPPORT/SECURITY TEAM

LAW
M203

M60

LAW
SAW

R/S
M16

ASST SQUAD LEADER
M203

Squad Antiarmor Ambush

At the Ambush Site. When the squad arrives at the ambush site, the leader reconnoiters and picks the kill zone. Good positions have the following attributes:

- Good fields of fire
- Cover and concealment
- An obstacle between the teams and the kill zone
- Covered and concealed withdrawal routes

Establishing an Antiarmor Ambush. Position a support-and-security team first, and provide security on both flanks. Position the Dragon and then the machine gun so they can cover the kill zone.

The leader initiates the ambush when the enemy enters the kill zone. A command-detonated antiarmor mine is an excellent means of initiating the ambush. The Dragon may be used to initiate the ambush, but it has a slow rate of fire, gives off a signature, and may not hit the target. When possible, the first and last vehicles of a column should be destroyed to keep other vehicles from escaping.

The rest of the squad opens fire when the ambush is initiated. Indirect fires should fall into the kill zone as soon as possible. If the kill zone is in range, squad members fire a LAW.

If enemy dismounted troops precede the armored vehicles, the squad leader must decide whether they pose a threat to the ambush. If they can outflank his squad before the enemy armor can be hit, he may decide to withdraw and set up another ambush somewhere else.

RAID

A raid is a combat operation to attack a position or installation followed by a planned withdrawal. Squads do not execute raids. The sequence of platoon actions for a raid is similar to that for an ambush. Additionally, the assault element of the platoon may have to conduct a breach of an obstacle. It may have additional tasks to perform on the objective; for example, demolition of fixed facilities.

TRACKING PATROL

Platoons and squads may receive the mission to follow the trail of an enemy unit. Even while tracking, they still gather information about the enemy, the route, and surrounding terrain.

Training

Soldiers must be taught to move stealthily and well trained in tracking techniques. Once soldiers are deployed into an area of operations, training continues so that the platoon can learn about local soil, climate, vegetation, animals, vehicles, footwear, and other factors.

Organization

When the platoon receives the mission to conduct a tracking patrol, it assigns the task of tracking to only one squad. The remaining squads and attachments provide security.

Trail Signs

Men, machines, and animals leave signs of their presence as they move through an area. These signs can be as subtle as an odor or as obvious as a well-worn path. All soldiers can read obvious signs such as roads, worn trails, or tracks in sand and snow; however, attention to detail, common sense, alertness, logic, and knowledge of the environment and enemy habits

R ●	PRIMARY TRACKER (point)
AR ●	SECURITY
WITHIN EYE CONTACT ↕	
SL ●	PATROL LEADER
TL ●	RATELO (recorder)
GRN ●	PACE MAN
TL ●	
AR ●	SECURITY
10–30 METERS ↕	
GRN ●	SECURITY
R ●	REAR SECURITY (cover trail)

Tracking Patrol

enable soldiers to obtain better information from signs they find in the battle area.

Trail and Sign Analysis
Once the first sign is discovered, it must not be disturbed or covered and should be analyzed carefully before the patrol follows the enemy. If the sign is found at the site of enemy activity, the exact occurrence can often be reconstructed. If a trail is the first sign found, the tracker can still determine such facts as the size and composition of the groups being tracked, their direction, and their general condition. The tracker must determine as much as possible about the enemy before following it, and his knowledge of the enemy continues to grow as he finds additional signs.

Finding the Trail
Finding the trail is the first task of the tracking team. The tracking team can reconnoiter around a known location of enemy activity when the trail cannot be found in the immediate area. There are two ways to hunt for a trail:
1. The tracking team can locate and follow the enemy's trail from a specific area or location where the enemy has been seen. This can be a camp or base or the site of an enemy attack or enemy contact.
2. The route of a friendly unit may cross a trail left by an enemy group. This can be by chance, or the team can deliberately take a route it believes will cut across one or more probable enemy routes.

Regaining a Lost Trail
If the tracker loses the trail, he immediately stops. The tracking team then retraces its path to the last enemy sign and marks this point. The team studies the sign and the area around it for any clue as to where the enemy went. It looks for signs that the enemy scattered, backtracked, doglegged, or used any other countertracking method. If the trail still cannot be found, the team establishes security in a spot that avoids destroying any sign. Then the tracker and an assistant look for the trail by "boxing" the area around the last sign. The tracking team always returns to the same path, away from the last sign, to create as few trails as possible.

PRESENCE PATROL
U.S. forces are deployed increasingly in support of stability and support operations (SASO) missions all around the world. The infantry platoon plans and conducts a presence patrol much the same as a combat patrol. The primary difference is that the patrol wants to be seen both as a show of force and to lend confidence and stability to the local population of the host nation

(HN). As its name implies, this patrol is constituted to achieve a presence. A presence patrol can be used only if a peace agreement has been negotiated between belligerents. The presence patrol is armed, and it conducts the planning and preparation necessary for combat operations at all times. The patrol would be used as a component of a larger force conducting stability and or support operations.

The platoon could be tasked to conduct mounted (if augmented with vehicles) or dismounted patrols planned by the higher headquarters to accomplish one or more of the following:
- Confirm or supervise an agreed cease-fire
- Gain information
- Cover gaps between OPs or checkpoints
- Show a stability force presence
- Reassure isolated communities
- Inspect existing or vacated positions of former belligerents
- Escort former belligerents or local populations through trouble spots

PATROL BASES
A patrol base is a position set up when a squad or platoon conducting a patrol halts for an extended period. When the unit must halt for a long time in a place not protected by friendly troops, it takes both active and passive security measures. Patrol bases should be occupied no longer than 24 hours, and the same patrol base is never used twice. Patrol bases are used for the following purposes:
- To avoid detection by stopping all movement
- For hiding during a long, detailed reconnaissance of an objective area
- To eat, clean weapons and equipment, and rest
- To plan and issue orders
- To reorganize after infiltrating an enemy area
- As a base from which to conduct several consecutive or concurrent operations such as ambush, raid, reconnaissance, or security

Site Selection
A tentative site is normally selected from a map or by aerial reconnaissance. Its suitability must be confirmed before occupation. An alternate site is selected in the event the first site is unsuitable or must be evacuated unexpectedly. The site should be on terrain of little tactical value to the enemy, off natural lines of drift, difficult for foot movement, and near a source of water; offer cover and concealment; and be defensible for a short period of time.

Occupation of the Patrol Base

The area is reconnoitered, and when it is determined to be secure, the patrol enters from a 90-degree turn. The platoon sergeant and the last fire team get rid of any tracks from the turn. A two-man OP is left at the turn. The platoon moves into the position with squad leaders moving to the left flank of their squad sector. The platoon leader checks the position, starting at 6 o'clock and moving in a clockwise direction. He meets each squad leader at the squad's left flank, adjusts the perimeter as needed, and repositions machine guns if he finds better locations.

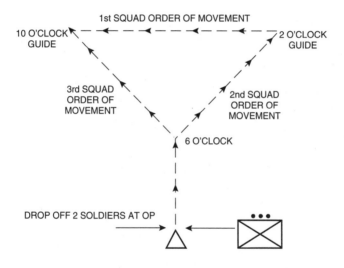

Occupation of a Patrol Base

When the perimeter is secure, the platoon leader directs each squad to conduct a reconnaissance to the front of its sector. Each squad sends out a team from the left flank of the squad sector, which moves a distance away from the position as directed by the platoon leader (200 to 400 meters, depending on terrain and vegetation). It then moves clockwise and reenters the patrol base at the right flank of the squad sector. The team looks for enemy, water, built-up areas, human habitat, roads, or trails. The platoon leader gathers information from the reconnaissance teams and determines the suitability of the area as a patrol base.

Patrol Base Activities

The considerations for a perimeter defense apply to establishing a patrol base. The leader assigns a priority of work, including the following.

Security

Each squad establishes an OP, and the soldiers quietly dig hasty fighting positions. Priorities of work can be accomplished by two-man positions, with one soldier on guard while the other soldier digs, conducts personal hygiene and maintenance, and eats. Noise and light discipline is enforced. Claymores are put out. Sector sketches and range cards are prepared. Soldiers should use only one point of entry and exit.

Alert Plan

The platoon leader states the alert posture (for example, 50 percent or 33 percent awake) and stand-to time for day and night. He prepares a roster for periodic checks of fighting positions and OPs and ensures that OPs are relieved periodically and that at least one leader is awake at all times. No more than half of the platoon eats at one time.

Withdrawal Plan

The platoon leader prepares a contingency plan for enemy contact, including a signal (for example, star cluster) to withdraw, order of withdrawal (squads not in contact move out first), and rendezvous point.

Maintenance

Leaders ensure that weapons and equipment are cleaned and maintained. Machine guns, radios, and night vision devices are not broken down at the same time. Weapons are not disassembled at night.

Field Sanitation and Personal Hygiene

Latrines are dug and trash points designated. Soldiers shave, wash, and brush teeth daily. A water party is organized to fill all canteens. No trash is left behind, and the position is sterilized upon departure.

8

Urban Operations

This chapter describes the basic techniques, procedures, and special considerations that platoons and squads will use throughout the planning and execution of operations in an urban environment along with some lessons learned during Operations Enduring Freedom and Iraqi Freedom. Remember, however, that in urban combat the principles and fundamentals of combat remain basically the same as in other combat operations.

According to the U.S. Army Center for Lessons Learned, only 5 percent of the casualties sustained during the October 3, 1993, raid by Task Force Ranger in Mogadishu, Somalia, occurred during the conduct of close quarters battle (CQB) inside buildings. The remaining 95 percent were sustained in the streets. Because of global urbanization, combat in built-up areas has become an important mission for the U.S. forces and thus, this type of combat cannot be avoided.

PRINCIPLES OF URBAN MOVEMENT

The principles of urban movement include security, coordinated fires and movement, communications, cover and concealment, speed, momentum, and violence of action.

Security. As with any combat operation, a 360-degree area of security is maintained at all times. In an urban environment the dimension of height must be considered due to the numerous multilevel buildings. This added dimension provides the enemy with more area in which to operate. In larger urban areas, security considerations become truly three-dimensional—subways, sewers, water mains, and other underground structures should be considered.

Coordinated Fires and Movement. Individuals and fire teams coordinate their fire and movements to maintain security. When moving down a street, overwatching fire teams provide suppressive fire for their fellow fire teams. This process is continuous as in the need for 360-degree, three-dimensional situational awareness.

During actual operations it is recommended that one to two light anti-tank weapons or antitank-4s (LAWs or AT-4s) be assigned per fire team to take out vehicles, fortified positions, or other obstacles. Remember that the fire team (four to five assaulters) is the smallest maneuver element. It must move quickly and together in order to handle all contingencies that can't be dealt with by one soldier.

Communications. Radio communications are maintained with the overwatching teams. Use of verbal and nonverbal (day and night) communications should be a part of the unit's standing operating procedure (SOP) and they should be rehearsed. Emphasis is placed on keeping radio traffic to a minimum during the operation and radio communication needs to be planned prior to the operation.

Cover and concealment. Cover is the use of objects, such as thick concrete walls or the engine of a vehicle, which can stop bullets. Concealment is the use of shadows, vegetation, or light structures such as wooden walls to limit the enemy's observation of your position. Do not silhouette yourself in interior doorways. When smoke is used to mask your patrols, remember that while the enemy cannot see you, you cannot see the enemy either. Smoke is more effective when an overwatch or sniper team in a higher position can see past the smoke and engage targets on the other side of the street. However, don't sacrifice speed to employ snipers. Smoke also identifies your position or that your element is active.

Speed. Speed is critical and also it is a form of security. Individual actions must be practiced until muscle memory has been developed through the use of battle drill rehearsals and other unit collective training. When moving outside, stay approximately 1 meter away from the walls of buildings or other structures because bullets that strike the wall travel down/along them.

Momentum. Continual movement of the assault force is a key to mission success. When an assault element stops, it gives the enemy time to go on the offensive and puts friendly forces in a reactive/defensive posture. Assault elements should continue to move and take ground in order to keep the enemy off balance. Offensive movements are better than defensive ones and when possible fight from the top (vertical) down.

Violence of action. Violence of action comes from a "never quit" attitude and in knowing you are better trained and equipped than your enemy. Violence of action also keeps the enemy off guard and unsure of his ability to defeat you.

OFFENSIVE OPERATIONS IN URBAN AREAS

While operating in urban areas, the major offensive collective tasks of a platoon and squad are attacking and clearing buildings. This involves isolating the objective, suppressing the enemy, advancing the assault element, assaulting the building, clearing the building, and consolidating and reorganizing the force. Regardless of the type of urban area or its structural characteristics, there are six interrelated requirements for attacking a defended building:

- Isolation of objective
- Supporting fires
- Tactical movement
- Conducting the breach
- Conducting the assault
- Consolidation and reorganization

Proper application and integration of these requirements reduces casualties and hastens accomplishment of the mission. The type of building to be assaulted, the rules of engagement (ROE), and the nature of the surrounding urban area will determine the method of execution. Platoon and squad leaders consider the assigned task, its purpose, and the method they will use to achieve the desired results. You do not always have to commit your troops to an assigned building, area, or sector. An unmotivated enemy with low morale may surrender before you have to commit troops, while simple negotiations or use of PSYOPS may give the desired results. On the other hand, a motivated and well-trained enemy may require you to commit direct and indirect fire assets into the area (ROE allowing) and this alone may cause a surrender; again keeping you from committing your troops.

Task Organization (Platoon Attack of a Building)

The platoon normally operates as part of a company force in urban operations. However, this chapter will focus on the platoon as if it is acting alone or has become isolated from the rest of the company. The platoon leader normally will organize his platoon into at least two elements: an *assault* element and a *support* element. If engineers are available, they are normally attached to the assault element and they will usually perform breaching tasks. If engineers are not available, the platoon leader may designate a breaching team from within either the assault or the support element or he may task organize a separate breach element. The size of these elements is METT-TC dependent.

Assault Element. The purpose of the assault element is to kill, capture, or force the withdrawal of the enemy from any urban objective and to seize key terrain. The assault element of a platoon may consist of one, two, or three squads. Squad leaders normally organize their two fire teams into two

ASSAULT ELEMENT

PLT   PLT
LDR   RTO

HEADQUARTERS

SQD   TL   GRN   SAW   RFLM   TL   GRN   SAW   RFLM
LDR

ASSAULT SQUAD #1

SQD   TL   GRN   SAW   RFLM   TL   GRN   SAW   RFLM
LDR

ASSAULT SQUAD #2

SUPPORT ELEMENT

PLT   PLT   FO   FO   MG   AG   MG   AG
SGT   MED NCO RTO

HEADQUARTERS   SUPPORT

SQD   TL   GRN   SAW   RFLM   TL   GRN   SAW   RFLM
LDR

SUPPORT RESERVES

Task Organization—Platoon Attack of a Building

clearing teams or, in special circumstances, the squad may be kept as a single assault squad. The assault force could be divided into two clearing teams with a breaching element designated from within one or both teams. As the breaching element and one clearing team move into position at the initial entry point, the remaining clearing team provides additional fire support. Once the lead clearing team has gained a foothold in the building, the remaining clearing team enters and secures the foothold.

Support Element. Its purpose is to provide immediate suppressive fire support to enable the assault element to close with the enemy and to assist in the isolation of the building. The support element at platoon level may consist of the weapons squad (or machine gun teams and antiarmor gunners) and any personnel not designated as part of the assault element. This assistance includes, but is not limited to:

- Suppressing enemy weapons systems and obscuring the enemy's observation within the objective building(s) and adjacent structures
- Isolating the objective building(s) with direct fires to prevent enemy withdrawal, reinforcement, or counterattack
- Obscuring enemy observation of obstacles en route and at the entry point to the objective during breaching operations
- Destroying or suppressing enemy positions with direct fire weapons
- Engaging enemy armor with antitank (AT) weapons
- Securing cleared portions of the objective
- Providing replacements for the assault element
- Providing the resupply of ammunition and pyrotechnics
- Bringing up specific equipment that the assault element could not carry in the initial assault
- Evacuating casualties, prisoners, and civilians

Note: The platoon sergeant must be prepared to rapidly evacuate the wounded from the objective area to the company casualty collection point (CCP). Barricades, rubble in the streets, and demolition of roads may impede ground ambulances; therefore, litter teams may be needed.

Breach Team. The purpose of the breach team is to clear and mark lanes through obstacles during movement and to provide the assault element with access to an urban objective. The platoon leader organizes the force to ensure that breaching teams are identified.

Tactical Movement
When moving in an urban area, squads and platoons use modified variations of the traveling, traveling overwatch, and bounding overwatch movement techniques. Leaders must be aware of the three-dimensional aspect of urban terrain such as streets, buildings, subsurface, and airspace. Because of sniper

Three-Dimensional Urban Terrain

vulnerability, countersniper techniques must be well rehearsed and implemented. Elements move in a manner that prevents the entire force from becoming decisively engaged at one time.

The assault force minimizes the effects of the enemy's defensive fires during movement by using covered and concealed routes, moving only after enemy fires have been suppressed or enemy observation obscured, moving at night or during periods of reduced visibility, selecting routes that will not mask friendly suppressive fires, crossing open areas quickly under the concealment of smoke and suppression provided by the support element, and moving on rooftops not covered by enemy fires. To avoid exposure on the street or to provide mutual support, if possible, the infantry squads may attempt moving through the buildings. The platoon moves along streets and alleys with two squads (one on either side of the street) leading and the third squad in the overwatch. The squads should move using bounding overwatch to quickly locate, identify, engage, and eliminate all enemy weapons systems.

Isolate the Objective or Building

When planning the isolation, leaders determine a three-dimensional and in-depth isolation of the objective (front, flanks, rear, upper stories, and rooftops). They should employ all available direct and indirect fire weapons allowed by the rules of engagement (ROE), including attack helicopters and close air support. Isolating the objective also involves seizing terrain that dominates the area so that the enemy cannot supply, reinforce, or withdraw its defenders. It also includes selecting terrain that provides the ability to place suppressive fire on the objective. (This step may be taken at the same time as securing a foothold.) If isolating the objective is the first step, speed is necessary so that the defender has no time to react.

Assault a Building

The assault element must quickly and violently execute the assault and subsequent clearing operations. The momentum is maintained to deny the enemy time to organize a more determined resistance on other floors or in other rooms.

Approaches. All routes to the breach and or entry point are planned in advance. The best route is confirmed and selected during the leaders' reconnaissance. The route should allow the assault element to approach the breach (entry) point from the blind side, if possible.

Order of March. The method of breach usually determines the order of march. Establishing an order of march aids the team leader with command and control (C^2) and minimizes exposure time in open areas and at the entry point. If the breach has been conducted prior to its arrival, the assault team quickly moves through the breach (entry) point. If a breach has not been made prior to its arrival at the breach (entry) point, and depending on the type of breach to be made, the team leader conducts the breach himself or signals forward the breach man or element.

Conduct of the Breach. Soldiers may be fighting just to get to the breach point; therefore, proper fire and movement will be required all the way to the breach (entry) point. All members not conducting the breach will provide internal support and suppressive fires onto enemy targets and probable enemy positions using direct fire and grenades (ROE dependent). Additionally, the rest of the squad or platoon will provide support to secure (left, right, up, and down) the assault element in the three-dimensional environment. Until an entry point into the building is established, all possible enemy positions and entry ways are watched and suppressed as necessary for potential enemy and booby traps. If possible, the breach is conducted in such a manner as to allow the assault element to continue movement without having to wait at the breach (entry) point. Deception (by use of fragmentation grenades, concussion grenades, or stun grenades in an area other than the actual breach or entry point) should be used to confuse the enemy as to the location of the primary entry point.

Breaching Methods. The three breaching methods discussed here are explosive, ballistic, and mechanical.

1. *Explosive Breach*. This method of breaching requires the use of an explosive composition such as C4, trinitrotoluene (TNT), or a manufactured shape charge directed against the target.

2. *Ballistic Breach*. This method requires the use of a weapon firing a projectile at the breach point.

3. *Mechanical Breach*. This method requires increased physical exertion by one or more soldiers using hand tools such as axes, saws, crowbars, hooligan's tools, or sledgehammers. The mechanical breach is not the preferred primary breaching method because it may be time consuming and defeat the element of surprise. However, the ROE and the situation may require the use of these tools, so soldiers should be proficient in their use.

Breach Locations. The success of the assault element often depends on the speed with which they gain access into the building. It is important that the breach location provide the assault element with covered or concealed access, fluid entry, and the ability to be overwatched by the support element.

Security. Because of the three-dimensional enemy associated with urban terrain, the assault element must maintain 360-degree security during movement to the breach (entry) point. If the assault element is to stop in the vicinity of the breach (entry) point to wait for the breach element to complete its task, the support element must maintain suppressive fire to protect the assault element.

Assault Location. The assault may begin from the top or bottom of the building. Entering at the top and fighting downward is the preferred method of clearing a building. This method is only feasible, however, when the platoon can gain access to an upper floor or rooftop by ladder; from the windows or roofs of adjoining, secured buildings; or by helicopter. Entry at the bottom is common and may be the only option available. When entering from the bottom, breaching a wall is the preferred method because doors and windows may be booby-trapped and covered by fire from inside the structure. If the assault element must enter through a door or window, it should enter from a rear or flank position.

Suppressive Fires during the Assault. The support force provides suppressive fire while the assault force systematically clears the building. It also provides suppressive fire on adjacent buildings to prevent enemy reinforcements or withdrawal. The support force destroys or captures any enemy personnel trying to exit the building. The support force also must deal with civilians displaced by the assault.

Clearing Rooms. The platoon leader must ensure that the clearing squads carry enough room marking equipment and plainly mark cleared rooms from the friendly side in accordance with unit SOPs. Markings must be visible to friendly units even if the operation occurs during limited visibility. The support force must understand which markings will be used and ensure that suppressive fires do not engage cleared rooms and floors. Maintaining awareness of where the assault teams are and which rooms and floors have been cleared is imperative and a key C^2 function for the platoon leader. (See Enter Building and Clear a Room Battle Drill in chapter 4 as an example.)

Direction of Assault Technique of Direct Fire Planning and Control. In this technique, building numbers are assigned in a consistent pattern in relation to the direction of assault. In the example shown below, the buildings are numbered consecutively in a counterclockwise manner. Additionally, the sides of the buildings are color-coded consistently throughout the objective area (WHITE = direction of assault side, GREEN = right side, BLACK = rear side, RED = left side, BLUE = roof). An odd shaped build-

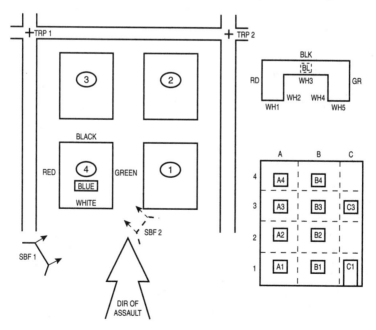

Direction of Assault Technique of Fire Control

ing is also shown. Note that a "four-sided" concept was retained to minimize confusion. Further designations of WHITE 1, WHITE 2, WHITE 3, and so on from left to right can be added to specify which wall will be engaged. Apertures on the buildings are also labeled consecutively using rows and columns, as shown. For example, "OBJ 4, WHITE, window A1" is the lower left-hand window on the direction-of-assault side of OBJ 4. All designations are labeled in relation to the direction of assault.

Enter and Clear a Building

Success or failure in urban terrain is often determined by actions taken instinctively by individual soldiers and fire teams as they encounter complex situations (such as the intermixing of combatants and civilians).

Principles. The principles of precision combat are surprise, speed, and controlled violence of action. These principles do not change regardless of ROE. The three principles of precision combat are each relative to one another, i.e., successful surprise allows increased speed; controlled violence coupled with speed increases surprise.

- *Surprise* is one of the elements necessary for a successful assault at close range. The assault team achieves surprise by attacking at a time and location unexpected by the defender using hand grenades, concussion grenades, or stun grenades. An explosive or ballistic breach will also provide the element of surprise by stunning the occupants of a room.
- *Speed* provides a measure of security to the clearing unit. Speed allows soldiers to use the first few seconds provided by surprise to their advantage. In urban combat, speed is not careless, but careful and deliberate.
- *Controlled violence of action* eliminates or neutralizes the enemy and decreases his chances of inflicting friendly casualties and it involves soldiers with the ability to maintain control of the situation.

Fundamentals of Clearing Operations

Some actions soldiers will take while moving along confined corridors to the room to be cleared, while preparing to enter the room, during room entry and target engagement, and after contact are:

- Move tactically while securing the corridors to the room to be cleared and minimize the equipment soldiers carry to eliminate noise and fatigue.
- If possible, arrive undetected at the entry to the room and in the correct order of entrance.

- Ensure security is maintained outside the room to protect the assault team inside the room.
- Enter quickly and dominate the room.
- Eliminate all enemy soldiers within the room with quick, accurate, and discriminating fires.
- Gain and maintain immediate control of the situation and all personnel in the room.
- Confirm whether enemy casualties are wounded or dead. Search all enemy casualties; disarm them, and segregate the wounded.
- Immediately perform a cursory search of the room and determine if a detailed search is required.
- Evacuate all wounded as quickly as possible. Friendly wounded should be evacuated as soon as they are out of direct small-arms fire. Evacuate any friendly dead.
- Mark the room as cleared in accordance with unit SOP using simple, clearly identifiable markings.
- Provide a situation report (SITREP) in accordance with the unit SOP when the room is cleared.
- Maintain security at all times and be prepared to react to more enemy contact at any moment. Do not neglect rear security.
- Rotate clearing teams to maintain the momentum of the attack.

Clearing Techniques

Methods of movement, firing techniques, weapon positioning, and reflexive shooting are fundamentals used in urban combat. Special clearing techniques may be required when highly restrictive ROE are in effect. The enemy situation may require that the units clear only a few selected buildings methodically to accomplish their mission rather than using firepower to suppress and neutralize buildings in the objective area. On the other hand, a robust ROE may favor the use of overwhelming firepower and units should employ direct and indirect fires, demolitions, and fragmentation or concussion grenades as necessary to assist in clearing an objective defended by an alert and determined force without noncombatants.

Consolidation and Reorganization

The squad and platoon will conduct consolidation and reorganization immediately after each action where soldiers are engaged and ammunition is expended. Consolidation in an urban environment must be quick in order to repel enemy counterattacks and to prevent the enemy from infiltrating back into cleared buildings or floors. Reorganization occurs after consolidation.

These actions prepare the unit to continue the mission by ensuring key leadership positions are filled and important weapon systems are manned. Many reorganization actions occur simultaneously during the consolidation of the objective. For more information, see chapters 4 and 5 on consolidation and reorganization.

DEFENSIVE OPERATIONS IN URBAN AREAS

This section covers the basic planning considerations, weapons selection, preparations, and the construction of a platoon defensive position on urbanized terrain.

Planning the Defense

Leaders plan an urban defense that uses terrain wisely, designates a point of main effort, uses defensive positions that force the enemy to make costly attacks or conduct time-consuming maneuvers to avoid them, and one that achieves surprise. Civilians, ROE, limited collateral damage, and coordination with adjacent units to eliminate the probability of fratricide must be considered.

The squad and platoon's focus for defending in an urban area is the retention of terrain. The platoon will be given either an area of operations (AO) to defend or a battle position to occupy. By using the terrain and fighting from well prepared and mutually supporting positions, a defending force can delay, block, fix, or inflict heavy losses on a much larger attacking force. In urban operations, the platoon is often a strongpoint defense of a building, part of a building, or a group of small buildings that is normally integrated into the company's mission. Weapon systems and personnel are positioned to maximize their capabilities personnel. Supporting fires are incorporated into the overall defensive plan to provide depth to the engagement area (EA). The platoon leader organizes the defense into a series of individual, team, and squad fighting positions located to cover avenues of approach and obstacles and to provide mutual support to repel the enemy advance.

The platoon and squad leader have only two choices in an urban defense—*hasty* or *deliberate*. Time to plan and prepare and knowledge of the enemy is really the only difference between a hasty and deliberate defense. All the troop-leading procedures (TLPs) are the same, many of the priorities of work of the two defense types will be the same, and the two may even take place concurrently. Units are deployed, key weapons emplaced, and fighting positions prepared in accordance with the amount of time available to the unit.

Occupation and Preparation of Positions

Normally, when occupying defensive positions, the platoon takes advantage of the cover and concealment already present and will continue to make improvements to the positions given more time and materials.

The platoon first positions crew-served weapons. Normal defensive priorities of work apply (see chapter 5). Fighting positions in buildings are constructed in the shadows of the room, away from windows and other openings, using appliances, furniture, and other convenient items and materials. Some of the more common fighting positions in an urban area are corners of buildings, behind walls, windows, unprepared loopholes, and the peak of a roof.

Firing Around Cover

Firing From Window

Firing From Loophole

Firing From Peak of Roof

Initial Firing Positions

Priorities of Work

In addition to general defensive priorities of work, special attention is to be given the following in the urban environment:

1. Select key weapons positions (for Javelins and M240B MGs) to cover likely mounted and dismounted avenues of approach. Position

the Javelins where flank engagements will occur inside buildings with adequate space and ventilation for backblast (on upper floors, if possible, for long-range shots). Position squad automatic weapons (SAWs) and machine guns (MGs) near ground level to increase grazing fires or in upper levels if ground rubble obscures grazing fire.

2. Ensure the positions are free of noncombatants. Remove them from the AOs before occupation of the position.
3. Clear fields of fire by utilizing loopholes, aiming stakes, sector stakes, and target reference point (TRP) markings. Construct positions with overhead cover and camouflage (inside and outside).
4. Identify and secure subterranean avenues of approach (sewers, basements) as well as stairwells and rooftops.
5. Stockpile ammunition, food, fire-fighting equipment, and drinking water throughout the depth of your defense.
6. Construct barriers and emplace obstacles to deny the enemy access to streets, underground passages, and buildings, and to slow his

Obstacles Blocking Street

movement. Erect the obstacles in an irregular pattern to hinder enemy movement. Employ the obstacles in depth (if possible). Tie the obstacles in with existing obstacles and cover all obstacles with fire and observation.

7. Improve and mark movement routes between positions and to alternate and supplementary positions. This is accomplished by digging trenches, using sewers and tunnels, creating mouseholes, and emplacing ropes for climbing and rappelling and ladders for ascent and descent.

Other Typical Tasks

Additional defensive preparation tasks may be required in basements, on ground floors, and on upper floors.

Basements and Ground Floors. Basements require preparation similar to that of the ground floor. Any underground system not used by the defender that could provide enemy access to the position must be blocked. Unused doors should be locked or nailed shut as well as blocked and reinforced with furniture, sandbags, or other field expedients. If not required for the defender's movement, hallways should be blocked with furniture and tactical wire. Unused stairs should be blocked with furniture and tactical wire or removed. If possible, all stairs should be blocked, and ladders should be used to move from floor to floor and then removed. Remove all window glass and block unused windows with boards or sandbags to prevent observation and access. Make fighting positions in the floors. If there is no basement, fighting positions can give additional protection from heavy direct-fire weapons. Erect support for ceilings that cannot withstand the weight of rubble from upper floors. Block rooms not required for defense with tactical wire.

Upper Floors. Upper floors require the same preparation as ground floors. Windows need not be blocked, but should be covered with wire mesh, canvas, ponchos, or other heavy material to prevent grenades from being thrown in from the outside. The covering should be loose at the bottom to permit the defender to drop grenades.

Interior Routes. Routes that permit defending forces to move within the building to engage enemy forces from any direction are required. Plan and construct escape routes to permit rapid evacuation of a room or a building. Mouseholes easily identified and marked should be made through interior walls to permit movement between rooms.

Fire Prevention. Buildings that have wooden floors and rafter ceilings require extensive fire prevention measures. Cover the attic floor and other wooden floors with about one to two inches of sand or dirt and position buckets of water for immediate use. Place fire-fighting materials (dirt, sand, fire extinguishers, and blankets) on each floor for immediate use. Fill water basins and bathtubs as a reserve for fire fighting. Turn off all electricity and gas.

Communications. Be aware that structures and a high concentration of electrical power lines may degrade radio communication in built-up areas. Visual signals are often not effective because of the screening effects of buildings and walls and they can signal location and intent to the enemy. Signals must be planned, widely disseminated, and understood by all assigned and attached units. Increased noise makes the effective use of sound signals difficult. Messengers and wire can be used as other means of communication.

Rubbling. Rubbling parts of the building may provide additional cover and concealment for weapons emplacements or serve as an obstacle against the enemy. Ensure you know what you are doing and get permission from higher headquarters.

Rooftops. Platoons must position obstacles on the roofs of flat-topped buildings to prevent helicopters from landing and to deny troops access to your building and adjacent buildings from the roof.

Obstacles. Position obstacles adjacent to buildings to stop or delay vehicles and infantry. Save time and resources by using available materials such as cars, and other available obstacles. The principles of mining are the same except the ground is much harder to deal with and may require special equipment.

Fields of Fire. Selectively clear fields of fire in accord with the weapon capabilities. Designate primary and alternate sectors of fire.

Antitank Weapons Positions. Employ AT weapons in areas that maximize their capabilities. Position AT weapons in upper stories and in pairs (if possible) to allow the same target to be engaged at the same time by pair firing. Ensure the AT systems are secured by additional positions and personnel.

Conduct of the Defense

The conduct of the defense in an urban area is similar to the conduct of the defense in any other area. The process of consolidation and reorganization in an urban area is similar to the process in any other area. Both are discussed in chapter 5.

Javelin Position

COMBAT MULTIPLIERS

An important lesson learned from recent urban operations is the need for a fully integrated combined arms team. The nature of urban operations makes it mostly an infantry operation, however, the more additional combat multipliers the better. The integration of armor and engineers increases lethality and these additional assets must be supported by integrated aviation, field artillery, communications, and logistical elements.

Armored Vehicles

This information is contained in chapter 9.

Engineers

Normally an engineer squad will be attached to an infantry company. Most engineer manual-labor tasks (for example, preparing fighting positions) will have to be completed by infantry units with reinforcing engineer heavy-equipment support and technical supervision.

On offensive missions in support of an infantry platoon, engineers may be required to use explosives to destroy fortifications and strong points that cannot be reduced with the maneuver unit's organic assets, locate and/or remove mines that may hamper the unit's movement, and conduct breaching operations.

On defensive missions in support of an infantry platoon, engineers may be required to construct complex obstacle systems, and/or assist in the preparation of defensive positions and strong points.

Mortars
Mortars are the most responsive indirect fires available to infantry commanders and leaders. Their mission is to provide close and immediate fire support to the maneuver units. Mortars are well suited for combat in urban areas because of their high rate of fire, steep angle of fall, and short minimum range. Platoon leaders and FOs must plan mortar support with the fire support element (FSE) as part of the total fire support plan.

Field Artillery
During urban combat, FA provides direct support, general support, and general support reinforcing to infantry units. In addition to its FA indirect fire support, field artillery is well suited to utilizing their guns in direct fire mode in urban operations. Employing artillery in the direct-fire mode to destroy fortifications should be considered, especially when assaulting well-prepared enemy positions. However, restrictive fire support coordination measures, such as a restrictive fire areas or no-fire areas, may be imposed to protect civilians and critical installations.

Attack Helicopters
Infantry units may receive support by a variety of attack helicopters, including (but not limited to) the AH-64A, AH-64D, OH-58D, and MH-6. Attack helicopters can provide area fire to suppress targets and precision fire to destroy specific targets or breach structures. Attack helicopters provide real-time reconnaissance information through direct viewing of the AO.

9

Combat Support and Combat Service Support

Combat support is any external support provided by the battalion antitank (AT) and mortar platoons, field artillery (FA), close air support (CAS), air defense artillery (ADA), military intelligence (MI), and combat engineers.

INDIRECT FIRE
Normally, the company plans most of the indirect fires and assigns platoons specific responsibilities. The platoon is limited by its ability to observe and initiate fires.

Field Artillery
FA can provide indirect fires to suppress, neutralize, or destroy enemy targets. Because it can mass fire quickly, FA produces more devastating effects on targets than mortars do.

Mortars
Mortars are organic to the battalion and the company and at times may be attached to or in direct support of platoons. They provide responsive fire against closer and smaller targets. Mortars can be used to do the following:
- Attack infantry in the open
- Attack infantry in positions without overhead cover (using variable time [VT] fuses) or with light overhead cover (using delay fuses).
- Suppress enemy positions and armored vehicles
- Obscure the enemy's vision (using white phosphorus)
- Engage the enemy on reverse slopes and in gullies, ditches, built-up areas, and other defilade areas
- Provide continuous battlefield illumination

- Provide obscuring smoke (smoke on the enemy positions) or screening smoke (smoke between the enemy and friendly units)
- Mark enemy locations for direct fire or CAS

DIRECT FIRE

Direct-fire support can be provided by tanks, antitank weapons (TOW, Dragon/Javelin, MK19), and attack helicopters. Leaders can direct tank or antitank and MK19 fires by radio, by phone, or face-to-face. They can identify the target location by target reference point (TRP) or tracer fire, or give the direction, description, and range. Another technique uses the gun barrel or heavy antitank missle (TOW) launcher with the clock method as a baseline for direction—for example, "Enemy tank, 10 o'clock, 1,200 meters." The gun barrel is at 12 o'clock when pointing directly forward from the vehicle or launcher, and it is at 6 o'clock when pointing directly to the rear.

Attack Helicopters

Attack helicopters are mainly antiarmor weapons, but they do have antipersonnel ability with rockets. Aeroscouts usually arrive ahead of the attack aircraft and set up communication with the ground force.

Close Air Support

The U.S. Air Force provides CAS on a preplanned or immediate-need basis. A forward air controller (FAC), on the ground or in the air, acts as a link between the ground force and the aircraft. Friendly positions must always be marked during close air strikes. Smoke grenades, flares, signal mirrors, strobe lights, vehicle lights, and thermal sources are commonly used as markers.

AIR DEFENSE ARTILLERY

Divisional air defense weapons may support and be positioned with infantry units. All ADA fires are controlled by orders and procedures established by higher headquarters.

MILITARY INTELLIGENCE

Ground surveillance radar and remote sensor teams from the division MI battalion may be attached to or support infantry units.

COMBAT ENGINEERS

Engineers are a valuable asset, and higher commanders determine their priority. Engineers can help the infantry prepare obstacles or positions by providing technical advice or the skills to do work beyond the ability of infantry units.

COMBAT SERVICE SUPPORT AT PLATOON LEVEL

Combat service support (CSS) operations at platoon level are a vital part of infantry operations. They consist of logistical, personnel, and health service functions. CSS is integrated into the tactical planning process from the starting phases of operations. Well-planned and -executed CSS is a large part of mission accomplishment and success of combat operations. Like CS, CSS is a combat multiplier. Soldiers well supplied with food, water, ammunition, shelter, and medical care are more successful in accomplishing their missions than those who are not. At platoon level, the platoon sergeant is the key CSS operator. He consolidates information and needs from the squad leaders, requests support from the executive officer (XO) or first sergeant, and assigns responsibilities to squads.

Individual Responsibilities for CSS

This paragraph focuses on specific individual responsibilities within the platoon's CSS chain.

Platoon Sergeant. As the platoon's main CSS operator, the PSG executes the platoon's logistical plan based on platoon and company standing operating procedures (SOPs). The PSG's CSS duties include:

- Participating in CSS rehearsals at the company level and integrating CSS into the platoon's maneuver rehearsals.
- Receiving, consolidating, and forwarding all administrative, personnel, and casualty reports to the first sergeant as directed or in accordance with unit SOP.
- Obtaining supplies, equipment (except Class VIII), and mail from the supply sergeant and ensuring proper distribution.
- Supervising evacuation of casualties, enemy prisoners of war (EPWs), and damaged equipment.
- Maintaining the platoon's manning roster.

Squad Leader. Each squad leader's CSS duties include:

- Ensuring soldiers perform proper maintenance on all assigned equipment.
- Compiling personnel and logistics reports for the platoon and submitting them to the PSG as directed or in accordance with unit SOP.
- Obtaining supplies, equipment (except Class VIII), and mail from the PSG and ensuring proper distribution.

Platoon Medic. The platoon medic is detached from the battalion medical platoon and attached to the rifle platoon to provide emergency medical treatment (EMT) for sick, injured, or wounded platoon personnel, to include treatment of trauma, opening an airway, starting intravenous fluids, controlling hemorrhage, preventing or treating for shock, splinting fractures or suspected fractures, and providing relief for pain. The EMT performed by the platoon medic is under the supervision of the battalion surgeon or physician's assistant (PA).

The platoon medic is responsible for:
- Triaging injured, wounded, or ill friendly and enemy personnel for priority of treatment.
- Conducting sick call screening for the platoon.
- Evacuating sick, injured, or wounded personnel under the direction of the PSG.
- Assisting in the training of the platoon's combat lifesavers in enhanced first-aid procedures.
- Requisitioning Class VIII supplies from the battalion aid station (BAS) for the platoon according to the tactical SOP (TSOP).
- Recommending locations for platoon casualty collection points (CCPs).
- Providing guidance to the platoon's combat lifesavers as required.

Resupply Operations
Platoon resupply is mainly a "push" system. The platoon receives a standard package of supplies based on past usage factors and planning estimates. Whatever supply technique is directed, leaders must ensure security. This involves security at the resupply point and rotating personnel to ensure continuous manning of crew-served weapons and OPs, leader availability, and unit preparedness in case of enemy attack. Platoons use backhauling to remove residue, casualties, damaged equipment, or excess ammunition to the rear. During each resupply operation, the platoon must plan for backhauling of excess items. Backhauling can be by manpack, vehicles, or aircraft. Effective backhauling lessens the platoon's need to bury, camouflage, or otherwise dispose of unneeded material.

In-Position or Tailgate Technique
The company brings forward supplies, equipment, or both to individual fighting positions. This technique is used when an immediate need exists to resupply single classes of supplies during contact or when contact is imminent. It enables leaders to keep squad members in their fighting positions.

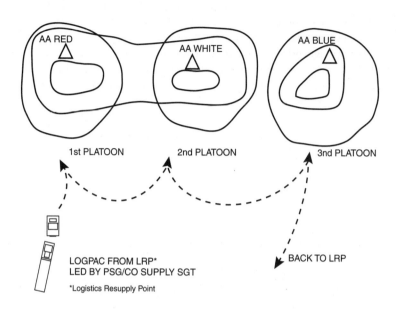

1st PLATOON 2nd PLATOON 3nd PLATOON

LOGPAC FROM LRP*
LED BY PSG/CO SUPPLY SGT

*Logistics Resupply Point

BACK TO LRP

In-Position or Tailgate Resupply Technique

Out-of-Position or Service Station Technique

To use this technique, soldiers must leave their fighting positions. Selected soldiers move to a company resupply point to the rear of the platoon positions, conduct resupply, and return to their fighting position. This technique is used when contact is not likely and for one or several classes of supplies.

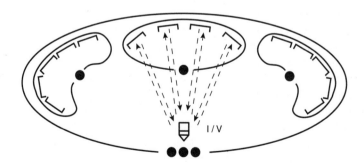

Out-of-Position or Service Station Technique

Preposition Technique

In this technique, the company prepositions supplies and equipment along a route to or at a platoon's destination. The company then directs the platoons to the sites. Although this method is often used during defensive operations to position supplies and equipment in subsequent battle positions (BPs), it can be equally effective in other operations as a cache.

Aerial Resupply

Aerial resupply is not a resupply technique, but it is often used to get supplies and equipment to the platoon. Helicopters are usually more precise than fixed-wing aircraft in delivering supplies, and they are used to deliver supplies and equipment to landing zones (LZs); fixed-wing aircraft are used for drop zones (DZs).

Personnel Service Support

The main platoon combat personnel service support functions are strength accounting and casualty reporting. The platoon leader and NCOs are also responsible for handling EPWs and for programs to counter the impact of stress and continuous operations. Platoon leaders coordinate personnel service support provided by the battalion adjutant (S1), personnel and administration center (PAC), and chaplain through the company headquarters.

Strength Accounting

Leaders use battle rosters to keep up-to-date records of their soldiers and to provide reports to the company at specific intervals. During combat, leaders also provide hasty strength reports upon request or when important strength changes occur.

Killed in Action

The platoon leader designates a location for the collection of KIAs. All personal effects remain with the body; however, the squad leader removes and safeguards any equipment and issue items. He keeps these until he can turn the equipment and issue items over to the platoon sergeant. The PSG turns over the KIA to the 1SG. As a rule, the platoon should not transport KIA remains on the same vehicle as wounded soldiers. KIAs are normally transported to the rear on empty ammunition resupply trucks, but this depends on unit SOP.

Casualty Reporting

During lulls in the battle, platoons give by-name (roster line number) casualty information to the company. Forms are completed to report KIAs who were not recovered, as well as missing or captured soldiers. A separate form is used to report KIAs who have been recovered and soldiers who have been wounded.

Handling Enemy Prisoners of War

EPWs are treated in accordance with international law. They are allowed to keep personal protective equipment, are not physically or mentally abused, and are treated humanely. If they cannot be evacuated within a reasonable time, they are given food, water, and, if necessary, first aid.

The five-S procedure reminds soldiers of the basic principles for handling EPWs, which include tagging prisoners and all captured equipment and materiel. The five Ss are: search, segregate, silence, safeguard, and speed to the rear.

Other Services

Other personnel service support functions include awards, leaves, mail, financial matters, legal assistance, rest and recreation, and other services related to the morale and welfare of soldiers.

Health Service Support

Health service support consists of the prevention, treatment, and evacuation of casualties.

Injury Prevention

Prevention is emphasized; soldiers can lose their combat effectiveness because of nonhostile injuries or disease. Observing field hygiene and sanitation, preventing weather-related injuries, and considering the soldier's overall condition can cut back on the number of casualties.

Treatment and Evacuation

Initial Steps: When combat begins and casualties occur, the platoon first must provide initial care to those wounded in action (WIA). Casualty evacuation is accomplished through the administration of first aid (self-aid/buddy aid), enhanced first aid (by the combat lifesaver), and EMT (by the trauma specialist/platoon medic). Casualties are cared for at the point of injury or under nearby cover and concealment. During the fight, casualties should remain under cover where they received initial treatment. As soon as the situation allows, squad leaders arrange for casualty evacuation to the platoon casualty collection point (CCP). The platoon normally sets up the CCP in a covered and concealed location to the rear of the platoon position. At the CCP, the platoon medic conducts triage on all casualties, takes steps to stabilize their conditions, and starts the process of moving them to the rear for advanced treatment. Before the platoon evacuates casualties to the CCP or beyond, leaders should remove all key operational items and equipment from each person. This includes signal operating instructions (SOI), maps, position-locating devices, and laser pointers. Every unit should establish an SOP for handling the weapons and ammunition of its WIA.

Movement: CASEVAC (casualty evacuation) is the term used to refer to the movement of casualties by air or ground on nonmedical vehicles or aircraft. CASEVAC operations normally involve the initial movement of wounded or injured soldiers to the nearest medical treatment facility. Casualty evacuation operations may also be employed in support of mass casualty operations. Medical evacuation includes the provision of in route medical care, whereas CASEVAC does not provide any medical care during movement.

Timely movement of casualties from the battlefield is important. Squad leaders are responsible for casualty evacuation from the battlefield to the platoon CCP. At the CCP, the senior trauma specialist assists the platoon sergeant and first sergeant in arranging evacuation by ground or air ambulance or by nonstandard means. From the platoon area, casualties are normally evacuated to the company CCP and then back to the battalion aid station (BAS). The company 1SG, along with the PSG, is normally responsible for movement of the casualties from the platoon and company CCP. The unit SOP should address this activity, including the marking of casualties during limited visibility operations. Once the casualties are collected, evaluated, and treated, they are prioritized for evacuation back to the company CCP. Once they arrive, the above process is repeated while awaiting their evacuation back to the BAS or to other medical facilities. When the company is widely dispersed, the casualties may be evacuated directly from the platoon CCP by vehicle or helicopter if they are able to fly. Coordination is made for additional transportation assets as necessary. The senior military person present determines whether to request medical evacuation and assigns precedence. Casualties will be picked up as soon as possible, consistent with available resources and pending missions. The following are categories of precedence and the criteria used in their assignment:

- **Priority I–Urgent:** Assigned to emergency cases that should be evacuated as soon as possible and within a maximum of two hours in order to save life, limb, or eyesight; to prevent complications of serious illness; or to avoid permanent disability.
- **Priority IA–Urgent–Surgery:** Assigned to patients who must receive far forward surgical intervention to save their lives and to stabilize them for further evacuation.

- **Priority II–Priority:** Assigned to sick and wounded personnel requiring prompt medical care. The precedence is used when the individual should be evacuated within four hours or his medical condition could deteriorate to such a degree that he will become an URGENT precedence, whose requirements for special treatment are not available locally, or who will suffer unnecessary pain or disability.
- **Priority III–Routine:** Assigned to sick and wounded personnel requiring evacuation but whose condition is not expected to deteriorate significantly. The sick and wounded in this category should be evacuated within 24 hours.
- **Priority IV–Convenience:** Assigned to patients for whom evacuation by medical vehicle is a matter of medical convenience rather than necessity.

ARMORED VEHICLE SUPPORT

Based on the considerations of the METT-TC analysis and the operational rules of engagement (ROE), a situation may arise that requires the attachment of tanks. The following are considerations for task-organizing mechanized, tanks, and (SBCT) units with infantry platoons.

Maneuver

Maneuver by the infantry is enhanced by support from the armored vehicles. The infantry assists the heavy forces by infiltrating to clear obstacles or key enemy positions and to disrupt the enemy defense. It provides security for the armored vehicles by detecting and suppressing or destroying enemy AT weapons. It designates targets and spots the impact of fires for tanks, Bradley fighting vehicles (BFVs), or Stryker mobile gun system (MGS) vehicles. Mechanized forces support the infantry by moving with it along an axis of advance and providing a protected, fast moving assault weapons system. They suppress fire from and destroy enemy weapons, bunkers, and tanks by fire and maneuver. They also provide transport when the enemy situation permits. Armored vehicles should never be maneuvered individually. The smallest maneuver level for armor is a section (two vehicles).

Command and Control

The platoon leader is responsible for incorporating elements in direct support into his C^2 functions. Tanks and mechanized infantry must work closely at platoon level. In most operations in which they work together, infantrymen must establish direct communication with individual vehicles to ensure quick and accurate response to directions given. Infantrymen and vehicle crews must know how to communicate by radio, telephone, and visual signals. For immediate, direct communication with the M1A1/A2 tank, the crew can run communication wire from the AM-1780 through the loader's hatch or vision block and be connected to a field phone attached to the outside of the tank. During the planning phase of an operation, infantry and armor leaders must allocate sufficient time for the conduct of detailed briefbacks and rehearsals.

Weapon Systems Considerations
The infantry leader must be knowledgeable of the capabilities, limitations, dangers, and effects of the armor weapon systems in support of his missions. The figure below shows the difference in the capabilities of the BFV and the M1A1/A2 tank in regard to fields of fire on urban terrain. Note that the BFV can engage a target 9 to 10 stories high at 20 meters, whereas an M1A1/A2 tank requires 90 meters.

Bradley Fighting Vehicles. The primary role of the BFV in most environments is to provide suppressive fires, breach exterior walls, destroy enemy fortifications, and provide shock to the enemy. The vehicle's armorpiercing rounds can penetrate concrete up to 16 inches thick and can easily penetrate brick structures. It is highly effective against earthen- and sandbag-reinforced structures. The BFV can elevate its 25-mm gun to about +60 degrees and depress the gun to about -10 degrees. The crew has limited visibility to the sides and rear and no visibility to the top when buttoned up. The BFV can be outfitted with an external phone hookup for communications with accompanying infantry. The 25-mm gun, firing armor piercing (AP), high explosive (HE), and even target practice–tracer (TP-T) rounds, can be used effectively against enemy-occupied buildings and fortifications.

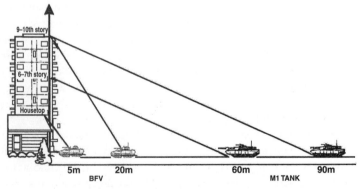

Fields of Fire in Urban Terrain

M1-Series Tanks. Normally, the primary ammunition for the main gun in the urban and restricted terrain environments is the high-explosive anti-tank (HEAT) round. It is the most effective round against masonry and will penetrate all but the thickest reinforced concrete. A HEAT round will create a hole in masonry or concrete large enough for a man to fit through but will not cut the reinforcing steel bars. HEAT is also effective against earthen- and sandbag-reinforced strong points, most bunkers, and fighting positions. Multipurpose antitank (MPAT) rounds will penetrate masonry and concrete but are less effective than HEAT rounds against heavier structures. Sabot ammunition has limited use against nonvehicular targets, and its discarding petals endanger accompanying infantry. Sabot petals create a hazard area extending 70 meters on either side of the gun target line for a distance of one kilometer. The external M2 heavy barrel (HB) cal. 50 MG can elevate to +36 degrees; however, to fire the cal. 50 on the M1A2 Abrams, the tank commander must be exposed to enemy fire.

Mobile Gun System. The thermal sights on the MGS vehicle can detect enemy activity through darkness and smoke, conditions that may limit even the best equipped infantry. The MGS vehicle can deliver devastating fires; is fully protected against antipersonnel mines, fragments, and small arms; and has excellent mobility along unblocked routes. The MGS vehicle projects a psychological presence, an aura of invulnerability that aids the friendly forces in deterring violence. Mounted patrols by MGS vehicles can monitor large areas of a city while making their presence known to the entire populace, both friendly and unfriendly. The mobile, protected firepower of MGS vehicles can add security to resupply convoys. The MGS vehicle's smoke-generation capability can aid in extracting wounded personnel and other small-unit actions. Crewmen in MGS vehicles have poor all-round vision through their vision blocks; they are easily blinded by smoke or dust. MGS vehicle gunners cannot easily identify enemy targets unless the commander exposes himself to fire by opening his hatch or other infantrymen direct the gunner to the target. Heavy fires from MGS vehicles cause unwanted collateral damage and can destabilize basic structures.

Infantry Carrier Vehicle (ICV) Striker. The ICV can provide protection to the infantry by negating the effects of enemy small-arms weapons, either by driving soldiers up to a building or by acting as a shield while the infantry moves behind it along a street or in restricted terrain. ICVs can resupply units quickly and with more ammunition than by foot. Because of their armor protection, ICVs can be used to conduct CASEVAC under fire. If buttoned up, crewmen in ICVs have poor all-round vision through their vision blocks; they are easily blinded by smoke or dust. The ICV has only a local defense weapon system mounted. Once the infantry has dismounted and is not supporting the vehicle, its firepower is diminished. The ICV is vulnerable to most weapons systems other than small arms and is particularly vulnerable to AT weapons.

Infantry Riding on Armored Vehicles

An additional maneuver consideration for a light/mechanized or mechanized/light operation is the decision of whether to move infantrymen on tanks. This mode of transportation can be difficult but is not impossible. It does, in fact, afford some significant advantages. The mounted infantry can provide additional security for the company. When the team conducts a halt or must execute a breach or other tactical tasks, infantry assets are readily available to provide support and security. The commander must weigh the potential dangers of carrying tank-mounted infantrymen against the advantages of mobility and security they can provide. Some of the safety considerations involved in mounting infantry on tanks are:

1. When mounting an armored vehicle, soldiers must always approach the vehicle from the front to get permission from the vehicle commander to mount. They then mount the side of the vehicle away from the coaxial machine gun and in view of the driver.

BUSTLE RACKS

Required Items:
Snap link: 9 each (SSSC* item)
1/2 inch rope: (SSSC item)
    Three—20-foot lengths
STEP HERE   Nine—6-foot lengths
*Self-service supply center

NOTE: Soldiers sit facing out, Personal gear is carried in company trains.

Mounting and Riding on an M-1 Tank

2. If the vehicle has a stabilization system, squad leaders ensure it is off before giving the okay for the vehicle to move.
3. The infantry must dismount as soon as possible when tanks come under fire or when targets appear that require the tank gunner to traverse the turret quickly to fire.
4. All soldiers must be alert for obstacles that can cause the tank to turn suddenly and for trees that can knock riders off the tank.
5. The M1 tank is not designed to carry riders easily. Riders must not move to the rear deck. Engine operating temperatures make this area unsafe for them. Other tank safety measures include the following:

   - One infantry squad can ride on the turret. The soldiers must mount in such a way that their legs cannot become entangled between the turret and the hull by an unexpected turret movement. Rope may be used as a field-expedient infantry rail to provide secure handholds.
   - Everyone must be to the rear of the smoke grenade launchers. This automatically keeps everyone clear of the coaxial machine gun and laser range finder.
   - The infantry must always be prepared for sudden turret movement.
   - Leaders should caution solders about sitting on the turret blowout panels, because 250 pounds of pressure will prevent the panels from working properly. If there is an explosion in the ammunition rack, these panels blow outward to lessen the blast effect in the crew compartment.
   - If enemy contact is made, the tank should stop in a covered and concealed position and allow the infantry time to dismount and move away from the tank. This action needs to be practiced before movement.
   - The infantry should not ride with anything more than their battle gear. Personal gear should be transported elsewhere.

PART TWO

Soldier Combat Skills

10

Call for and
Adjust Indirect Fire

A call for fire is a concise message prepared by an observer (a person need-ing indirect fire support). Either a soldier or a forward observer (FO) can prepare and request a call for fire. However, to receive immediate indirect fire support, the observer must plan targets and follow proper call-for-fire procedures. A call for fire must be sent quickly but clearly enough that it can be understood, recorded, and read back to the observer without error, by the fire direction center (FDC). The call for fire must contain all of the infor-mation needed by the artillery or mortar FDC to bring indirect fires on the target. The call for fire must include the following **required** elements and may include some optional elements:

REQUIRED ELEMENTS OF A CALL FOR FIRE
Observer Identification and Warning Order (WARNO)
Observer identification (your call sign) tells the fire direction center (FDC) who is calling. It also clears the net (frequency) for the duration of the call. The WARNO tells the FDC the type of mission and the method of locating the target. The types of indirect fire missions are:
- **Adjust fire**—Use this command when uncertain of target location. The observer announces "Adjust fire."
- **Fire for effect**—Use this command for rounds on target; no adjust-ment. This is used when the observer is certain that the target loca-tion is accurate and that the first volley of fire should have the desired effects on the target with little or no adjustment required. The observer announces "Fire for effect."

- **Suppression**—Use this command to obtain fire quickly on a target that is not active (followed by the target identification).
- **Immediate suppression**—Use this command to indicate the friendly unit is already being engaged by the enemy (must give target identification).

Method of Target Location

When locating a target for engagement, the observer must determine which of the following target location methods he will use:

- Grid
- Polar
- Shift from a known point.

Grid Mission. The observer sends the target location as a six-digit grid. Before the first adjusting rounds are fired, the FDC must know the direction from the observer's location. The observer sends observer-target (OT) direction (to the nearest 10 mils) from his position to the target. OT is the direction in mils from the observer to the target.

Grid Request

Polar Mission. The observer sends a direction, distance, and an up or down measurement (vertical shift) to the target. The word **polar** in the warning order alerts the FDC that the target will be located with respect to the observer's position, which must be known by the FDC. A vertical shift tells the FDC how far in meters, the target is located above or below the observer's location.

FORWARD OBSERVER

INITIAL FIRE REQUEST

"Z56, this is Z31, fire for effect, polar, over"

"This is Z56, fire for effect, polar, out"

"Direction 4520, distance 2300, down 35, over"

"Direction 4520, distance 2300, down 35, out"

"Infantry company in open, ICM, over"

"Infantry company in open, ICM, out"

MESSAGE TO OBSERVER

"Y, VT, 3 rounds, target, AF2036, over"

"Y, VT, 3 rounds, target, AF2036, out"

FDC

Polar Request

Shift from a Known Point. In a shift from a known-point mission, the point or target from which the shift will be made is sent in the warning order. Both the observer and the FDC must know the point. The observer sends a target/registration point number, an OT direction, a right or left correction (lateral shift), an add or drop correction to the nearest 100 meters (range shift), and an up or down correction (vertical shift) from the known point to the target. Normally, the OT direction is sent in mils, but the FDC can accept degrees or cardinal direction if that is all the observer can send. The lateral shift is how far left or right the target is from the known point. The range shift is how much farther (add) or closer (drop) the target is from the known point. The vertical shift is how much the target is above (up) or below (down) the altitude of the known point, to the nearest 5 meters (the vertical shift is ignored unless it exceeds 30 meters).

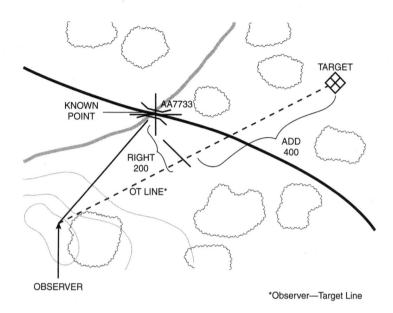

*Observer—Target Line

Lateral and Range Shifts From a Known Point

Target Description

The observer needs to give enough target detail so the FDC can determine the amount and type of ammunition to use. Give a brief description of the target using the acronym SNAP:

- *Size and/or Shape.* If these are significant, use an example such as: "rectangular, 400 meters by 200 meters; circular, radius 200 meters."
- *Nature and/or Nomenclature.* The number of elements in the unit, and other identifying characteristics such as infantry; armor; mechanized, supply trucks; or unit insignia.
- *Activity.* What is the target doing (digging in, assembly area activities, tactical movement, etc.)?
- *Protection and/or Posture.* In the open, in foxholes, in bunkers, in buildings, overhead protection, etc.

FORWARD OBSERVER

INITIAL FIRE REQUEST

"H66, this is H44, adjust fire, shift 732, over"

"This is H66, adjust fire, shift 732, out"

"Direction 5210, left 380, add 400, over"

"Direction 5210, left 380, add 400, out"

"Combat OP in open, ICM I/C, over"

"Combat OP in open, ICM I/C, out"

MESSAGE TO OBSERVER

"Charlie, one round, over"

"Charlie, one round, out"

FDC

Shift Request

Optional Elements of a Call for Fire

The normal observer who needs a call-for-fire mission will usually need to use only the required elements in the preceding paragraphs. However, the trained observer's call for fire mission might also include the following optional elements of information:

Method of Engagement

The observer may indicate how he wants to attack the target. The method of engagement consists of danger close (if applicable) and distribution, ammunition, and trajectory (DAT).

Type of Adjustment

Two types of adjustment may be employed—*precision* and *area*. Unless precision fire is specified, area fire will be used. Precision fire is conducted with one weapon on a point target. It is used either to obtain registration corrections or to destroy a target. If the target is to be destroyed, the observer announces "Destruction." Area fire is used to attack an area target.

Danger Close

"Danger close" is included in the method of engagement when the target is (rounds will impact) within 600 meters of friendly troops for mortar and artillery, 750 meters for naval guns 5-inch and smaller, and 1,000 meters for naval guns larger than 5-inch. For naval 16-inch improved conventional munition (ICM), danger close is 2,000 meters.

In the event that fire is required within 600 meters of friendly troops, the following guidelines apply:

- Announce "Danger close" to the FDC.
- The initial target location is reported on the enemy side of the target.
- Creeping procedures are used to adjust danger-close fire. Range corrections should not exceed 100 meters. Do *not* bracket. It could cause friendly casualties.

Mark

"Mark" is included in the method of engagement to indicate that the observer is going to call for rounds to orient himself in his zone of observation or to indicate targets to ground troops, aircraft, or fire support.

Trajectory

Low-angle fire is standard for field artillery. If high-angle fire is desired, it is requested immediately after the type of engagement. If high angle is not specified, low angle will (normally) be used. If the firing unit determines that high angle must be used to attack a target, the unit must inform the observer that high angle will be used. Mortars fire only high angle.

Ammunition

The observer may request any type of ammunition during the adjustment or the fire for effect (FFE) phase of his mission. Shell high explosive (HE) with fuse quick is normally used in adjustment. If that is what the observer desires, he need not request it in his call for fire. Examples of requests for other than HE projectiles are "illumination," "ICM," and "smoke."

Volume of Fire

The observer may request the number of rounds to be fired by the weapons firing in effect. For example, "3 rounds" indicates that the firing unit will fire three volleys. When a battery has six guns, each gun will fire three rounds.

Method of Fire and Control

The method of fire and control indicates the desired manner of attacking the target, whether the observer wants to control the time or delivery of fire, and whether he can observe the target. The observer announces the appropriate method of fire and control. "At my command" (AMC) and "Time on target" (TOT) are very useful methods of controlling mass fires. Some methods and their meanings follow:

At My Command

If the observer wishes to control the time of delivery of fire, he includes "At my command" in the method of control. When the pieces are ready to fire, the FDC announces "Platoon [or battery or battalion] is ready, over" (call signs are used). The observer announces "Fire" when he is ready for the pieces to fire. "At my command" remains in effect throughout the mission until the observer announces "Cancel. At my command. Over."

Cannot Observe

"Cannot observe" indicates that the observer cannot see the target (because of vegetation, terrain, weather, or smoke); however, he has reason to believe that a target exists at the given location and that it is important enough to justify firing on it without adjustment.

Time on Target

The observer may tell the FDC when he wants the rounds to impact by requesting "Time on target [so many] minutes from now, over" or "Time on target 0859, over." The FO must conduct a time check to ensure that 0859 on his watch is 0859 on the FDC's watch.

Check Firing

"Check firing" is used to cause an immediate halt in firing.

Repeat

"Repeat" can be given during adjustment or FFE missions. During adjustment, "repeat" means fire another round(s) with the last data and adjust for any change in ammunition, if necessary. During FFE, "Repeat" means fire the same number of rounds using the same method of FFE as last fired.

Corrections of Errors

Errors are sometimes made in transmitting data or by the FDC personnel in reading back the data. If the observer realizes that he has made an error in his transmission or that the FDC has made an error in the readback, he announces "Correction" and transmits the correct data.

Refinement and End of Mission

The observer should observe the results of the fire for effect (FFE) and then take one of the following actions to complete the mission:

- Correct any adjustments
- Record as target
- Report battle damage assessment

ADJUSTING FIRE

To adjust fire onto a target, use the *bracketing* method of adjustment. Spot each round when it impacts as over or short, right or left of the target. When the first range spotting is observed, make a range correction that would result in a range spotting in the opposite direction. For example, if the first round is short, add enough range to get an *over* on the next round.

Use the following guide to establish a bracket:

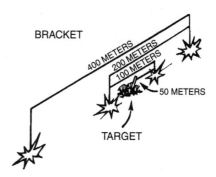

Successive Bracketing

Round Impact from Target	Add or Drop + or -
Over 400 meters	800 meters + or -
200–400	400 meters + or -
100–200 meters	200 meters + or -
Less than 100 meters	100 meters

1. *Deviation.* Measure the horizontal angle in mils, using either fingers or the reticle pattern in the binoculars. Estimate the range to the target and divide by 1,000. This is the observer target (OT) factor. If the OT distance is 1,000 meters or greater, the OT factor is expressed to the nearest whole number. If the OT distance is less than 1,000

Fingers Pattern

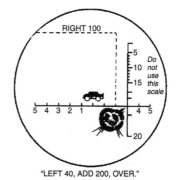

"LEFT 40, ADD 200, OVER."

Reticle Pattern

meters, the OT factor is expressed to the nearest tenth. For example, 800 = 0.8. Multiplying the OT factor by the deviation measured in mils produces deviation in meters.

For example, if we measure the round 100 mils right of the target and estimate the range to be 2,200 meters, the OT factor is 2. For adjustment purposes, we express the OT factor to the nearest whole number. Example: 1.1 would be 1; 1.8 would be 2; 2.5 would be 2. Multiplying the angle (100 mils) by the OT factor (2), we get the deviation in meters (200 meters right).

2. *Transmit corrections to the FDC in meters.* The initial correction should bracket the target in range. Deviation correction should be made to keep the rounds on the observer target line. The accompa-

MILS x OT = SHIFT
50 x 2 = 100 METERS
"RIGHT 100, DROP 400, OVER."

Initial Round Impact

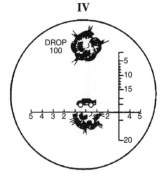

"LEFT 40, ADD 200, OVER."

Adjustment

"DROP 100, OVER."

Adjustment (continued)

"ADD 50, FIRE FOR EFFECT, OVER."

Final Adjustment

nying figure shows the impact of the initial round. Since the round is beyond the target, you must drop. You estimate that the round is 250 meters beyond the target. Therefore, a 400-meter drop will give you a bracket. The round impacted 50 mils left of the target. With an OT factor of 2, the round impacted 100 meters left. Your correction to the FDC is "Right 100, drop 400, over."

3. *Continue splitting the range bracket until a 100-meter bracket is split or a range correct spotting is observed, maintaining deviation on line.*

4. *Initiate fire for effect.* When a 100-meter bracket is split or a range correct spotting is made, the fire-for-effect phase is entered, and the call is "Fire for effect."

5. *Observe the results of fire for effect and report the results.* When the smoke clears, tell the FDC what the results are. Such things as the number of casualties, damaged equipment, stalled tracks, and so forth are important.

LESSONS LEARNED DURING OPERATION ENDURING FREEDOM

The following text comes from a series of small infantry unit After Action Reviews on indirect fire support in Afghanistan.

Mortars at Company and Battalion Level

Despite the desire to go in light, mortars are essential for mountain warfare. Mortars were used to destroy visible targets at long ranges, immediate target engagement, and to cover the abundance of dead space. Mortar platoon members in some units carried 5 rounds per person and every soldier carried 2 rounds. Since the mortars were not static, but had to move positions (sometimes rapidly) several leaders remarked that it worked well in their situation to not have everyone drop off all their rounds at the mortar position. In other words, if the rounds were immediately brought to the mortar position, when they moved it would have been impossible to relocate them with the tubes.

Prior to departure, work out with the artillery three or four easily recognizable target reference points (TRPs). Arrange to communicate directly with the artillery to get rapid action on requests for smoke (for orientation) and supporting fire.

From a Company First Sergeant

I recommend all squad leaders and platoon leaders carry binoculars with the mil reticule. Countless times team leaders and squad leaders had the opportunity to call in mortars and the binoculars are needed. More importantly is that leaders and soldiers know how to use them. Contrary to popular belief it's not the platoon leader who's going to call it in, it's the soldier in the position who will. Range estimation is probably the most important or critical thing you do. If you close on your estimation you'll get the target. We all carried in 2 mortar rounds apiece and that was more then enough. We took mix of everything; the only thing we used was WP [white phosphorus] and HE [high explosive]. All together our company took in at least 120 rounds.

11

Camouflage, Concealment, and Decoys

Camouflage, concealment, and decoys (CCD) all involve the use of materials and techniques to hide, blend, disguise, decoy, or disrupt the appearance of military targets and/or their backgrounds. CCD helps prevent an enemy from detecting or identifying friendly troops, equipment, activities, or installations. Properly designed CCD techniques take advantage of the immediate environment and natural and artificial materials. Good CCD is an action that makes soldiers, equipment, and units difficult to locate.

Each soldier is responsible for camouflaging himself, his equipment, and his position. CCD reduces the probability of an enemy placing aimed fire on a soldier. The soldier uses natural and artificial materials for CCD. Natural CCD includes defilade, grass, bushes, trees, and shadows. Artificial CCD for soldiers includes battle dress uniforms (BDUs), lightweight camouflage nets, skin paint, and natural materials removed from their original positions. To be effective, artificial CCD must blend with the natural background.

Noise, movement, and light discipline all contribute to individual CCD. Effective noise discipline muffles and eliminates sounds made by soldiers and their equipment. Movement discipline minimizes movement within and between positions and limits movement to routes that cannot be readily observed by the enemy. Light discipline controls the use of lights at night. Examples are not smoking in the open or walking around with a lit flashlight.

Dispersal, the spreading of soldiers and equipment over a wide area, is a key individual survival technique. It creates a smaller target mass for enemy sensors and weapon systems. Dispersal, therefore, not only reduces casualties and losses in the event of an attack but also makes enemy detection efforts more difficult.

Camouflage

CCD CONSIDERATIONS
Movement
Movement draws attention, whether it involves vehicles on the road or individuals walking around. The naked eye, as well as infrared and radar sensors, can detect movement. Soldiers should minimize movement while they are in the open. They should remember that darkness does not prevent observation by an enemy equipped with modern sensors. When movement is necessary, slow, smooth movement attracts less attention than quick, irregular movement.

Shape
The soldier should use CCD materials to break up the shapes, outlines, and shadows of positions and equipment, as all three are revealing. As shadows can visually mask objects, soldiers should stay in shadows whenever possible, especially when moving. When conducting operations close to the enemy, disguise or distort the shape of the helmet and the human body with

artificial camouflage materials, as they are easily recognized by the enemy at close range.

Shine and Light

Gloss or shine can also attract attention. Pay particular attention to gloss and shine caused by light reflecting from smooth or polished surfaces, such as mess kits, mirrors, eyeglasses, watch crystals, windshields, and starched uniforms. Plastic map cases, dust goggles worn on top of the helmet, and clear plastic garbage bags also reflect light almost as well as windshields and mirrors. Cover or remove these items from exposed areas. Vehicle headlights, taillights, and safety reflectors reflect not only light but also laser energy used in weapon systems. Cover this equipment when the vehicle is not in operation. Red filters on vehicle dome lights and flashlights, while designed to protect the soldier's night vision, are extremely sensitive to detection by night vision devices. A tank's red dome light, reflecting off the walls and out through the sight and vision blocks, can be seen from as far away as 4 kilometers with a starlight scope. Red-lensed flashlights, as well as cigarettes and pipes, are equally observable. To reduce the chances of detection, soldiers should replace red with blue-green filters and practice strict light discipline. Soldiers should also use measures to prevent shine at night, because moonlight and starlight can be reflected as easily as sunlight.

Color

The contrast of skin, uniforms, and equipment with the background helps the enemy detect opposing forces. Individual CCD should blend with the surroundings; at a minimum, objects must not contrast with the background.

| Sand and Light Green for Desert and Dry Areas | Loam and White for Snow Covered Areas | Loam and Light Green for Vegetated Areas |

Colors Used in CCD

Therefore, the proper camouflage technique is to blend colors with the background or to hide objects with contrasting colors.

CCD EMPLOYMENT

Before applying CCD to himself, his equipment, and his position, a soldier should study the nearby terrain and vegetation. His reconnaissance should incorporate an analysis of the CCD considerations listed above. He then chooses CCD materials that best blend with the area. When moving from one area to another, change CCD as required. What works well in one location may draw fire in another.

Skin

Exposed skin, even very dark skin, reflects light. CCD paint sticks cover these oils and provide blending with the background. Avoid using oils or insect repellent to soften the paint stick, because doing so defeats the purpose by making the skin shiny. Soldiers applying CCD paint should work in pairs and help each other. Self-application may leave gaps, such as behind the ears. Paint high, shiny areas (forehead, cheekbones, nose, ears, and chin) a dark color. Paint low, shadow areas a light color. Paint the exposed skin on the back of the neck, arms, and hands with an irregular pattern. When CCD paint sticks are not available, use field expedients such as burnt cork, bark, charcoal, lampblack, or mud. Mud contains bacteria, so consider it a last priority for field-expedient paint.

Uniform

BDUs, which have a CCD pattern, often require additional CCD, especially when operating very close to the enemy. Soldiers should attach leaves, grass, small branches, or pieces of lightweight camouflage screening system (LCSS) to their uniforms and helmets. These items assist in distorting the shape of the soldier and in blending colors with the natural background. The BDU provides visual as well as near infrared (NIR) CCD. Do not starch BDUs; doing this counters the infrared properties of the dyes. Replace excessively faded and worn BDUs, because they lose their CCD effectiveness as they wear.

Equipment

Soldiers should inspect their personal equipment to ensure that shiny items are covered or removed. Take corrective action on items that rattle or make other noises when moved or worn. Soldiers assigned equipment such as vehicles or generators should be knowledgeable of their appropriate CCD techniques.

Individual Fighting Position

While building a fighting position, soldiers should camouflage it and carefully dispose of the earth spoil. They must also remember that too much CCD material applied to a position can actually disclose it. Soldiers should obtain CCD materials from a dispersed area to avoid drawing attention to the position due to the stripped area around it.

Camouflage the position as it is built. To avoid disclosing a fighting position, soldiers should observe the following guidelines:

- Do not leave shiny or light-colored objects exposed.
- Do not remove shirts while in the open.
- Do not use fires.
- Do not leave tracks and other signs of movement.
- When aircraft fly overhead, refrain from looking up, as one of the most obvious features on aerial photographs is the upturned faces of soldiers.

When CCD is complete, inspect the position from the enemy's viewpoint. Check CCD periodically to see that it stays natural looking and conceals the position. When CCD materials become ineffective, change or improve them.

12

Land Navigation
and Map Reading

COMPASS

Compasses are the primary tools to use when moving in an outdoor world where there is no other way to find directions. The lensatic compass is the most common and simplest instrument for measuring direction. The lensatic compass consists of the following major parts:

- The *cover* protects the floating dial. It contains a sighting wire and two luminous sighting slots or dots used for night navigation.
- The *base* or body of the compass contains a thumb loop and moving parts that include the floating dial, which is mounted on a pivot and rotates freely when the compass is held level. Printed on the dial in luminous figures are an arrow and the letters *E* and *W*. The arrow always points to magnetic north, and the letters rest at east (90 degrees) and west (270 degrees). There are two scales, the outer denoting mils and the inner (normally in red) denoting degrees. Encasing the floating dial is a glass containing a fixed, black index line.
- The *bezel ring* is a ratchet device that clicks when turned. It will make 120 clicks when rotated fully; each click is equal to 3 degrees. A short, luminous line that is used in conjunction with the north-seeking arrow is contained in the glass face of the bezel ring.
- The *lens* is used to read the dial. It contains the rear-sight slot used in conjunction with the front sight for sighting on objects. The rear sight must be opened more than 45 degrees to allow the dial to float freely.

Lensatic Compass

Handling the Compass

The compass is a delicate instrument and should be closed and in its case when not being used. Metal objects and electricity can affect the performance of a compass. Nonmagnetic metals and alloys do not affect the compass. To ensure its proper functioning, observe these suggested safe distances:

High-tension power lines	55 meters
Field gun, truck, or tank	18 meters
Telegraph or telephone wires and barbed wire	10 meters
Machine gun	2 meters
Steel helmet or rifle	0.5 meter

Using the Compass

The compass must always be held level and firm when sighting on an object. Some of the techniques are as follows:

Centerhold

Open the compass to its fullest so that the cover forms a straight edge with the base. Place your thumb through the thumb loop, form a steady base with your third and fourth fingers, and extend your index finger along the side of the compass. Place the thumb of the other hand between the lens (rear sight)

Compass Centerhold

and the bezel ring; extend the index finger along the other side of the compass and the remaining fingers around the fingers of the other hand. Pull your elbows in firmly to your sides—this places the compass between your chin and belt. To measure an azimuth, simply turn your entire body toward the object, pointing the compass cover directly at the object. Then look down and read the azimuth from beneath the fixed, black index line.

Compass-to-Cheek
Open the cover of the compass containing the sighting wire to a vertical position, and fold the rear sight slightly forward. Look through the rear-sight slot, and align the front-sight hairline with the desired object in the distance. Then glance down at the dial through the eye lens to read the azimuth.

Compass-to-cheek

Presetting a Compass and Following an Azimuth

In Daylight or with a Light Source

Hold the compass level in the palm of the hand. Rotate it until the desired azimuth falls under the fixed, black index line. Turn the bezel ring until the luminous line is aligned with the north-seeking arrow. The compass is now preset.

To follow the azimuth, use the centerhold technique and turn your body until the north-seeking arrow is aligned with the luminous line. Then proceed forward in the direction of the front cover's sighting wire, which is aligned with the fixed, black index line.

Presetting a Compass

In Darkness or Limited Visibility

Set the azimuth by the click method (each click equals a 3-degree interval). Rotate the bezel ring until the luminous line is over the fixed, black index line. Find the desired azimuth and divide it by three. The result is the number of clicks that you have to rotate the bezel ring. If the desired azimuth is smaller than 180 degrees, the number of clicks on the bezel ring should be counted in a counterclockwise direction. If the desired azimuth is larger than 180 degrees, subtract the number of degrees from 360 degrees and divide by three to obtain the number of clicks. Count them in a clockwise direction. For example, if the desired azimuth is 330 degrees, then 360-330 = 30 divided by 3 = 10 clicks clockwise.

With the compass preset, use the centerhold technique and rotate your body until the north-seeking arrow is aligned with the luminous line on the bezel. Then proceed forward in the direction of the front cover's luminous dots, which are aligned with the fixed, black index line.

Offset

A deliberate offset is a planned magnetic deviation to the right or left of an azimuth to an objective. It is used when the objective is located along or in the vicinity of a linear feature such as a road or stream. Because of errors in reading the compass or map, you may reach the linear feature without knowing whether the objective lies to the right or left. A deliberate offset by a known number of degrees in a known direction compensates for possible errors and ensures that upon reaching the linear feature you will know whether to go left or right.

Orienting Compass and Map

Place the compass on the map so that the cover of the compass is pointing toward the top of the map. Align the sighting wire or the straight edge of the compass over a north-south grid line, and rotate the map and compass together until the north arrow of the compass points in the same direction and number of degrees as shown in the current, updated grid-magnetic angle.

FIELD EXPEDIENT METHODS
Using the Sun and Stars

When a compass is not available, different techniques should be used to determine the four cardinal directions.

Shadow-Tip Method

This simple and accurate method of finding direction by the sun consists of four basic steps:

Step 1. Place a stick or branch into the ground at a level spot where a distinctive shadow will be cast. Mark the shadow tip with a stone, twig, or other means. This first shadow mark is always the west direction.

Step 2. Wait 10 to 15 minutes until the shadow tip moves a few inches. Mark the new position of the shadow tip in the same way as the first.

Step 3. Draw a straight line through the two marks to obtain an approximate east-west line.

Step 4. Standing with the first mark (west) to your left, the other directions are simple; north is to the front, east is to the right, and south is behind you.

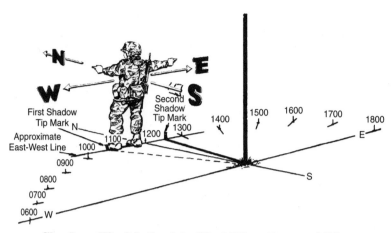

Shadow-Tip Method to Find Direction and Time

A line drawn perpendicular to the east-west line at any point is the approximate north-south line. If you are uncertain which direction is east and which is west, observe this simple rule—the first shadow-tip mark is always in the west direction, everywhere on earth.

The shadow-tip method can also be used as a shadow clock to find the approximate time of day (see the figure).

To find the time of day, move the stick to the intersection of the east-west line and the north-south line, and set it vertically in the ground. The west part of the east-west line indicates 0600 hours, and the east part is 1800 hours, anywhere on earth, because the basic rule always applies.

The north-south line now becomes the noon line. The shadow of the stick is an hour hand in the shadow clock, and with it you can estimate the time using the noon line and the 6 o'clock line as your guides. Depending on your location and the season, the shadow may move either clockwise or counterclockwise, but this does not alter your manner of reading the shadow clock.

The shadow clock is not a timepiece in the ordinary sense. It makes every day 12 unequal hours long, and always reads 0600 hours at sunrise and 1800 hours at sunset. The shadow clock time is closest to conventional clock time at midday, but the spacing of the other hours compared with conventional time varies somewhat with the locality and the date. However, it does provide a satisfactory means of telling time in the absence of properly set watches.

The shadow-tip system is not intended for use in polar regions, which the Department of Defense defines as being above 60° latitude in either hemisphere.

Watch Method

A watch can be used to determine approximate true north and true south. In the north temperate zone only, the hour hand is pointed toward the sun. A south line can be found midway between the hour hand and 1200 hours, standard time. If daylight saving time is in effect, the north-south line is found between the hour hand and 1300 hours. If there is any doubt as to which end of the line is north, remember that the sun is in the east before noon and in the west after noon.

A watch may also be used to determine direction in the south temperate zone, but the method is different. The 1200-hour dial is pointed toward the sun, and halfway between 1200 hours and the hour hand is the north line. If on daylight saving time, the north line lies midway between the hour hand and 1300 hours.

Watch Method

The watch method can be in error, especially in the lower latitudes, and may cause circling. To avoid this, make a shadow clock and set your watch to the time indicated. After traveling for an hour, take another shadow-clock reading. Reset your watch if necessary.

Star Method

Less than 60 of approximately 5,000 stars visible to the eye are used by navigators. The stars we see when we look up at the night sky are not evenly scattered across the whole sky; they are grouped in constellations. Which constellations we see depends on where we are, the time of the year, and the time of the night. The night sky changes with the seasons because the earth

Determining Direction by the North Star and Southern Cross

revolves around the sun, and it also changes from hour to hour because the rotation of the earth makes some constellations seem to travel in a circle. But the North Star, also known as the Polar Star or Polaris, is in almost exactly the same place in the sky all night long every night. The North Star is less than 1 degree off true north and does not move because the axis of the earth is pointed toward it. The North Star is the last star in the handle of the Little Dipper. Two stars in the Big Dipper are a help in finding the North Star. They are called the Pointers, and an imaginary line drawn through them five times their distance points to the North Star. There are many stars brighter than the North Star, but none is more important. However, the North Star can be seen only in the Northern Hemisphere, so it cannot serve as a guide south of the equator. The farther north one goes, the higher the North Star is in the sky; above latitude 70 degrees, it is too high in the sky to be useful.

Depending on the star selected for navigation, azimuth checks are necessary. A star near the north horizon serves for about a half hour. When moving south, azimuth checks should be made every 15 minutes. When traveling east or west, the difficulty of staying on azimuth is more likely caused by the star climbing too high in the sky or disappearing below the horizon than by the star changing direction angle. When this happens, it is necessary to choose another guide star.

The Southern Cross is the main constellation used as a guide south of the equator, and the general directions above for using north and south stars are reversed. When navigating using the stars as guides, the user must know the different constellation shapes and their locations throughout the world.

GLOBAL POSITIONING SYSTEM

The AN/PSN-11 GPS is a satellite-based, radio navigational system. It consists of a constellation with 24 active satellites that interface with a ground-, air-, or sea-based receiver. Each satellite transmits data that enables the GPS receiver to provide precise position and time to the user. The GPS receivers

AN/PSN-11 GPS

come in several configurations, hand-held, vehicular-mounted, aircraft-mounted, and water craft–mounted.

The most common GPS used by the U.S. Army is the Precision Lightweight Global-Positioning System Receiver (PLGR). PLGR is a highly accurate satellite signal navigation set. It calculates the user's position on earth by measuring the distance from a group of satellites in space to the user's location. The AN/PSN-11 is designed for battlefield use anywhere in the world. It is sealed watertight for all-weather day or night operation. The AN/PSN-11 is held in the left hand and operated with the thumb of the left hand. The AN/PSN-11 is operated stand-alone using prime battery power and integral antenna. It can be used with an external power source and external antenna.

Capabilities
The AN/PSN-11 provides worldwide, 24-hour, all-weather, day or night coverage when the satellite constellation is complete. The AN/PSN-11 can locate the position of the user accurately to within 21 meters—95 percent of the time. However, the AN/PSN-11 has been known to accurately locate the position of the user within 8 to 10 meters. It can determine the distance and direction from the user to a programmed location or the distance between two programmed locations called waypoints.

Characteristics
The AN/PSN-11 is 9.5 inches long, 4.1 inches wide, and 2.6 inches deep. It weighs 2.75 pounds with all batteries in place. The small size and light weight make the set easy to carry and use. The durable plastic case is sealed for all-weather use. The AN/PSN-11 features make it easy to use. (These features are highlighted in the physical description.)

Users of the AN/PSN-11 GPS should refer to operator's manual: TB 11-5825-291-10-2, *Soldier's Guide for the Precision Lightweight GPS Receiver (PLGR)* for proper setup and use.

MAP READING
To be in the right place at the right time is essential on the battlefield, so map-reading and land-navigation skills are important for every soldier.

Military Grid System
A military grid system is a network of squares formed by north-south and east-west grid lines placed on a map. The distance between grid lines represents 1,000 or 10,000 meters, depending on the scale of the map. A grid system enables the map reader to locate a point on a map quickly and accurately.

A grid line is identified by a specific number printed in the margin directly opposite the line it indicates. Any point on a map can be identified by coordinates. Following are rules for reading grid coordinates:

1. Large, bold-faced numbers in the margin label each grid line.
2. Starting at the lower left-hand corner of the map, read right and up.
3. Write the coordinates as a continuous series of numbers. The first half of the total number of the digits represents the "right" reading; the last half represents the "up" reading.

Examples (using a map with 1,000-meter grid squares):

- Location of a point within a 1,000-meter grid square is used to designate an object that is easily identifiable within a large area. Identify the grid square by using the numbers of the two grid lines intersecting at the lower left-hand corner, e.g., 9176.
- Location of a point within 100 meters. Use the appropriate corner of a coordinate scale that breaks the 1,000-meter square into 10 equal parts along each side (100-meter segments are indicated by longer

(100-METER SQUARE)

THE 6-DIGIT COORDINATE 915761 LOCATES SPOT ELEVATION (SE)696 TO WITHIN 100 METERS

1/25,000 MAP

The Six-Digit Coordinate

lines on the coordinate scale). Place the coordinate scale along the east-west grid at the lower left-hand corner of the grid square, then slide it eastward to the center of the object. Location is expressed as a six-digit coordinate. The third digit is the longer line nearest grid line 91, and the sixth digit is the longer line nearest the spot elevation (SE), e.g., 915761.

- Location of a point within 10 meters. The short lines divide 100-meter segments into 20-meter segments. To read to the nearest 10 meters, interpolate along the scale. The coordinate will be an eight-digit coordinate, e.g., 91547614.

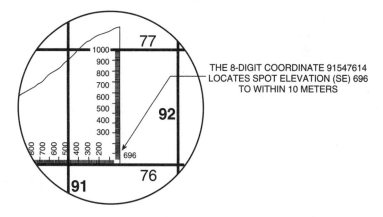

THE 8-DIGIT COORDINATE 91547614
LOCATES SPOT ELEVATION (SE) 696
TO WITHIN 10 METERS

The Eight-Digit Coordinate

Scale

Scale is defined as the fixed relationship between map distance (MD) and the corresponding ground distance (GD). It is expressed as a representative fraction (RF):

$$RF = \frac{MD}{GD}$$

The RF appears in the margin of the map as 1/25,000 or 1:25,000, each of which means that one unit of measure on the map represents 25,000 similar units of measure on the ground.

The graphic scale is printed in the margin as a special ruler and is used to measure ground distances on a map. Military maps normally have three graphic scales, expressed in miles, meters, and yards.

Direction
Direction is defined as an imaginary straight line on the map or ground and is expressed as an azimuth.

Azimuth
An azimuth is a horizontal angle measured clockwise from a north baseline. All directions originate from the center of an imaginary circle called the azimuth circle. This circle is divided into 360 equal units of measurement, called degrees. The degrees are numbered in a clockwise direction, with east at 90 degrees, south at 180 degrees, west at 270 degrees, and north at 360 or 0 degrees. Distance has no effect on azimuth.

Back Azimuth
The back azimuth of a line differs from its azimuth by exactly 180 degrees. The rules for determining back azimuth are as follows:
- If the azimuth is less than 180 degrees, the back azimuth is the value of the azimuth *plus* 180.
- If the azimuth is more than 180 degrees, the back azimuth is the value of the azimuth *minus* 180.
- If the azimuth is 180 degrees, the back azimuth is 0 degrees or 360 degrees.

Measuring Azimuths on a Map
Map azimuths are measured with a protractor. The issue protractor (MR-1) is graduated in two scales—0 to 180 degrees, and 180 to 360 degrees—to represent the complete azimuth circle.
   To read a map azimuth between any two points:
- Draw a line connecting the two points.
- Place the index at the point from which you are measuring, ensuring that the baseline of the protractor is on or parallel to a north-south grid line.
- Read the azimuth at the point where the line intersects the scale.

To plot an azimuth on a map:
- Place the protractor on the map with the index at the initial point and baseline parallel to a north-south grid line.
- Place a dot on the map at the desired azimuth reading.
- Remove the protractor; connect the initial point and the dot with a line.

APPROXIMATE MEAN
DECLINATION 1948
FOR CENTER OF SHEET

Draw this current G-M angle.

From the base of the G-M angle, draw a line to the right; this line represents any azimuth.

To use the G-M angle diagram in working with a map having an EAST G-M angle:

1. Convert magnetic azimuth to grid azimuth.

MAGNETIC AZIMUTH = 200°
G-M ANGLE = 16°E
GRID AZIMUTH = 216°

2. Then convert grid azimuth to magnetic azimuth.

GRID AZIMUTH = 216°
G-M ANGLE = 16°E
MAGNETIC AZIMUTH = 200°

When working with a map having a WEST G-M angle:

1. Convert magnetic azimuth to grid azimuth.

MAGNETIC AZIMUTH = 200°
G-M ANGLE = 16°W
GRID AZIMUTH = 184°

2. Then convert grid azimuth to magnetic azimuth.

GRID AZIMUTH = 184°
G-M ANGLE = 16°W
MAGNETIC AZIMUTH = 200°

Converting Between Grid and Magnetic Azimuth

Base Direction

There are three base directions: true north, grid north, and magnetic north.

1. *True North.* Direction to the north pole. The symbol is a star.
2. *Grid North.* Direction of the north-south grid lines. The symbol is GN.
3. *Magnetic North.* Direction in which the magnetic arrow of a compass points. The symbol is a half arrow.

The angular relationships among these three directions are shown by a declination diagram in the margin of a map.

Grid-Magnetic Angle

To understand the grid-magnetic (G-M) angle, you must know the meaning of azimuth. Map readers are concerned with two base directions: grid north, from which we read grid azimuths (protractor and map), and magnetic north, from which we read magnetic azimuths (compass and ground).

Grid azimuth is a horizontal angle measured clockwise from grid north. *Magnetic azimuth* is a horizontal angle measured clockwise from magnetic north. *G-M angle* is the angular difference between grid north and magnetic north, measured from grid north.

To use a grid azimuth in the field with a compass, you must first change it to a magnetic azimuth. To plot a magnetic azimuth on a map, you must first change it to a grid azimuth. To make either of these changes, you must use a G-M angle diagram as shown in the diagram.

You should construct and use the G-M angle diagram *each time* conversion of azimuths is required. As a time-saving procedure when working frequently with the same map, construct a G-M angle conversion table on the margin. The following is an example, using a map having a G-M angle of 16 degrees east:

For Conversion of:

Magnetic azimuth to grid azimuth: Add 16 degrees
Grid azimuth to magnetic azimuth: Subtract 16 degrees

Intersection

Distant or inaccessible objects can be located on a map by intersecting lines from two known points. For example, a magnetic azimuth from a known observation post (OP) to a distant point is converted to a grid azimuth and drawn on the map. Another magnetic azimuth from another OP to the same distant point is converted to a grid azimuth and drawn on the same map. The intersection of the two lines on the map is the location of the known point.

Resection

The resection method lets you locate your position on a map. Take magnetic azimuths to two distant points on the ground that can be identified on the map. Change these azimuths to back azimuths, convert to grid azimuths, and draw the *converted* azimuths from the known points on the map. Your location is where these two lines intersect. To verify and make a final determination of your position, compare ground features with those shown on the map.

Modified Resection

Modified resection is a method of locating your position on a map when you are on a road, stream, or other linear feature identified on the map. Take a magnetic azimuth to a distant point that can be identified both on the ground and on the map. Change this to a back azimuth, and convert to a grid azimuth. Draw this *converted* azimuth on the map from the known point. Your position is where the azimuth line on the map crosses or intersects the linear feature.

Elevation and Relief (Contour Lines)

On a standard topographical map, contour lines are the most common method of showing relief and elevation. A contour line represents an imaginary line on the ground, above or below sea level. All points on the contour line are at the same elevation. The elevation represented by contour lines is the vertical distance above or below sea level. The three types of contour lines used on a standard topographic map are as follows:

- *Index:* Starting at zero elevation or mean sea level, every fifth contour line is a heavier line. These are known as index contour lines. Normally, each index contour line is numbered at some point. This number is the elevation of that line.
- *Intermediate:* The contour lines falling between the index contour lines are called intermediate contour lines. These lines are finer and do not have their elevations given. There are normally four intermediate contour lines between index contour lines.
- *Supplementary:* These contour lines resemble dashes. They show changes in elevation of at least one-half the contour interval. These lines are normally found where there is very little change in elevation, such as on fairly level terrain.

Contour Interval

Before the elevation of any point on the map can be determined, the user must know the contour interval for the map he is using. The contour interval measurement given in the marginal information of the map is the vertical distance between adjacent contour lines. To determine the elevation of a point on the map you must:

  1) Determine the contour interval and the unit of measure used for your map (in the marginal data), for example, feet, meters, or yards.
  2) Find the numbered index contour line nearest the point of which you are trying to determine the elevation.
  3) Determine if you are going from lower elevation to higher, or vice versa. In the figure, point (a) is between the index contour lines. The lower index contour line is numbered 500, which means any point on that line is at an elevation of 500 meters above mean sea level. The upper index contour line is numbered 600, or 600 meters. Going from the lower to the upper index contour line shows an increase in elevation.
  4) Determine the exact elevation of point (a), start at the index contour line numbered 500 and count the number of intermediate contour

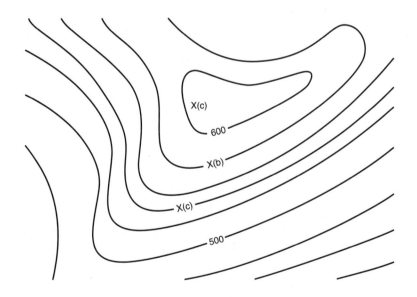

Points on Contour Lines

lines to point (a). Locate point (a) on the second intermediate contour line above the 500-meter index contour line. The contour interval is 20 meters (see figure), thus each one of the intermediate contour lines crossed to get to point (a) adds 20 meters to the 500-meter index contour line. The elevation of point (a) is 540 meters; the elevation has increased.

5) Determine the elevation of point (b). Go to the nearest index contour line. In this case, it is the upper index contour line numbered 600. Locate point (b) on the intermediate contour line immediately below the 600-meter index contour line. Below means downhill or a lower elevation. Therefore, point (b) is located at an elevation of 580 meters.

6) Determine the elevation to a hilltop point (c). Add one-half the contour interval to the elevation of the last contour line. In this example, the last contour line before the hilltop is an index contour line numbered 600. Add one-half the contour interval, 10 meters, to the index contour line. The elevation of the hilltop would be 610 meters.

Slope

Depending on the military mission, soldiers may need to determine not only the height of a hill, but the degree of the hill's slope as well. The rate of rise or fall of a terrain feature is known as its slope. The speed at which equipment or personnel can move is affected by the slope of the ground or terrain feature. This slope can be determined from the map by studying the contour line; the closer the contour lines, the steeper the slope; the farther apart the contour lines, the gentler the slope.

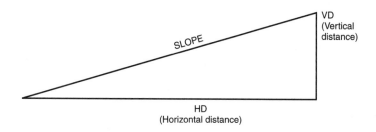

Slope Diagram

Percentage of Slope

The speed at which personnel and equipment can move up or down a hill is affected by the slope of the ground and the limitations of the equipment. It is often necessary to have a more exact way of describing a slope.

- Slope may be expressed in several ways, but all depend upon the comparison of vertical distance (VD) to horizontal distance (HD). Before we can determine the percentage of a slope, we must know the VD of the slope. The VD is determined by subtracting the lowest point of the slope from the highest point. Use the contour lines to determine the highest and lowest point of the slope.
- To determine the percentage of the slope in meters between points (a) and (b), determine the elevation of point (b) (590 meters). Then determine the elevation of point (a) (380 meters). Determine the vertical distance between the two points by subtracting the elevation of point (a) from the elevation of point (b).The difference (210 meters) is the VD between points (a) and (b). Then measure the HD between the two points on the map. After the horizontal distance has been determined, compute the percentage of the slope by using the formula shown in the illustration.

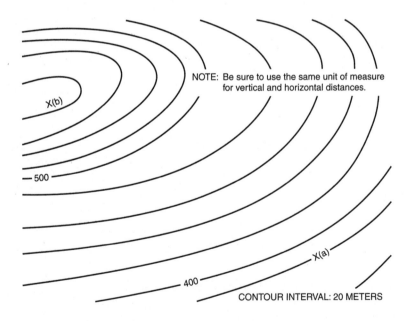

Contour Line Around a Slope

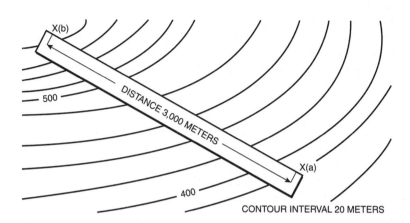

CONTOUR INTERVAL 20 METERS

Measuring Horizontal Distance

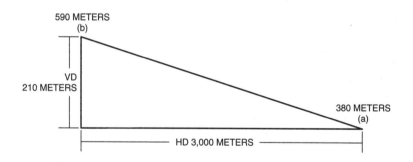

VD = b − a = 210 METERS
HD = 3,000 METERS

$$\% \text{ SLOPE} = \frac{VD \times 100}{HD} \text{ or } \frac{(VD)\ 210 \times 100}{(HD)\ 3,000} = \frac{21,000}{3,000} = 7\%$$

Multiply the distance by 100. Divide the total by the
horizontal distance. The result is the percentage of slope.

Percentage of Slope in Meters

TERRAIN FEATURES

All terrain features are derived from a complex landmass known as a mountain or **ridgeline.** The term ridgeline is not interchangeable with the term ridge. A ridgeline is a line of high ground, usually with changes in elevation along its top and low ground on all sides from which a total of 10 natural or man-made terrain features are classified.

Ridgeline

Terrain Features

Hilltop

(On Map)
Last closed contour.

(On Ground)
When you are located on a hilltop,
the ground slopes down in all directions.

Ridge

 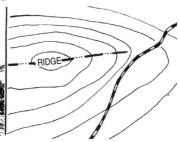

(On Ground)
When you are located on a ridge,
the ground slopes down in three
directions and up in one direction.

(On Map)
U- or V-shaped contours with the base
of the U or V pointing away from
higher ground.

Saddle

(On Map)
Hourglass or figure eight–
shaped contours.

(On Ground)
When you are located in a saddle,
there is higher ground in two directions
and lower ground in two directions.

Primary Terrain Features

Valley

(On Ground)
Reasonably level ground bordered on side by higher ground. Generally has maneuver room and may contain streams.

(On Map)
Contour lines form U. Lines tend to parallel stream before crossing. Contour lines crossing a stream always point uphill.

Depression

(On Map)
Indicated by depression contours.

(On Ground)
Low point or hole in the ground with high ground on all sides.

Draw

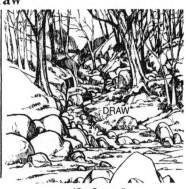

(On Map)
Like a valley, but normally has less developed stream course. No level ground and little or no maneuver room. Ground slopes upward on the sides and toward the head of the draw.

(On Ground)
Contour lines are V-shaped with the point of the V toward the head of the draw (high ground).

Spur

(On Ground)
Short, continuously sloping line of higher ground jutting out of the side of a ridge. Often formed by parallel streams cutting draws down a ridge.

(On Map)
Contour lines depict a spur with the U or V pointing away from high ground.

Cliff

(On Ground)
A vertical or near vertical slope.

(On Map)
Contour lines are close together or a ticked or "carrying" contour line (ticks point to lower ground).

Cut or Fill

Cuts are manmade features resulting from cutting through high ground, usually to form a level bed for a road or railroad track. Fills are manmade features resulting from filling a low area, usually to form a level bed for a road or railroad track.

GROUND NAVIGATION

Before you can navigate on the ground you first must determine your location on the map and on the ground by using the following procedure: Orient the map to the north. Inspect the surrounding area or ground to determine all distinct terrain features. On the map, look for an area having the same types of features in the same relative positions as those observed on the ground. Through comparing the map to the ground and using a process of elimination, isolate the terrain feature on which you are located. Confirm this terrain feature by assuring that the direction to, distance from, and difference in elevation from all adjacent terrain features are identical on the map and on the ground. Determine your exact location on the isolated terrain feature by a detailed analysis of all the immediate terrain features.

Ground navigation is movement between two points in which an individual, using terrain features as guides, knows both his map and ground location throughout the movement. Ground navigation demands a thorough knowledge of terrain features as they appear on the map and on the ground. Since terrain features are used as guides during movement, use of the compass is minimal. Two basic rules must always be applied:

1. Begin from a known location on both the map and the ground.
2. Then orient the map to the ground and keep it oriented throughout the movement.

With the basic rules established, the following steps outline the ground (land) navigation procedure:

1. Through a map study of the terrain, determine the most practical route to your destination, and select terrain features along this route to guide your movement.
2. Determine the general direction of movement.
3. Begin movement, considering the horizontal and vertical distances between terrain features along the route.
4. Confirm your location at selected terrain features (checkpoints) along the route.
5. Upon arrival at the final destination, confirm your location by a detailed comparative analysis between the ground position and the plotted map position.

Mounted Navigation

With the addition of more combat vehicles to the Army, your chances of having to navigate while mounted are increasing. The major difference between navigating while mounted and while dismounted is the speed at which you travel. When moving mounted, it is important to designate a navigator who makes sure that the correct distance and direction are followed

NOTE: All azimuths in this figure are grid.

Mounted Movement

and recorded, beginning with the leg from the start point to the first prominent feature and then to subsequent easily identifiable features on the ground. The navigator prepares a log to record azimuths and distances for each leg of the movement. During movement, the navigator must face in the direction of travel to keep his map oriented and to identify terrain features.

Mounted navigation with a compass requires determination of the amount of deviation caused by the vehicle. This can be done in the following manner:

1. The navigator dismounts and moves 50 meters in front of the vehicle.
2. The navigator determines an azimuth from his position to a fixed object at least 50 meters to his front.
3. The driver moves the vehicle forward, keeping it centered on the navigator, and stops as close to him as safely possible.
4. The navigator then gets back into the vehicle and measures the azimuth to the fixed object from the vehicle. The vehicle's engine must be running. The difference between the two azimuths is the

deviation. The deviation is logged and added to or subtracted from the azimuth to be followed. This procedure should be followed for any change of direction of 10 degrees or more.

Be aware that distance measured on a vehicle's odometer during mounted movement may be greater than that measured on the map, since the map measurements do not take into consideration the rise and fall of the land.

How to Fold a Map

Use the following steps to fold a map:

1. Lay the map flat, faceup, north at the top. Fold it in half, turning the bottom edge up to the top.
2. Crease map into three equal parts parallel to the center fold just made.
3. Open the map completely, faceup. Turn it so east is at the top.
4. Repeat the folding procedures of steps 1 and 2.
5. Open the map again, faceup, placing north at the top. With a sharp blade, neatly cut the map as shown in sketch 1, along heavy lines.

SKETCH 1

SKETCH 2

SKETCH 3

Folding a Map Sheet

6. Grasp as in sketch 2, drawing paper up at the crease. Fold over toward the top edge.
7. Repeat step 6 with the second crease from the bottom, folding to meet the top edge of the map. Fold up the remaining flap. The edge view of the map should look like sketch 3.
8. From the center V, open the map to center section without unfolding the remainder. Turn the map so east is at the top.
9. Follow the same creasing and folding procedures as in steps 6 and 7.
10. Again open the map at the center V without unfolding the rest, exposing the center section.
11. Without unfolding the map, carefully glue or tape together the eight places where the edges you have cut come together.
12. You now have three sections, each of which may be used like a book map. You can fold the entire map so that only the desired "book" is exposed for use.

13

Fighting Positions

The defensive plan normally will require building fighting positions. Fighting positions protect soldiers. They provide *cover* from direct and indirect fires, and they provide *concealment* through proper positioning and camouflage.

PRINCIPLES
Leaders follow three basic principles to effectively and efficiently prepare fighting positions:
1. Site positions to best engage the enemy
2. Prepare positions by stages
3. Inspect all positions.

Site Positions to Best Engage the Enemy
The most important aspect of a fighting position is that it be tactically well positioned. Leaders must be able to look at the terrain and quickly identify the best locations for fighting positions that allow:
- Soldiers to engage the intended enemy element within their assigned sectors of fire.
- Soldiers to fire out to the maximum effective range of their weapons with maximum grazing fire and minimal dead space.
- Grenadiers to be placed in positions to cover dead space.

Additionally, leaders site fighting positions to provide mutually supporting, interlocking fires so they can cover the platoon's sector from multiple positions. When possible, they site positions behind natural cover and in easily camouflaged locations. The enemy must not be able to identify the position until it is too late and he has been effectively engaged.

Prepare Positions by Stages

Leaders and soldiers prepare fighting positions based on the situation. Soldiers prepare fighting positions every time the platoon makes an extended halt. Usually half of the platoon digs in or conducts various priorities of work while the other half maintains security. Soldiers prepare positions in stages and a leader inspects the position at each stage before the soldiers move to the next stage.

Stage 1. The leader checks fields of fire from the prone position. For a stage 1 position, the soldiers:

- Emplace sector stakes.
- Stake the primary sector.
- Position grazing-fire log or sandbag between the sector stakes.
- Place the aiming stake(s), if required, to allow limited visibility engagement of a specific target.
- Scoop out elbow holes.
- Trace the outline of the position on the ground.
- Clear the fields of fire for both the primary and secondary sectors of fire.
- Ensure the leader inspects the position before they move to stage 2.

Stage 1

Stage 2. Soldiers prepare retaining walls for the parapets. They ensure the following:

- There is a minimum distance (equal to the width of one helmet) from the edge of the hole to the beginning of the front, flank, and rear cover.
- The cover to the front consists of sandbags (or logs), two to three high, and for a two-soldier position, about the length of two M203 rifles (about 7 feet).
- The cover to the flanks is the same height, but only one M203 rifle length (about 3.5 feet).
- The cover to the rear is one sandbag high and one M203 long (about 3.5 feet).
- If logs are used, they must be held firmly in place with strong stakes.
- The leader inspects the retaining wall before they begin stage 3.

FRONT WALL
Two sandbags high by two M203s long

Armpit deep by two helmets wide
by two M203s long

FLANK WALL
Two sandbags high
by one M203 long

FLANK WALL
Two sandbags high
by one M203 long

REAR WALL
One sandbag high by one M203 long

KEVLAR HELMET (1 FT)   M203 (3.5 FT)

Stage 2

Stage 3. Soldiers dig the position and throw dirt forward of the parapet retaining walls and pack it down hard. They:

- Dig the position armpit (of the tallest soldier) deep.
- Fill the parapets in order of front, flanks, and rear.
- Camouflage the parapets and the entire position.
- Dig grenade sumps and slope the floor toward them.
- Dig storage areas for two rucksacks into the rear wall if needed.
- Ensure the leader inspects the work.

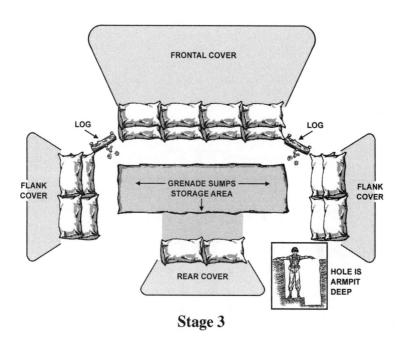

Stage 3

Stage 4. Soldiers prepare the overhead cover. They:
- Always provide solid support for overhead cover. They build the support with 4- to 6-inch logs on top of each other running the full length of the front and rear cover.
- Place five or six logs 4 to 6 inches in diameter and two M203s long (about 7 feet) over the center of the position, resting them on the overhead cover support, not on the sandbags.
- Place waterproofing (plastic bags, ponchos) on top of these logs.
- Put a minimum of 18 inches of packed dirt or sandbags on top of the logs.
- Camouflage the overhead cover and the bottom of the position.
- Ensure the leader inspects the position.

Stage 4

Inspect All Positions
Leaders must ensure their soldiers build fighting positions that are both effective and safe. An improperly sited position cannot be used and an improperly constructed position is a danger to its occupants. Leaders should inspect the progress of the fighting position at each stage in its preparation.

TYPES OF FIGHTING POSITIONS

There are many different types of fighting positions. The number of personnel, types of weapons, time available, and terrain are the main factors that dictate the type of position.

Hasty Fighting Position

Soldiers use this type of position when there is little or no time to prepare. They locate it behind whatever cover is available. It should give frontal protection from direct fire while allowing fire to the front and obliquely. A hasty position may consist simply of a rucksack placed beside a tree or large rock. For protection from indirect fire, a hasty fighting position should be in a small depression or hole at least 18 inches deep. The term *hasty position* does not mean that there is no digging. In only a few minutes, a prone shelter can be scraped out or dug to provide some protection. This type of position is well suited for ambushes or for protection of overwatching elements during raids and attacks. Hasty positions can also be the first step in the construction of more elaborate positions.

Hasty Fighting Position

One-Soldier Fighting Position
Positions that contain a single soldier are the least desirable, but they are useful in some situations. One-soldier positions may be required to cover exceptionally wide frontages. They should never be positioned out of sight of adjacent positions. The one-soldier fighting position should allow the soldier to fire to the front or to the oblique from behind frontal cover.

One-Soldier Fighting Position

Two-Soldier Fighting Position

A two-soldier fighting position can be prepared in close terrain. It can be used where grazing fire and mutual support extend no farther than to an adjacent position. It can be used to cover dead space just in front of the position. One or both ends of the hole are extended around the sides of the frontal cover. Changing a hole this way allows both soldiers to see better and have greater sectors of fire to the front. Also, during rest or eating periods, one soldier can watch the entire sector while the other sleeps or eats. If they receive fire from the front, they can move back to gain the protection of the frontal cover. By moving 1 meter, the soldiers can continue to find and hit targets to the front during lulls in enemy fire. This type of position requires more digging and is harder to camouflage. It is also a better target for enemy hand grenades.

Cutaway View of Two-Soldier Position

Modified Two-Soldier Fighting Position

A modified two-soldier fighting position may be prepared in close terrain, where grazing fire and mutual support extend no farther than to an adjacent position, or it can be prepared to cover dead space just in front of the position. This is done by extending one or both ends of the hole around the sides of the frontal cover.

Positions on Steep Terrain

On a steep slope, a soldier in a hole behind frontal cover cannot shoot attackers without standing up and exposing himself. To overcome this, the hole is dug and firing ports are dug out at each end of the hole. The ground between the firing ports then serves as frontal cover for the position.

Steep Terrain Position

Three-Soldier Fighting Position

A three-soldier position has several advantages over the other positions. There is a leader in each position, which makes command and control easier. It supports continuous, secure operations better than other positions. One soldier can provide security; one can do priority work; and one can rest, eat, or perform maintenance. It allows the platoon to maintain combat power and security without shifting personnel or leaving positions unmanned. It provides 360-degree observation and fire.

The leader must consider the following with three-person positions:

- Either the distance between positions must be increased or the size of the squad's sector reduced. The choice depends mainly on visibility and fields of fire.

- Because the squad leader is in a fighting position that will most likely be engaged during the battle, he cannot exert personal control over the other two positions. The squad leader keeps control over the battle by:
  — Clearly communicating plans and intent to his squad, including control measures and fire plans
  — Using prearranged signals such as flares, whistles, or tracers
  — Positioning key weapons in his fighting position
  — Placing his fighting position so that it covers key or decisive terrain
  — Placing his fighting position where his team might be able to act as a reserve

The three-soldier emplacement is the T-position. This basic design can be changed by adding or deleting berms, changing the orientation of the T, or shifting the position of the third soldier to form an L instead of a T. Berms, camouflage, and overhead cover are similar to other fighting positions.

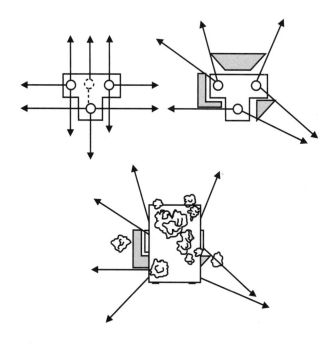

Three-soldier T-position

MACHINE GUN POSITIONS

The primary sector of fire is usually situated obliquely so that the gun can fire across the platoon's front. The tripod is used on the side with the primary sector of fire, and the bipod legs are used on the side with the secondary sector. When changing from primary to secondary sectors, the machine gun is moved, but the tripod is left in place. Dig a trench for the bipod legs in the secondary sector. After the platoon leader positions the gun and assigns sectors of fire, mark the position of the tripod legs and the limits of the sector of fire. Then trace the outline of the hole and the frontal cover.

Machine Gun Position Preparation

The gun is lowered by digging down the firing platforms where the gun will be placed. The platforms must not be so low that the gun cannot be traversed across the sector of fire. Lowering the gun reduces the profile of the gunner when he is shooting and reduces the height of the frontal cover needed. Dig the firing platform first, to lessen the gunner's exposure in case firing is required before the position is completed.

After the firing platforms have been dug, dig the hole, placing the dirt first where frontal cover is needed. The hole is dug deep enough to provide protection and still let the gunner shoot, usually about armpit deep. When the frontal cover is high and thick enough, the rest of the dirt is used to build the flank and rear cover. Three trench-shaped grenade sumps are dug at various points so that grenades can be kicked into them. Overhead cover is constructed following the steps of stage 4.

Note: If only a primary sector of fire is given, dig only half the position.

Machine Gun Position (continued)

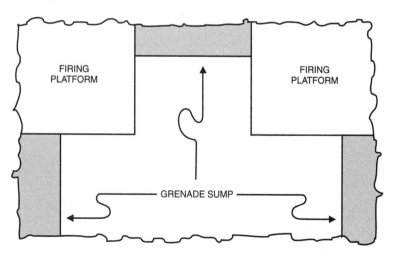

Machine Gun Position (continued)

JAVELIN POSITION

The Javelin can be employed from initial or completed positions. However, some changes are required:

1. The gunner must keep the weapon at least 6 inches above the ground to allow room for the stabilizing fins to unfold. The hole is only waist deep to allow the gunner to move while tracking a target. Because the Javelin gunner must be above ground level, the frontal cover should be high enough to hide his head and, if possible, the backblast of the Javelin. A hole is dug in front of the position for the bipod legs.

Javelin in an Individual Fighting Position

2. When the Javelin can be fired in one direction only, the position is adjusted to provide cover and concealment from all other directions, and the Javelin should be fired to the oblique. This protects the position from frontal fire and allows engagement of the target from the flank. Both ends of the launcher must extend out over the edges of the hole.
3. Overhead cover must be built on the flanks. Cover must be large enough for the gunner, the tracker, and the missiles. Overhead cover that allows fire from underneath can be built if the backblast area is clear. Overhead cover must be well camouflaged.

TOP VIEW JAVELIN FIGHTING POSITION

Standard Javelin Position

4. The Javelin is an important weapon and is easy to detect, therefore selection and preparation of alternate positions have a high priority. When preparing an alternate position, the gunner should select and improve a covered route to it so he can move to the position under fire.

Flush Position. The flush position is a hasty position that does not provide overhead protection for the Javelin gunner during firing. The position is basically a hole dug to approximately armpit depth. Overhead cover can be prepared either to the center or the flanks of the position.

Flush Fighting Position

AT4 POSITION

The AT4 can be fired from infantry fighting positions. If the AT4 is to be fired from a two-soldier position, the gunner must ensure the other soldier is not in the backblast area. Assume the basic standing position, but instead of stepping forward, lean against the back wall of the fighting position. Ensure that the rear of the weapon extends beyond the rear of the fighting position.

MORTAR POSITIONS

The standard dug-in mortar position has three stages of construction:

1. Mortar pit
2. Personnel shelters
3. Ammunition bunker

A dug-in position for 81-mm or 60-mm mortars is the same as for 4.2-inch mortars, with only slight changes in dimensions. The standard mortar position should be constructed on reasonably flat ground. It can be constructed totally below, partially above, or completely above ground, depending on the time and material available and the composition of the ground.

Stage 1. After the general location is selected, the exact baseplate position is marked, and construction of the mortar pit is begun.

Stage 2. As soon as the mortar pit is completed and as time allows, personnel shelters with overhead cover are constructed. Firing ports should be built into the personnel shelter and positioned as determined by assigned sectors of fire. There should be a blast barrier at least two sandbags thick separating the personnel shelters from the mortar pit.

Mortar Position
Three stages of construction: (1) mortar pit;
(2) personnel shelters; (3) ammunition bunker

Stage 3. If time and resources permit, ammunition bunkers are constructed. Each bunker is divided into four sections for each type of ammunition: white phosphorus (WP), illumination, final protective fire (FPF), and high explosive (HE).

Camouflaging the position is done in conjunction with construction through all stages.

VEHICLE POSITIONS

The deliberate position is constructed in four parts: hull defilade, concealed access ramp or route, hide location, and turret defilade. The access ramp from the hide location to the hull defilade usually provides turret defilade for a vehicle at some point on the ramp. This location is marked to allow the driver to drive to it during daylight and darkness.

Vehicle Position

14

First Aid

Soldiers may have to depend on their first-aid knowledge and skills to save themselves or other soldiers. They may be able to save a life, prevent permanent disability, or reduce long periods of hospitalization by knowing what to do, what not to do, and when to seek medical assistance. Most injured or ill soldiers are able to return to their units primarily because they are given appropriate and timely first aid followed by the best medical care possible.

The U.S. Army Combat Lifesaver Program trains nonmedical unit members in medical training beyond basic first aid (referred to as enhanced first aid). A minimum of one individual per squad, crew, team, or equivalent-sized unit should be trained as a combat lifesaver. The primary duty of this individual does not change. The additional duty of combat lifesaver is to provide enhanced first aid for injuries based on his training before the trauma arrives. This is a great program that all units should strive to include in their units.

EVALUATING A CASUALTY
All casualties should be evaluated in eight steps, checking for:
1. Responsiveness
2. Breathing
3. Pulse
4. Bleeding
5. Shock
6. Fractures
7. Burns
8. Head injury

Seek medical aid as soon as possible, but do not stop treatment. If the situation allows, send another person to find medical aid. If there are any signs of chemical or biological poisoning, immediately mask the casualty.

If it is nerve agent poisoning, administer the appropriate antidote, using the casualty's injector. Remember that in a chemical environment, the service member should not evaluate the casualty until the casualty has been masked.

Likewise, the prevalence of various body armor systems currently fielded to U.S. service members, and those in development for future fielding, may present a temporary obstacle to effective evaluation of an injured service member. You may have to carefully remove the body armor from the injured service member to complete the evaluation or administer first aid. Begin by removing the outer—most hard or soft body armor components (open, unfasten, or cut the closures, fasteners, or straps), then remove any successive layers in the same manner. Be sure to follow other notes, cautions, and warnings regarding procedures in contaminated situations and when a broken back or neck is suspected. Continue to evaluate according to the following steps.

1. RESPONSIVENESS
Check the casualty for responsiveness by gently shaking or tapping him while calmly asking, "Are you okay?" Watch for a response. If the casualty does not respond, go to step 2. If the casualty responds, you can assume that he is breathing and has a pulse and continue the evaluation at step 4. If the casualty is conscious, ask him where he feels different from usual or where it hurts. Ask him to identify the location of pain if he can, or to identify the area in which there is no feeling.

2. BREATHING
Check for breathing. If the casualty is breathing, proceed to step 4. If the casualty is not breathing, stop the evaluation and begin treatment. Lack of oxygen intake (because of a blocked airway or inadequate breathing) can lead to brain damage or death in only a few minutes.

Open the Airway

Head-Tilt/Chin-Lift Technique
In most cases, the airway can be cleared by simply using the head-tilt/chin-lift technique. Place one hand on the casualty's forehead and apply firm, backward pressure with the palm to tilt the head back. Place the fingertips of the other hand under the bony part of the lower jaw and lift, bringing the chin forward. The thumb should not be used to lift the chin. If the casualty does not resume breathing, give mouth-to-mouth resuscitation.

Once the rescuer uses one of the techniques to open the airway, he should maintain that head position to keep the airway open. If the casualty does not promptly resume adequate spontaneous breathing after the airway is open, rescue breathing (artificial respiration) must be started.

Give Artificial Respiration
Rescue breathing, or artificial respiration, is performed at the rate of about one breath every 5 seconds (12 breaths per minute), with rechecks for pulse and breathing after every 12 breaths. Rechecks can be accomplished in 3 to 5 seconds. Continue rescue breathing until the casualty starts to breathe on his own, until another person relieves you, or until you are too tired to continue.

Mouth-to-Mouth Method

While maintaining an open airway, take a deep breath and place your mouth (in an airtight seal) around the casualty's mouth. Blow two full breaths into the casualty's mouth (1 to $1^{1}/_{2}$ seconds per breath), taking a breath of fresh air before each blow. Watch out of the corner of your eye for the casualty's chest to rise. If the chest rises, sufficient air is getting into the casualty's lungs. After giving two breaths that cause the chest to rise, attempt to locate a pulse on the casualty. If a pulse is found and the casualty is not breathing, continue rescue breathing.

PRESS CHEEK FIRMLY AGAINST NOSE, OPEN YOUR MOUTH WIDE, AND BLOW UNTIL CHEST RISES, LISTEN AND LOOK FOR SIGNS OF THROAT OBSTRUCTION OR CLOGGED AIR PASSAGE.

Mouth-to-Mouth Resusitation Method

Mouth-to-Nose Method

The mouth-to-nose method is performed in the same way as the mouth-to-mouth method, except that you blow into the nose while you hold the lips closed with one hand at the chin. You then remove your mouth to allow the casualty to exhale passively. It may be necessary to separate the casualty's lips to allow the air to escape during exhalation.

OPEN YOUR MOUTH WIDE AND BLOW INTO NOSE UNTIL CHEST RISES. LISTEN AND LOOK FOR SIGNS OF THROAT OBSTRUCTION OR CLOGGED AIR PASSAGE.

Mouth-to-Nose Method

3. PULSE
If a pulse is present and the casualty is breathing, proceed to step 4. If a pulse is not found, seek medically trained personnel for help.

4. BLEEDING
Look for spurts of blood or blood-soaked clothes. Also check for both entry and exit wounds. If the casualty is bleeding from an open wound, stop the evaluation and begin first-aid treatment.

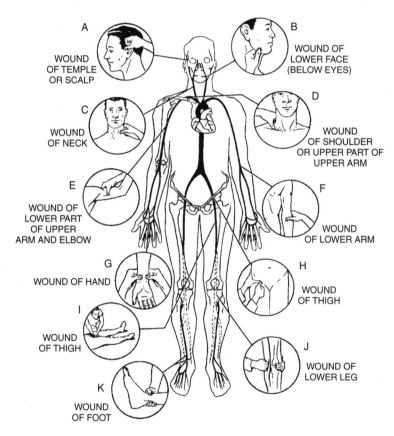

**Pressure Points for Temporary Control of
Arterial Bleeding**

Arm or Leg Wound

Use the casualty's first-aid dressing; remove it from the wrapper and pull the dressing open with the white side down. Place the dressing directly over the wound without touching the sterile white side of the dressing. Wrap both tails of the dressing around the injured limb in opposite directions until the edges of the dressing are sealed. Leave enough tail for a knot. Tie the knot over the outer edge of the dressing but not directly over the wound. The dressing should be tied firmly enough to stop the bleeding, but without causing a tourniquet-like effect.

If the bleeding continues after applying field dressing, apply firm pressure with the hand over the dressing for 5 to 10 minutes, or have the casualty do it if he is conscious. Elevate the wound slightly above the heart to stop the bleeding.

If the bleeding continues, use a pressure dressing (a wad of padding or cloth). Place it directly over the wound and use a cravat or improvised dressing to wrap the padding tightly over the previously placed field dressing. Tie the ends together in a nonslip knot directly over the wound site. Continue to elevate the wound.

Place Dressing Directly Over Wound

Tie Tails Into Nonslip Knot
(Not Over Wound)

Tourniquet

If the bleeding still continues and all other measures have failed, or if the limb is severed, apply a tourniquet. A tourniquet is a constricting band placed around an arm or leg to control bleeding. A soldier whose arm or leg has been completely amputated may not be bleeding when first discovered, but a tourniquet should be applied anyway. If the pressure dressing under firm hand pressure becomes soaked with blood and the wound continues to bleed, apply a tourniquet. If left in place too long, a tourniquet can cause loss of an arm or leg. Once applied, however, it must stay in place, and the casualty must be taken to the nearest medical treatment facility as soon as

1. Tourniquet placed 2 to 4 inches above wound   2. Rigid object on top of half knot

3. Full knot over rigid object   4. Twist the stick and align it lengthwise with the limb

5. Free ends looped and tied off

Applying a Tourniquet

possible. Do not loosen or release a tourniquet after it has been applied and the bleeding has stopped.

In the absence of a specially designed tourniquet, one can be made from strong, pliable material such as gauze or muslin bandages, clothing, or kerchiefs. An improvised tourniquet is used with a rigid sticklike object. To minimize skin damage, ensure that the improvised tourniquet is at least 2 inches wide. Place the tourniquet around the limb, between the wound and the body trunk (or between the wound and the heart). Place the tourniquet 2 to 4 inches from the edge of the wound site. Never place it directly over a wound or fracture or directly on a joint (wrist, elbow, or knee). For wounds just below a joint, place the tourniquet just above and as close to the joint as possible. The tourniquet should have padding underneath. If possible, place the tourniquet over the smoothed sleeve or trouser leg to prevent the skin from being pinched or twisted. If the tourniquet is long enough, wrap it around the limb several times, keeping the material as flat as possible. Damaging the skin may deprive the surgeon of skin required to cover an amputation. Protection of the skin also reduces pain.

Open Abdominal Wound

Position the Casualty
Place and maintain the casualty on his back with his knees in an upright (flexed) position, unless other wounds prevent such action. The knees-up position helps relieve pain, assists in the treatment of shock, prevents further exposure of the bowel (intestines) or abdominal organs, and helps relieve abdominal pressure by allowing the abdominal muscles to relax.

Expose the Wound
Remove the casualty's loose clothing to expose the wound. However, *do not* attempt to remove clothing that is stuck to the wound; it may cause further injury. Gently pick up any organs that may be on the ground. Do this with a clean, dry dressing or with the cleanest available material. Place the organs on top of the casualty's abdomen.

Apply the Field Dressing
If the field dressing is not large enough to cover the entire wound, the plastic wrapper from the dressing may be used to cover the wound first (placing the field dressing on top). If necessary, other improvised dressings may be made from clothing, blankets, or the cleanest materials available. Field dressings can be covered with improvised reinforcement material (cravats, strips of torn T-shirt, or other cloth), if available, for additional support and protection.

Do not give casualties with abdominal wounds food or water, although moistening the lips is allowed.

1. Place the casualty on his back with knees flexed

2. Before applying dressings, carefully place protruding organs near the wound to protect them and control contamination

3. Dressing applied and tails tied with nonslip knot (side of wound)

4. Field dressing covered with improvised material and loosely tied (opposite side)

Open Abdominal Wound

Open Chest Wound

Expose the Wound
Follow the same procedure as for an open abdominal wound. Expose the wound. Listen for sucking sounds to determine if the chest wall is punctured. If there is an object extending from (impaled in) the wound, *do not* remove it. Apply a dressing around the object and use additional improvised bulky materials or dressings (use the cleanest materials available) to build up the area around the object. Apply a supporting bandage over the bulky materials to hold them in place.

Dress the Wound
The field dressing plastic wrapper is used with the field dressing to create an airtight seal. If a plastic wrapper is not available or if an additional wound needs to be treated, cellophane, foil, the casualty's poncho, or similar material may be used. The covering should be wide enough to extend 2 inches or more beyond the edges of the wound in all directions.

1. Open chest wound sealed with plastic wrapper

2. Field dressing placed on plastic wrapper

3. Tails of dressing tied into nonslip knot over center of dressing

Open Chest Wound

5. SHOCK

Signs of shock are sweaty but cool (clammy) skin, paleness of skin, restlessness or nervousness, thirst, loss of blood, confusion, faster than normal breathing rate, blotchy or bluish skin, especially around the mouth, and nausea and/or vomiting.

In the field, the procedures to treat shock are identical to those used to prevent shock:

- Move the casualty to cover.
- Lay the casualty on his back. If shock occurs after a heart attack, chest wound, or breathing difficulty, the casualty may breathe easier in a sitting position. If this is the case, allow him to sit upright, but monitor him carefully in case his condition worsens.
- Elevate the casualty's feet higher than the level of his heart.
- Loosen clothing at the neck, waist, or wherever it may be binding.
- Prevent chilling or overheating.
- Calm the casualty.

Do not give a shock casualty any food or drink. If you must leave the casualty or if he is unconscious, turn his head to the side to prevent him from choking should he vomit.

6. FRACTURES

Signs of a broken bone include tenderness over the injury with pain on movement, inability to move the injured part, unnatural shape, swelling, and discoloration of the skin. All these signs may or may not be present with a fracture; if you are not sure, give the patient the benefit of the doubt and treat it as a fracture.

Handle with care. Prevent shock and further injury. Broken ends of bone can cut nerves, blood vessels, and so on. Do not move the patient unless necessary. If he must be moved, splint the fracture first.

If there is a wound, apply dressing as for any other wound. If there is bleeding, it must be stopped. If a tourniquet is necessary, do not place it over the site of the fracture. If time permits, improvise splints (sticks, blankets, poncho, and the like); if a weapon is used for a splint, unload it first. Pad splints well with soft material to prevent pressure and rubbing. The splint should extend from above the joint above the fracture to below the joint below the fracture. Bind splints securely at several points, but not so tightly as to interfere with blood flow (check pulse).

One of the quickest ways to splint a broken leg is by tying it to the uninjured leg (do not use narrow materials such as wire). Use padding between the legs, and tie at several points above and below the break. Tie the feet together.

Support a fracture of the arm or shoulder with a sling (do not try to bend an injured elbow if it is straight).

Back and Neck Injuries
Check for signs or symptoms of a back or neck injury, such as pain or tenderness, cuts or bruises, numbness, and inability to move (paralysis). Look for unusual body or limb position. Unless there is immediate life-threatening danger, *do not* move a casualty who has a suspected back or neck injury. Movement may cause permanent paralysis or death.

Spinal Column Fractures
If a casualty does not have any feeling in his legs and cannot move them, he has a severe back injury that should be treated as a fracture. If the casualty is lying faceup, slip a blanket or other like material under the arch of his back to support the spinal column in a swayback position. If he is lying facedown, *do not* put anything under any part of his body.

If the casualty must be transported to a safe location and is in a faceup position, transport him by litter or use a firm substitute. Loosely tie the casualty's wrists together over his waistline and his feet together to avoid accidental shifting of the body. Lay a folded blanket or substitute across the litter

In this position, bone fragments may bruise or cut the spinal cord

Blankets in place

Broken Back

where the arch in the back is to be placed. Use a four-man team and place the casualty on the litter without bending his spinal column or his neck. If the casualty is in a facedown position, he must be transported in this same position. Keep the spinal column in a swayback position, and use a blanket or substitute placed on the litter where the chest will be placed to maintain this position.

Neck Fractures

A fractured neck is extremely dangerous. Moving the casualty may cause death. *Leave him in the position in which he is found.* If his neck or head is in an abnormal position, immediately immobilize the neck and head. If he is lying faceup, raise his shoulders slightly, and slip a roll of cloth that has the bulk of a bath towel under his neck. The roll should be thick enough to arch his neck only slightly, leaving the back of his head on the ground. Place heavy objects such as rocks or the casualty's boots on each side of his head to immobilize it. If it is necessary to use boots, fill them with stones, gravel, sand, or dirt and tie them tightly at the top. *Do not* move the casualty in any way or place any objects under his neck if he is lying facedown.

Casualty with roll of cloth (bulk) under neck
and boots used to immobilize head

Broken Neck

7. BURNS

Look carefully for reddened, blistered, or charred skin; also check for singed clothing. If burns are found, stop the evaluation and begin treatment.

Minor burns (no charring or blistering) of small skin areas should be covered with a first-aid packet or other dry, sterile dressing. Otherwise, leave them uncovered.

If a burn is severe (blistered or charred or covers a large area of body), infection and shock must be prevented. Cover the burned area with a dry, sterile dressing. Do not touch the burn with anything but sterile dressings, except in the case of mass casualties. Then cover their burns with clean sheets, T-shirts, and the like. Leave a severe burn uncovered only as a last resort. Do not place the dressing over the face or genital area. Do not pull clothes over the burned area, try to remove pieces of cloth sticking to skin, try to clean the burned area, break a burn blister, or put grease, Vaseline, or ointment on a burn.

Prevent shock by placing the casualty's head and shoulders lower than the rest of the body and by replacing body fluids. If the casualty is conscious, is not vomiting, and has no belly wound, give small amounts of cool or cold water. Give a few sips every few minutes; increase amounts until one-third of a canteen cupful is drunk every hour. If the casualty vomits or acts as if he might, do not give him any more water. Do not use warm water, which can cause vomiting.

8. HEAD INJURY

A head injury may be opened or closed. In open injuries, there is a visible wound and the brain may be seen. In closed injuries, no visible injury is seen, but the casualty may experience the same signs and symptoms. If you suspect a severe head injury, evaluate the casualty for loss of consciousness, nausea or vomiting, convulsions, slurred speech and confusion, sleepiness, dizziness, clear or bloody fluid leaking from the ear or nose, headache, paralysis, black eyes, or other obvious signs.

The casualty should be continuously monitored for the development of conditions that might require basic lifesaving measures. Treat the injury as a suspected neck or spinal injury until proved otherwise. Place a dressing over the wounded area, and keep the casualty warm. Place the casualty in a position with the head slightly elevated if there is no accumulation of fluid or blood in the casualty's throat. When there is bleeding from the mouth and throat, place the casualty on his side or face so the blood can run out of the mouth. Remove all foreign objects and false teeth from unconscious casualties.

Jaw Wounds

Before applying a bandage to a casualty's jaw, remove all foreign material from the mouth. If the casualty is unconscious, check for obstructions in the airway. When applying the bandage, allow the jaw enough freedom to permit passage of air and drainage from the mouth. If the casualty is unconscious, place him on his belly or side with the head lower than the body and turned slightly to one side.

MISCELLANEOUS INJURIES

Foreign Bodies

In the Eye
Do not rub eye. Tears frequently flush out the particle. If not, pull the eyelid up or down and attempt to remove the particle with the corner of a moist, clean handkerchief. If unsuccessful, or if the foreign body is glass or metal, blindfold both eyes and evacuate to medical facilities.

In the Ear, Nose, or Throat
Never probe for a foreign object in the ear or nose. A live insect in the ear may be removed by attracting it with a flashlight or by pouring water into the ear to drown it and flush it out. Do not attempt to flush a foreign object out of the ear with water if the object will swell when wet.

Remove foreign objects from the nose by blowing.

Coughing frequently dislodges a foreign object from the throat. If this fails and the object can be reached, try to remove it with the fingers, but be careful not to push it deeper.

HEAT INJURIES
Heat injuries are disabling to varying degrees and can be fatal. They occur when water and salt lost in sweat are not replaced. Heat injuries are especially liable to occur in individuals who are not acclimatized (accustomed) to the heat and in those who are overweight, have fevers (sunburn, infection, reaction to immunizations), or are already dehydrated (have insufficient water in their bodies) because of diarrhea, alcohol consumption, or simply not having drunk enough water.

Sweating
The evaporation of sweat is the only way the body can cool itself when the temperature is above 95° Fahrenheit; evaporation is less efficient and more water intake is required in the humid jungle than in the dry desert. More than 3 gallons of water and salt may be lost and need to be replaced by soldiers working hard in the heat.

Water

It's best to replace water as it is lost—soldiers should drink when thirsty. There is no benefit in withholding water until later. It is impossible to train soldiers to get by on less water than the amount required to replace that lost in sweat. Water requirements can be reduced only if sweating is reduced by working during the cooler hours of evening, night, and early morning.

Salt

Extra salt is required when soldiers are sweating heavily. Salt tablets should *not* be used to prevent heat injury, however. Usually, eating field rations or liberal salting of the garrison diet provides enough salt to replace what is lost.

Heat Cramps

Heat cramps are cramps of the muscles of the belly, arms, or legs. They occur when a person sweats a lot and has not consumed extra water.

Heat Exhaustion

The victim of heat exhaustion may have a headache and be dizzy, faint, and weak. He has cool, pale (gray), moist (sweaty) skin and loss of appetite. Move him to a shady area or improvise shade and have him lie down. Loosen or remove clothing and boots, pour water on him, and fan him if it is hot. Elevate his legs, and have him slowly drink at least one canteen of water. The patient should not participate in further strenuous activity and should be evacuated if symptoms persist.

Heatstroke

Heatstroke is a medical emergency and can be fatal if not treated promptly and correctly. It is caused by failure of the body's cooling mechanisms. Inadequate sweating is a factor. The casualty's skin is flushed, hot, and dry. He may experience dizziness, confusion, headaches, seizures, and nausea, and his respiration and pulse may be weak. Cool the casualty immediately by moving him to a shaded area; remove outer clothing, pour water on him or immerse him in water, and fan him to permit the cooling effect of evaporation. Massage his skin, elevate his legs, and have him slowly drink water. Get him to a medical facility as soon as possible.

COLD INJURIES
Cold injuries are caused when the body loses heat. They can cause the loss of toes, fingers, feet, ears, and so on.

Frostbite
If body heat is lost quickly and the tissues actually freeze, the injury is called frostbite. Frostbite usually affects the face, hands, or feet. There may be no pain. Frostbitten parts of the body become grayish or white and lose feeling. Use a buddy system to keep watch on one another for signs of frostbite.

Treat frostbite by removing the casualty's clothing (boots, gloves, socks) and thawing the area by placing it next to a warm part of his or somebody else's body. Warm (not hot) water may be used. Remove constrictive clothing that interferes with circulation. Do not rewarm by walking, massage, exposure to open fire, cold water, or rubbing with snow. After the part has been warmed, protect it from further injury by covering it lightly with a blanket or dry clothing. Do not use ointments or other medications.

Trenchfoot (Immersion Foot)
Trenchfoot or immersion foot resembles frostbite but occurs when the feet are exposed to cold and wet conditions. (See the section on Foot Care.)

Prevention of Cold Injuries
Cold injuries can be prevented by proper leadership and by training in conserving body heat.

Leadership—command interest—is essential. Personnel must be taught how to prevent cold injuries. Reduce their exposure to cold, wet, and wind when possible. Rotate individuals and units to warming tents. Provide changes of dry clothing, hot food, and drinks.

Individuals can take the following steps:
- Do not stand in wet positions—build them up with branches and the like.
- Carry extra dry socks, and change after marching or standing.
- Remove cold and wet boots and socks before going to sleep.
- Sleep back to back with a buddy to prevent loss of body heat.
- Massage the feet several times daily, especially when changing socks.
- Do not touch bare metal with bare skin.

To dress properly, remember C-O-L-D:

C: Keep *clean.* Dirty clothing has less insulating quality.

O: Avoid *overheating.* Overheating causes sweating, and clothing wet from sweat causes cold injury.

L: Wear *loose* and in *layers.* Warm air is trapped between layers and acts as insulation. Tight clothing, boots, and gloves leave no room for a warm air layer or for the exercise of fingers and toes and may act as a tourniquet to shut off circulation.

D: Keep *dry.* Dry clothing retains heat; wet clothing conducts heat away from the body.

SNAKEBITES

Keep the bitten person quiet, and do not let him walk or run. Kill the snake, if possible, and keep it for identification. If the bite is on an extremity, do not elevate the limb; keep it level with the body. If the bite is on an arm or leg, place a constricting band (narrow gauze bandage) one to two finger widths above and below the bite. If the bite is on a hand or foot, place the band above the wrist or ankle.

The band should be tight enough to stop the flow of blood near the skin, but not so tight as to interfere with circulation. It should not have a tourniquet-like effect. Get the casualty to medical treatment as soon as possible.

FOOT CARE

Socks

Wash and dry socks daily. Start each day with a fresh pair. After crossing a wet area, dry your feet, put on foot powder, and change socks if the situation permits. Avoid worn or tight-fitting socks. Carry an extra pair in a pack or inside the shirt.

Blisters

Wash the area, open the blister, drain, and cover with adhesive tape.

Athlete's Foot

Keep feet clean and dry. Use foot powder.

15

Reporting Enemy Information

Commanders get information (intelligence) about the enemy from many sources, but especially from individual soldiers who collect information from battlefield operations, including:
- Prisoners of war (PWs)
- Captured documents
- Enemy activity
- Local civilians

WHAT TO REPORT
Report all information about the enemy to your leader *quickly*, *accurately*, and *completely*. Such reports should answer the questions Who, What, Where, and When. It is best to use the SALUTE format (Size, Activity, Location, Unit, Time, and Equipment) when reporting. Use notes and draw sketches as aids in remembering details.

Size
Report the number of soldiers and vehicles you saw. For example, report: "ten enemy infantrymen" (not "a rifle squad") or "three enemy tanks" (not "an enemy tank platoon").

Activity
Report what you saw the enemy doing—for example, "emplacing mines in the road."

Location
Report where you saw the enemy. If you have a map, try to give a six-digit coordinate, such as "GL567345." If you do not have a map, relate the location to some key terrain feature, such as "on the Hann Road, about 300 meters south of the Kelly River bridge."

Unit

If the enemy's unit is not known, report any distinctive features, such as bumper markings on trucks or type of headgear. Some armies have distinctive uniforms and headgear, or colored tabs on their uniforms, to identify types of units. A unit's action may also indicate its type. The kind of equipment observed may me peculiar to a certain type of unit. For example, a soviet vehicle used by reconnaissance units (BRDM) may indicate a reconnaissance unit.

Time

Report the time you saw the enemy activity, not the time you report it. Always report local or Zulu times.

Equipment

Report all of the equipment the enemy is wearing or using. If you do not recognize an item of equipment or a type of vehicle, sketch it and submit the sketch with the report

The following is an example of a SALUTE report:

"Combat OP [observation post] Foxtrot sighted four enemy tanks moving west along secondary road at grid NB612297 at 241730Z. Tanks traveling at approximately 5 KMH. Hatches are open, and visible enemy personnel are wearing protective masks."

PRISONERS OF WAR (PW) AND CAPTURED DOCUMENTS

Enemy prisoners of war (EPW) are a good source of information. They must be handled without breaking international law and without losing a chance to gain intelligence. Treat EPWs humanely. Do not harm them either physically or mentally. Do not give them candy, cigarettes, or other comfort items. EPWs who receive favors or are mistreated are poor interrogation subjects. In handling PWs, follow the five Ss:

- *Search* EPWs as soon as they are captured. Take their weapons and papers, except identification cards and protective masks. Give them a written receipt for any personal property and documents taken. When searching an EPW, have one man guard him while another searches him. A searcher must not get between the guard and the PW. To search a PW, have him spread-eagle against a tree or wall, or get him into a push-up position with his knees on the ground.
- *Segregate* PWs into groups by sex and into subgroups such as officers, enlisted, civilians, and political figures. This keeps the leaders from organizing escape efforts.

- *Silence* PWs and do not let them talk to each other. This keeps them from planning escapes and cautioning each other on security. Report anything an EPW says or does.
- *Speed* PWs to the rear. Turn them over to your leader. He or she will assemble them and move them to the rear for questioning by the S2.
- *Safeguard* PWs when taking them to the rear. Do not let anyone abuse them. Watch out for escape attempts. Do not let EPWs bunch up, spread out too far, or start diversions.

Identification

Before evacuating an EPW, attach a tag to him showing the date and time of capture, place, capturing unit, and circumstances.

Handling Captured Documents and Equipment

Enemy documents and equipment are good sources of information. Documents may be official (maps, orders, records, photos) or personal (letters, diaries).

If such items are not handled properly, the information in them may become outdated. Give them to your leader quickly. Tag each item with information on when and where it was captured; if it was found on a PW, include the PW's name on the tag.

16

Individual
Movement and Security

As a member of a fire team you may have to get close to an enemy position using the correct individual tactical fire and movement techniques dictated by METT-TC. All movement needs to be coordinated with other team/squad members in order for each of you to provide cover for one another. After analysis or orders, determine the correct individual movement technique(s) for each individual movement forward.

MOVEMENT SKILLS
Observe the following practices during movement:
- Camouflage yourself and your equipment.
- Tape your dog tags to each other and to the chain to prevent rattle. Tape or pad loose parts of your weapon and equipment so they do not rattle or get snagged. Jump up and down. Listen for rattles.
- Do not carry unnecessary equipment.
- Stop, look, and listen before moving. Be especially alert when birds or animals are alarmed (the enemy may be nearby). Look for your next position before leaving a position. Look for covered and concealed routes on which to move.
- Change direction from time to time when moving through tall grass.
- Use battlefield noises to conceal your movement noises.
- Cross roads and trails at places that have the most cover and concealment (large culverts, low spots, curves, or bridges).
- Avoid steep slopes and places with loose dirt or stones.
- Avoid cleared, open areas and tops of hills and ridges.

INDIVIDUAL MOVEMENT TECHNIQUES

Low Crawl

Select the low crawl when the route provides cover or concealment less than one foot high, visibility provides the enemy good observation, and speed is not required. The proper way to do the low crawl is (A) to keep your body as flat as possible to the ground. Hold your weapon by grasping the sling at the upper sling swivel, letting the handguard rest on your forearm and the butt of the weapon drag on the ground, thus keeping the muzzle off the ground. Move forward (B) by pushing both arms forward while pulling your right leg forward and then pull with both arms while pushing with your right leg (C). Continue these push-pull movements until you reach your next position, changing your pushing leg frequently to avoid fatigue.

Low Crawl

High Crawl

Select the high crawl when the route provides cover and concealment, poor visibility reduces enemy observation, and speed is required but the terrain and vegetation are suitable only for the low crawl. The proper way to do the high crawl is to keep your body off the ground while resting your weight on your forearms and lower legs. Cradle your weapon in your arms, keeping its muzzle off the ground. Keep your knees well behind your buttocks so they stay low and move forward by alternately advancing your right elbow and left knee, and left elbow and right knee.

High Crawl

Rush

Select the rush when you must cross open areas and time is critical. The proper way to do the rush is to move from your firing position by rolling or crawling because the enemy may have your current position identified. Start from the prone position and select your next position by slowly raising your head. Lower your head while drawing your arms into your body, keeping your elbows down, and pulling your right leg forward. Raise your body in one movement by straightening your arms and springing to your feet, stepping off with either foot. Run to the next position keeping your distance short and try not to stay up longer than 3 to 5 seconds. At your position, plant your feet and fall forward by sliding your right hand down to the heel of the butt of your weapon and break your fall with the butt of your weapon. Roll or crawl to a covered or concealed firing position.

(A) Seek next position.

(B) Raise up.

(C) Rush Forward.

(D) To stop—plant both feet.

(E) Fall forward—roll on your non-firing side.

(F) Assume prone firing position.

Rush

STEALTH

To move with stealth, use the following procedures:
1. Hold your rifle at port arms (ready position).
2. While stepping, make your footing sure and solid by keeping your body's weight on the leading foot.
3. Raise the moving leg high to clear brush or grass.
4. Gently let the moving foot down toe first, with your body's weight on the rear leg.
5. Lower the heel of the moving foot after the toe is in a solid place.
6. Shift your body's weight and balance to the forward foot before moving the rear foot.
7. Take short steps to help maintain balance.

NIGHT MOVEMENT

When moving through dense vegetation, avoid making noise. Hold your weapon in one hand and keep the other hand forward, feeling for obstructions.

When going into the prone position:
1. Hold your rifle with one hand, and crouch slowly.
2. Feel the ground with your free hand to make sure it is clear of mines, trip wires, or other hazards.
3. Lower your knees one at a time, until your body's weight is on both knees and your free hand.
4. Shift your weight to your free hand and opposite knee.
5. Raise your free leg up and back, and lower it gently to that side.
6. Roll quietly into a prone position.

When crawling at night:
1. Crawl on your hands and knees.
2. Hold your rifle in your firing hand.
3. Use your nonfiring hand to feel for and make clear spots for your hands and knees to move to.
4. Move your hands and knees to those spots, and put them down softly.

FLARES

If you are caught in the light of a ground flare, move quickly out of the lighted area. The enemy knows where the flare is and will be ready to fire into that area. Move well away from the lighted area, and look for other team members. If you hear the firing of an aerial flare while you are moving, hit the ground (behind cover, if possible) while the flare is rising and before it illuminates the area.

The sudden light of a flare may temporarily blind both you and the enemy. To protect your night vision, close one eye while the flare is burning.

If you are caught in the light of an aerial flare and you can easily blend with the background (in a forest), freeze in place until the flare burns out. If caught in the open, immediately crouch low or lie down.

SECURITY MEASURES

The enemy must not get information about your operations. This means that you and your fellow soldiers must do the following:
- Practice camouflage principles and techniques.
- Practice noise and light discipline.
- Practice field sanitation.
- Use proper radiotelephone procedures.
- Use the challenge and password properly.
- Not take personal letters or pictures into combat areas.
- Not keep diaries in combat areas.
- Be careful when discussing military affairs.
- Use only authorized codes.
- Abide by the Code of Conduct.
- Report any soldier or civilian who is believed to be serving or sympathetic with the enemy.
- Report anyone who tries to get information about U.S. operations.
- Destroy all maps or important documents if capture is imminent.

SURVIVAL

Continuous operations and fast-moving battles increase your chances of becoming separated from your unit. Your mission is to rejoin your unit. Survival is the action of staying alive in the field with limited resources. You must survive when you become separated from your unit, are evading the enemy, or are a prisoner.

Evasion

Evasion is the action you take to stay out of the hands of the enemy. There are several courses of action you may take:
- You may stay in your current position and wait for friendly troops to find you. This may be a good course of action if you are sure that friendly troops will continue to operate in the area, and if there are a lot of enemy units in the area.

- You may break out to a friendly area. This may be a good course of action if you know where a friendly area is, and if the enemy is widely dispersed.
- You may move farther into enemy territory to temporarily conduct guerrilla-type operations. This is a short-term course of action to be taken only when other courses of action are not feasible. This may be a good course of action when the enemy area is known to be lightly held or when there is a good chance of linking up with friendly guerrillas.
- You may combine two or more of the above. For example, you may stay in your current area until the enemy moves out of the area and then break out to a friendly area.

Enemy
There may be times when you will have to kill, stun, or capture an enemy soldier without alerting other enemy in the area. At such times, a rifle or pistol makes too much noise, and you will need a silent weapon. Some silent weapons are the bayonet, the garotte (a choke wire or cord with handles), and improvised clubs.

RESISTANCE
The Code of Conduct (at the front of this book) is an expression of the ideals and principles that traditionally have guided and strengthened American servicemembers. It prescribes the manner in which every soldier of the U.S. Armed Forces must conduct himself when captured or faced with the possibility of capture. You should never surrender of your own free will. Likewise, a leader should never surrender the soldiers under his command while they still have the means to resist. If captured, you must continue to resist in every way you can, remembering the following:
- Make every effort to escape and help others to escape.
- Do not accept special favors from the enemy.
- Do not give your word not to escape.
- Do nothing that will harm a fellow prisoner.
- Give no information except name, rank, social security number, and date of birth.
- Do not answer any questions other than those concerning your name, rank, social security number, and date of birth.

ESCAPE

Escape is the action you take to get away from the enemy if you are captured. The best time for you to escape is right after you are captured. You will probably be in your best physical condition at that time. The following are other reasons for making an early escape:

- Friendly fire or air strikes may cause enough confusion and disorder to provide a chance of escape.
- The first guards you have probably will not be as well trained as guards farther back.
- Some of the first guards may be walking wounded who are distracted by their own condition.
- You know something about the area where you are captured and may know the location of nearby friendly units.

The way you escape depends on what you can think of to fit the situation. The only general rules are to escape early and escape when the enemy is distracted.

Once you escape, it may not be easy to contact friendly troops, even when you know where they are. You should contact a friendly unit as you would if you were a member of a lost patrol. Time your movement so that you pass through enemy units at night and arrive at a friendly unit at dawn. A good way to make contact is to find a ditch or shallow hole to hide in where you have cover from both friendly and enemy fire. At dawn, attract the attention of the friendly unit by an action such as waving a white cloth, shouting, or showing a panel. When the friendly unit has been alerted, shout who you are and what your situation is, and ask for permission to move toward the unit.

NIGHT VISION DEVICES (NVD)

Units that train with individuals in the use of NVDs can dominate night operations, especially against a lesser-equipped enemy. From the 1960s until most recently, the military has gone from Generation I to the very sophisticated Generation IV NVDs. Generation III, though very good, can create some halo effects around light sources that could partially white out the view and such halos also make use of aiming devices less precise and reduce overall clarity. The newer Generation IV sees farther under equal light conditions, provides a clearer picture with greater detail, and makes sighting more precise. Some of the older and newer reconnaissance, surveillance, and target acquisition (RSTA) devices or NVDs available today include the following:

AN/PVS-4 Individual Weapon Night Vision Device. The AN/PVS-4 night vision sight is a portable, battery-operated, electro-optical instrument used for observation and aimed fire of weapons at night. It amplifies reflected light such as moonlight, starlight, and sky glow so that the viewed scene becomes clearly visible to the operator. It can be used on the M16A2 rifle, M4 carbine, M4 modular weapon system, M249 machine gun, M60 machine gun, M240B machine gun, M136 (AT4), and the M203 grenade launcher. It has a magnification of 3.6× and range of 400 to 600 meters (for man-sized target) in starlight and moonlight.

**AN/PVS-4
Individual Weapon NVD**

AN/PVS-5 Night Vision Goggles. This is both an active and a passive night vision device worn on the head. It has a built-in infrared light source for close-up viewing within 2 meters. This mode can be used to read maps, orders, and overlays or for vehicle maintenance. The goggles have a range of 150 meters in the passive mode. The AN/PVS-5 is an older, but still effective device.

**AN/PVS-5
Night Vision Goggles**

AN/PVS-7A and AN/PVS-7B Night Vision Systems. The AN/PVS-7A and AN/PVS-7B are self-contained night vision systems worn on the head or handheld. They provide improved night vision capabilities using available light from the sky and moonlight. The goggles enable the user to perform normal tasks such as reading, walking, driving, or surveillance during times of darkness. The goggles may be used with or without the standard battle helmet and provide capabilities for all infantry tasks. The head harnesses differ slightly. The 7B version has some improvements over the 7A version. The 7A version has an effective range of 100 meters, and the 7B version has an effective range of 300 meters under optimal conditions.

**AN/PVS-7A/B
Night Vision System**

AN/TAS-5 Dragon Thermal Night Vision Sight. This is a passive thermal imagery system with a range of 1,200 meters.

**AN/TAS-5
Dragon Thermal Sight**

AN/VVS-2 Night Vision Driver's Viewer. This image-intensification device is mounted in the Bradley driver's station and has a range in excess of 150 meters. It can observe rounds fired from the 25-mm gun and the 7.62-mm coaxial machine gun out to greater ranges.

**AN/VVS-2
Night Vision Driver's Viewer**

AN/PVS-14 Monocular NVD. The AN/PVS-14 is either a hand-held, helmet-mounted, head-mounted, or weapon-mounted night vision device that enables walking, driving, weapon firing, short-range surveillance, map reading, vehicle maintenance, or administering first aid in moonlight and starlight. Each unit allows for vertical adjustment (using head straps), fore and aft adjustment, objective lens focus, and eyepiece focus. The device is also equipped with an infrared light-emitting source with a vari-

**AN/PVS-14
Monocular NVD**

able gain control. It has a magnification of 1× or 3× with an optional magnifier. The AN/PVS-14 night vision device amplifies available ambient star, moon, or reflected light to produce an intensified image in the proper perspective.

AN/PAS-13 Medium Weapon Thermal Sight. The AN/PAS-13 (V2) medium weapon thermal sight (MWTS) and the AN/PAS-13 (V3) heavy weapon thermal sight (HWTS) are silent, lightweight, compact, and durable battery-powered infrared-imaging sensors that operate with low battery consumption. The MWTS has a 3.3× magnification and the HWTS has a 10× magnification. When firing your weapon with either weapon thermal sight (WTS), the fundamentals of marksmanship are the same as with each weapon system using the AN/PVS-4 minus certain techniques for the M203 and M2 HB .50 caliber.

AN/PAS-13(V2)
Medium Weapon Thermal Sight (MWTS)

AN/PAS-13 (V3)
Heavy Weapon Thermal Sight (HWTS)

AN/TVS-5 NVD. The AN/TVS-5 is a portable, battery-operated electro-optical instrument used for observation and aimed fire of weapons at night. It amplifies reflected light such as moonlight, starlight, and sky glow so that the viewed scene becomes clearly visible to the operator. The only two weapons that use the AN/TVS-5 are the M2 HB .50-caliber machine gun and the MK19 grenade launcher. By using this device, the gunner can observe the area and detect and engage any suitable target. It has a magnification: 5.6× and range of 1,000 to 1,200 meters for vehicle targets (under ideal conditions).

AN/TVS-5 NVD

AN/PVS-10 Night Vision Sniper Scope. The AN/PVS-10 night vision sniper scope, referred to as the sniper night scope (SNS), is an integrated weapon sight that provides both day and night operation in a single sight. The M3A scope is the primary day sight that snipers employ. All sniper marksmanship training is based on the M3A scope. The scope has an effective range in the day of 800 meters and night of 600 meters.

AN/PVS-10
Night Vision Sniper Scope

AN/PAQ-4C Laser Aiming Light. The AN/PAQ-4C aiming light projects an infrared laser beam that cannot be seen with the eye but can be seen with night vision devices. This aiming light works with the AN/PVS-7B/D series goggles and AN/PVS-14. The AN/PAQ-4C mounts on various weapons with mounting brackets and adapters. It has a range beyond 600 meters or more dependent on light level and night vision device used for observation.

AN/PAQ-4C
Laser Aiming Light

AN/PEQ-2A Laser Aiming Light. The AN/PEQ-2A is a Class IIIb laser that emits a highly collimated beam of infrared light for precise aiming of the weapon as well as a separate infrared illumination beam with adjustable focus. Both beams can be zeroed to the weapon and each other. The beams can be operated individually or in combination. The AN/PEQ-2A is for use in conjunction with night vision devices and can be used as either a handheld illuminator/pointer or can be weapon mounted with included brackets and accessory mounts. In weapon-mounted mode, the AN/PEQ-2A can be used to accurately direct fire as well as illuminate and designate areas and targets.

**AN/PEQ-2A
Laser Aiming Light**

M68 Close Combat Optic. The M68 Close Combat Optic (CCO) sight is a reflex (nontelescopic) sight. It uses a red aiming reference (collimated dot) and is designed for use with both eyes open. At ranges beyond 50 meters, the red dot remains fixed on the target no matter what angle is used and the gunner fires at the target. No centering is required. The best ranges fall between close combat and 300 meters.

M68, Close Combat Optic

M145 Telescope. The M145 telescope is a fixed 3.4-power, 28-mm optical sight that has been designed to engage targets accurately out to 1,200 meters. The optical sight weighs 24 ounces, is extremely rugged, has excellent vision in low light levels, and provides for rapid target acquisition. The M145 straight telescope mounts directly to the mounting rail on the M249 and M240B machine guns.

M145 Telescope

17

NBC (Nuclear, Biological, Chemical) Warfare

NBC weapons can cause casualties, destroy or disable equipment, restrict the use of terrain, and disrupt operations. The infantry platoon must be prepared to operate on an NBC-contaminated battlefield without degradation of the platoon's overall effectiveness.

CHEMICAL AGENTS
Chemical agents can cover large areas and may be delivered as a liquid, vapor, or aerosol and can be disseminated by artillery, mortars, rockets, missiles, aircraft spray, bombs, land mines, and covert means. The following table provides the characteristics of and the treatment for exposure to chemical agents.

BIOLOGICAL AGENTS
Protective measures against biological attack include up-to-date immunizations, good hygiene, area sanitation, physical conditioning, and water purification. Toxins and pathogens are the two types of biological agents. Toxins are poisonous substances produced from living organisms. They can be synthesized (artificially produced); they can mirror the symptoms of nerve agents. After about 8 to 12 hours, they are destroyed by the sun. Pathogen are infectious agents such as bacteria, viruses, and rickettsiae that cause disease in man and animals. Pathogens have a delayed reaction (incubation 1–21 days), can multiply and overcome natural defenses. When used in vectors (disease-infected insects), they can circumvent protective clothing and prolong hazards.

CHARACTERISTICS OF CHEMICAL AGENTS

AGENT	Nerve	Blood	Blister	Choking
PROTECTION	Mask and BDO*	Mask and BDO*	Mask	Mask
DETECTION	M8A1, M256A1, chemical agent monitor (CAM), M8 and M9 paper	M256A1, CAM, M8 and M9 paper	M256A1	Odor (freshly mowed hay)
SYMPTOMS	Difficult breathing, drooling, nausea, vomiting, convulsions, and blurred vision	Burning eyes, stinging skin, irritated nose	Convulsions and coma	Coughing, nausea, choking, headache, and tight chest
EFFECTS	Incapacitates	Blisters skin, damages respiratory tract	Incapacitates	Floods and damages lungs
FIRST AID	Mark 1 nerve agent antidote kit (NAAK)	As for 2nd and 3rd degree burns	None	Keep warm and avoid movement
DECON	M291 and flush eyes with water	M291 and flush eyes with water	None	None

*Battle Dress Overgarment

NUCLEAR WEAPONS

Soldiers should also know the effects of nuclear explosions—even accidental ones—and how to protect themselves from the effects of nuclear detona-
tions. The three principal effects of a nuclear weapon detonation are blast,
radiation, and electromagnetic pulse. Blast is the high-pressure shock wave
that crushes structures and causes missiling damage. Thermal radiation is
the intense heat and extremely bright light that cause burns, temporary blind-
ness, and dazzle. Nuclear radiation is energy released from nuclear detonation that produces fallout in the form of initial and residual radiation, both
of which can cause casualties. Electromagnetic pulse is the surge of electrical power that occurs within seconds of a nuclear detonation and damages
electrical components in equipment (radios, radar, computers, and vehicles)
and weapons systems (TOW, Javelin).

Cover and or shielding offers the best protection from the immediate
effects of a nuclear attack. This includes cover in fighting positions, culverts,
and ditches. Soldiers should cover exposed skin and stay down until the blast
wave passes and debris stops falling. Immediately after a nuclear attack, the
platoon leader should begin continuous monitoring for radiation using the
AN/VDR-2 radiacmeter.

TENETS OF NBC DEFENSE

Contamination Avoidance

Avoidance allows commanders to shield soldiers and units, thus shaping the
battlefield. It involves both active and passive measures. Passive measures
include training, camouflage, concealment, hardening positions, and dispersion. Active measures include detection, reconnaissance, alarms and signals, warning and reporting, marking, and contamination control.

NBC reconnaissance is the detection, identification, reporting, and
marking of NBC hazards. NBC reconnaissance consists of search, survey,
surveillance, and sampling operations.

Protection Against Contamination

Techniques that work for avoidance also work for protection (for example,
shielding soldiers and units and shaping the battlefield). Other activities that
comprise protection involve sealing or hardening positions, protecting soldiers, assuming MOPP (Mission Oriented Protective Posture), reacting to
attack, and using collective protection. Individual protective items include
the protective mask, battle dress overgarments (BDOs), green vinyl over-

MOPP Level Equipment	MOPP READY	MOPP 0 (ZERO)	MOPP 1	MOPP 2	MOPP 3	MOPP 4	Command (mask only)
Mask	Carried	Carried	Carried	Carried	Worn[1]	Worn	Worn
Overgarment	Ready[3]	Available[4]	Worn[1]	Worn[1]	Worn[1]	Worn	
Vinyl overboots	Ready[3]	Available[4]	Available[4]	Worn	Worn	Worn	
Gloves	Ready[3]	Available[4]	Available[4]	Available[4]	Available[4]	Worn	
Helmet protective cover	Ready[3]	Available[4]	Available[4]	Worn	Worn	Worn	
Chemical protective undergarment 2	Ready[3]	Available[4]	Worn[2]	Worn[2]	Worn[2]	Worn[2]	

[1]In hot weather, coat or hood can be left open for ventilation.
[2]The chemical protective undergarment is worn under the BDU (this primarily applies to armor vehicle crewmen and special operations forces).
[3]These items must be available to the soldier within two hours, with a second set available within six hours.
[4]These items must be positioned within arm's reach of the soldier.

MOPP LEVELS

boots, and gloves. Higher level commanders establish the minimum level of protection; subordinate units may only increase this level as necessary.

Individual Protective Gear

Currently, most active-duty military units have the Joint Service Lightweight Integrated Suit Technology (JSLIST) as a replacement for the old chemical protective suit or battle dress overgarment (BDO). When combined with the chemical protective mask, the JSLIST provides protection against chemical and biological agents, radioactive fallout particles, and battlefield contaminants. The JSLIST chemical protective overgarment is currently qualified by the military to meet the requirements for protection from chemical-warfare agents for up to 6 launderings, 45 days of wear, 120 calendar days after removal from the factory-sealed bag, or 24 hours after contamination, whichever comes first.

A complete chemical-warfare protective ensemble includes the following components: mask; chemical protective overgarment; chemical protective gloves; and chemical protective overboots compatible with the JSLIST chemical protective overgarment.

During Operation Iraqi Freedom, the lighter nature of the JSLIST allowed the soldiers to operate in temperatures approaching 100°F with only minimal degradation. This was a significant improvement over the BDO. However, the JSLIST proved to be not as durable as the BDO under the strenuous field conditions. Infantry soldiers easily tore many suits as they went about their day-to-day activities. It is recommended to be more careful and to have extra suits on hand.

DECONTAMINATION
Contamination forces units into protective equipment that degrades performance of individual and collective tasks. Decontamination restores combat power and reduces casualties that may result from exposure, thus allowing commanders to sustain combat operations.

Principles of Decontamination
Use the four principles of decontamination when planning decon operations:
1) Decon as soon as possible
2) Decon only what is necessary
3) Decon as far forward as possible (METT-TC dependent)
4) Decon by priority

Levels of Decontamination
The three levels of decontamination are immediate, operational, and thorough.
1) *Immediate*. Immediate decontamination requires minimal planning. It is a basic soldier survival skill and is performed in accordance with the current soldier manual. Personal wipedown removes contamination from individual equipment using the M291.
2) *Operational*. Operational decontamination involves MOPP gear exchange and vehicle spraydown. MOPP gear exchange should be performed within six hours of being contaminated when thorough decon cannot be performed.
3) *Thorough*. Thorough decontamination involves detailed troop decontamination (DTD) and detailed equipment decontamination (DED). Thorough decontamination is normally conducted by company-size elements as part of restoration or during breaks in combat operations. These operations require support from a chemical decontamination platoon.

Decontamination Planning Considerations
Leaders should include the following when planning for decontamination:
- Plan decon sites throughout the width and depth of the sector.
- Tie decon sites to the scheme of maneuver and templated NBC strikes.
- Apply the principles of decontamination.
- Plan for contaminated routes.
- Plan for logistics and resupply of MOPP, mask parts, water, and decon supplies.

COMPARISON DATA FOR DECONTAMINATION LEVELS

Level	Technique	Best Start Time	Responsibility	Advantages
Immediate	Skin decon	Within 1 minute of contamination	Individual	Prevents agents from penetrating*
	Personal wipedown	Within 15 minutes	Individual Or Crew	
	Operator spraydown	Within 30 minutes		
Operational	MOPP gear exchange**	Optimal within 6 hours, but no later than 24 hours	Contaminated Unit	Temporary relief from MOPP4
	Vehicle washdown***			Limit agent spread
Thorough	Detailed equipment decon (DED)	When mission allows/reconstitution	Decon PLT	Long-term MOPP reduction with minimal risk
	Detailed troop decon (DTD)		Unit	

*The techniques become less effective the longer they are delayed.
**Performance degradation and risk assessment must be considered when exceeding 6 hours. See FM 3-7 for information on BDO risk assessment.
***Vehicle washdown is most effective if started within one hour.

- Plan for medical concerns to include treatment and evacuation of contaminated casualties.
- Maintain site security.

MARKING CONTAMINATION

When contamination is found, it must be marked to prevent other soldiers from being exposed, and then reported. The only exception to marking an area is if the marking would help the enemy avoid contamination. If this exception is approved by the commander, the contaminated area must still be reported. When marking an area, place the markers facing away from the contamination. Markers are placed at roads, trails, and other likely points of entry.

NBC MARKERS

28cm

GAS — CHEMICAL
20cm 20cm   Yellow Background with Red Lettering

BIO — BIOLOGICAL
Blue Background with Red Lettering

ATOM — RADIOLOGICAL
White Background with Black Lettering

GAS MINES — CHEMICAL MINEFIELD
(UNEXPLODED MINES)
Red Background with Yellow Lettering and Stripe

FRONT SURFACE OF
MARKER FACES AWAY
FROM CONTAMINATION

NBC Contamination Marking Set

PASSING ALARMS AND SIGNALS

The vocal alarm for any chemical or biological hazard or attack is the word "gas." The person giving the alarm stops breathing, masks, and shouts "Gas" as loudly as possible. Everyone hearing this immediately masks and passes the alarm.

The first person to hear or see the M8 automatic chemical alarm sound or flash also stops breathing, masks, and yells "Gas."

The all-clear signal is given by word of mouth through the chain of command. The signal is given by leaders after testing for contamination proves negative.

TREATMENT OF CHEMICAL CASUALTIES
Soldiers check for casualties, give first aid, identify the agent, send reports to higher headquarters, request permission to move, schedule decontamination operations, and mark the area to warn friendly soldiers.

Antidote Treatment, Nerve Agent, Auto-injector (ATNAA)
The ATNAA is a new nerve agent antidote device that will be used by the Armed Forces in the treatment of nerve agent poisoning. The ATNAA is a multichambered device that consists of three components; the auto-injector tube, a spring-activated needle, and a safety cap. The device is packaged in a chemically hardened pouch.

Antidote Treatment, Nerve Agent, Auto-injector (ATNAA)

First Aid for Chemical Casualties
Soldiers must be able to treat themselves and each other after exposure to dangerous chemicals.

Self-Aid
If you experience most or all of the mild symptoms of nerve agent poisoning, you should immediately hold your breath. Do not inhale. Put on your protective mask and administer one ATNAA injection into your lateral thigh muscle or buttocks. Wait 10 to 15 minutes after giving yourself the first ATNAA injection because it takes that long for the antidote to take effect. If

you are able to ambulate and know who and where you are, you will not need a second ATNAA injection.

Warning. Giving yourself a second ATNAA injection may create a nerve agent antidote overdose, which could result in incapacitation. If symptoms of nerve agent poisoning are not relieved after administering one ATNAA injection, seek someone else to check your symptoms. A buddy must administer the second and third sets of injections, if needed.

Buddy Aid

If you encounter a service member suffering from severe signs of nerve agent poisoning, mask the casualty if necessary. Do not fasten the hood. Administer three ATNAAs in rapid succession. Follow administration procedures outlined below.

Combat Lifesaver Procedures

The combat lifesaver (CLS) must check to verify if the individual has received three ATNAAs. If not, the CLS performs first aid as described for buddy aid above. If the individual has received the initial three ATNAAs, then the CLS may administer additional atropine injections at approximately 15-minute intervals until atropinization is achieved (that is, a heart rate above 90 beats per minute, reduced bronchial secretions, and reduced salivations). Administer additional atropine at intervals of 30 minutes to 4 hours to maintain atropinization or until the casualty is placed under the care of medical personnel. Check the heart rate by carefully lifting the casualty's mask hood and feeling for a pulse at the carotid artery. Request medical assistance as soon as the tactical situation permits.

Trauma Specialist/Medic

When a casualty has received three ATNAAs but atropinization has not been achieved, administer additional atropine at approximately 15-minute intervals until atropinization is achieved. Administer additional atropine at intervals of 30 minutes to 4 hours to maintain atropinization or until the casualty is evacuated to a medical treatment facility (MTF). Check the heart rate by lifting the casualty's mask hood and feeling for a pulse at the carotid artery. Provide assisted ventilation for severely poisoned casualties if equipment is available. Monitor the patient for development of heat stress.

Administering Nerve Agent Antidotes

The injection site for administering the ATNAA is normally in the outer thigh muscle. The thigh injection site is the area about a hand's width above the knee to a hand's width below the hip joint. It is important that the injections be given into a large muscle area. If the individual is thinly built, then the injections should be administered into the upper outer quarter (quadrant) of the buttocks. Injecting in the buttocks of thinly built individuals avoids injury to the thigh bone. (See figures.)

Thigh Injection Site

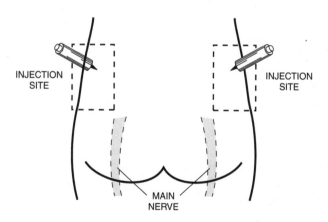

Antidote Buttocks Injection Site

18

Radio Sets, Procedures, and Field Antennas

Radios, the most common means of military communication, are particularly suited for use when you are on the move. Small handheld or backpack radios that communicate for only short distances are found at squad and platoon levels. As the need grows to talk over greater distances and to more units, the size and complexity of radios increase.

From brigade level to the squad level, the Army primarily uses FM (frequency modulating) single-channel radios as its primary means of communication. The FM radio has a range of approximately 35 to 40 kilometers, which covers a brigade/battalion maneuver area. FM radio transmissions are normally line-of-sight (LOS), so large terrain features can block transmission.

ENVIRONMENT
Factors that affect the range of radios are weather, terrain, power, antenna, and the location of the radio. Man-made objects such as bridges and buildings may affect radio transmission. Interference may also come from power lines, electrical generators, bad weather, other radio stations, and enemy jamming. You can correct many of the causes of poor radio communications by using common sense. For example, make sure you are not trying to communicate from under a steel bridge.

RULES FOR RADIO USE
Observe the following rules for radio use:
- Listen before transmitting.
- Avoid excessive radio checks.
- Make messages clear and concise. If possible, write them out before transmitting.
- Speak clearly, slowly, and in natural phrases, and enunciate each word. If the receiving operator must write, allow time for writing.

- Always assume the enemy is listening.
- If jammed, notify higher headquarters by established procedures.
- Maintain whip antennas in a vertical position.
- Make sure the radio is turned off before starting a vehicle.

PROWORDS

Common prowords are those words that are used on a regular basis while conducting radio operations. Prowords are not interchangeable as the meanings are specific and clear to the receiver. An example is "Say again" versus "Repeat." "Say again" means to repeat the last transmission, while "Repeat" means to fire the last artillery fire mission again. The following are frequently used prowords:

All After—I refer to the entire message that follows. . .

All Before—I refer to the entire message that precedes. . .

Break—I now separate the text from other parts of the message.

Correction—There is an error in this transmission. Transmission will continue with the last word correctly transmitted.

Groups—This message contains the number of groups indicated by the numeral following.

I Say Again—I am repeating transmission or part indicated.

I Spell—I shall spell the next word phonetically.

Message—A message that requires recording is about to follow. (Transmitted immediately after the call.) This proword is not used on nets primarily employed for conveying messages. It is intended for use when messages are passed on tactical or reporting net.

More to Follow—Transmitting station has additional traffic for the receiving station.

Out—This is the end of my transmission to you and no answer is required or expected.

Over—This is the end of my transmission to you and a response is necessary. Go ahead: transmit.

Radio Check—What is my signal strength and readability, i.e., How do you hear me?

Roger—I have received your last transmission satisfactorily, radio check is loud and clear.

Say Again—Repeat all of your last transmission. Followed by identification data means "repeat - (portion indicated)."

This Is—This transmission is from the station whose designator immediately follows.

Time—That which immediately follows is the time or date-time group of the message.

Wait—I must pause for a few seconds.

Wait-Out—I must pause longer than a few seconds.

Wilco—I have received your transmission, understand it, and will comply, to be used only by the addressee. Since the meaning of ROGER is included in that of WILCO, the two prowords are never used together.

Word After—I refer to the word of the message that follows.

Word Before—I refer to the word of the message that precedes.

SECURITY

Radio is one of the least secure means of communicating. Each time you talk, your voice travels in all directions. The enemy can listen to your transmissions to get information about you and your unit, or to locate your position to destroy you with artillery fire. Communications security keeps unauthorized persons from gaining information of value from radio and telephone transmissions. It includes the following:

- Using authentication to make sure that the other communicating station is a friendly one.
- Using only approved codes.
- Designating periods when all radios are turned off.
- Restricting the use of radio transmitters and monitoring radio receivers.
- Operating radios on low power.
- Enforcing net discipline and radiotelephone procedure (all stations must use authorized prosigns and prowords and must transmit official traffic only).
- Using radio sites with hills or other shields between them and the enemy.
- Using directional antennas when feasible.

RADIO SETS AND RECEIVER-TRANSMITTERS

SINCGARS Ground Combat Net Radio

The bulk of U.S. Army active and reserve component forces are likely to be supplied with one or more versions of the single-channel ground and airborne radio (SINCGARS). The older versions are the Receiver-Transmitter (RT) 1523A/B models. The newer versions are the SIP (Systems Improvement Program) ground combat radio RT-1523C/D models and the even newer SINCGARS ASIP (Advanced Systems Improvement Program) ground combat radio or RT-1523E model. These RT-1523A–D radio systems look very much alike, but the newer version has better technology for electronic warfare and better data transfer rates.

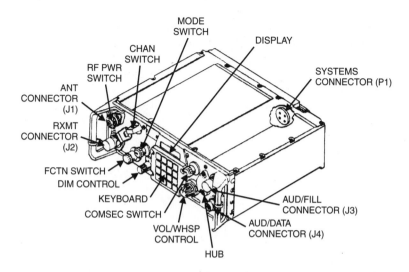

Receiver-Transmitter (RT-1523 A–D Series)

The newer SINCGARS ASIP is a user-owned-and-operated solid-state frequency modulated (FM) combat net radio (CNR). It operates in the 30.000 to 87.975 MHz frequency range in the single-channel (SC) or frequency-hopping (FH) mode. The ASIP replaces the RT-1523A and RT-1523B model SINCGARS. The ASIP is compatible with the older SINCGARS and with NATO forces in SC, squelch-off mode. It provides electronic warfare (EW) protection and a reduced electromagnetic signature in the FH mode. Maintenance procedures are the same for the older SINCGARS radio. The SINCGARS has eight preset channels in SC mode and six for FH mode. The cue and manual frequencies are included in the eight single-channel frequencies. It is designed for secure voice and data communications and is an antijam radio. The individual components are interchangeable from one radio to the next.

As mentioned above, the primary component of the SINCGARS is the receiver-transmitter or RT-1523 Series A through E. The RT-1523 series and necessary additional components make up either a dismounted or a mounted configuration.

The radio appearance of the RT-1523 Series A through D is basically the same (see figure).

The front panels and keyboards for the RT-1523 Series differ depending on the versions (see figures).

RT-1523-E Series ASIP Model

RT-1523C/D FRONT PANEL

RT-1523C/D KEYBOARD

**RT-1523 C/D Series
SIP Front Panel and Keyboard**

RT-1523 A/B FRONT PANEL

RT-1523 A/B KEYBOARD

RT-1523 A/B Series
Front Panel and Keyboard

RT-1523E Front Panel

GENERAL CHARACTERISTICS AND CAPABILITIES
SINCGARS

Operating Voltage:	Manpack: 13.5 volts from primary battery.
	Vehicular: 27.5 volts from vehicular battery.
Frequency Range:	30 MHz to 87.975 MHz.
Number of Operating Frequencies:	2320.
Channel Spacing:	25 kHz.
Frequency Stability:	Plus or minus 5 parts per million.
Frequency Offset Ability (SC):	Plus or minus 5 and 10 kHz.
Type of Modulation:	FM.
Audio Response Capability:	300–3000 Hz.
Types of Operation:	Push-to-talk (PTT) and release to receive.
	Retransmit: automatic.
	Remote: push-to-talk, release to receive.
	Data: automatic via data device.
Modes of Operation:	Voice: SC and FH.
	Retransmit: SC to SC, SC to FH, FH to FH.
	Digital data: SC, FH.
	Remote: with AN/GRA-39, CM, or RCU.
	Plain-text or cipher text.
Tuning:	Electronic SC frequency entered manually by using keyboard. Up to eight SC channels and six FH channels can be loaded and later selected using CHAN (channel) switch.

Components

A few components make up the basic radio sets. This simplifies the radio's installation, its tailoring for specific missions, and the maintenance support system. The RT-1523 is the main component of all radio sets. The components make the two primary radio configurations: *dismounted configuration* and *vehicle-mounted configuration*.

Dismounted Configuration (Manpack Radios)

The term "manpack" is the common name for the soldier-carried AN/PRC-119A/D/F. The "A/D/F" indicates this is an ICOM (Integrated COMSEC [communications security]) radio. Dismount is the term used to indicate that

SINCGARS Receiver/Transmitter
RT-1523 A/B or C/D

Battery

Battery box

Latches

Binding Post
Connector

RT

P1 RT System
Connector

Holding Battery Decal
(Bottom of RT)

SINCGARS Rucksack
slots in the top flap

Manpack
Antenna

Handset

AN-PRC 119A/D/F
SINCGARS Manpack System

the equivalent of a manpack radio is included within the components of selected vehicular radios. Once assembled, there is no difference between a radio referred to as manpack and one called dismount.

General Information for Manpack Components:
- *Antenna, manpack radio:* may be AS-3683/PRC or AS-4266/PRC (long antenna)
- *Receiver-Transmitter (RT):* may be RT-1523 Series
- *Handset:* H-250/U or new Handheld Remote Control Radio Device (HRCRD) (C-12493/U)
- *Battery Box:* may be CY-8523A/B (CY-8523C is used with the HRCRD). Not required for ASIP RT
- *Battery, main power:* may be Battery, Nonrechargeable, BA-5590/U; Battery, Rechargeable, BB-590/U; or Battery, Rechargeable, BB-390/U
- *Carrying Case*

Vehicular Radios (Mounted Configuration)

There are six configurations of vehicular radios:

1) Short-Range (SR) Radio (AN/VRC-87A/D/F*)
2) Short-Range Radio with Dismount (AN/VRC-88/A/D/F)
3) Long-Range (LR) Radio (AN/VRC-90A/D/F)
4) Short-Range/Long-Range Radio (AN/VRC-89A/D/F)
5) Short-Range/Long-Range Radio with Dismount (AN/VRC-91A/D/F)
6) Long-Range/Long-Range Radio (AN/VRC-92A/D/F)

*The "A/D/F" in SINCGARS radio nomenclature means that these are ICOM (secure) radios. The "C" in radio nomenclature indicates Single

Receiver-Transmitter,
Radio RT-1523(C)/U Series

Amplifier-Adapter Vehicular
AM-7239/VRC Series

Mounting Base,
Electrical Equipment
MT-6352/VRC
MT-6352A/VRC

Amplifier,
Radio Frequency
AM-7238/VRC Series

Mounting Base,
Electrical Equipment
MT-6353/VRC

Handset
H-250/U

Loudspeaker—
Control Unit
LS-671/VRC

Cable Assembly,
Radio Frequency
(W2)

Antenna,
Vehicular
AS-3900/VRC

Antenna,
Vehicular
AS-3900A/VRC

Antenna,
Vehicular
AS-3916/VRC

Cable Assembly,
Special Purpose
Electrical

Receiver-Transmitter,
Radio RT-1523E(C)/U

Control-Monitor
C-11291/VRC

SINCGARS Vehicle-Mounted
Radio Components

Radio Mount (SRM) radios. The components that are used in all vehicular radio configurations are shown in the graphic.

Common components are the key to tailoring the radio sets for specific missions. The components included in the radio set determine its capabilities. The number of RTs and amplifiers, an installation kit, and a backpack determine the model. The RT is the basic building block for all mounted radio configurations.

Mounted Configurations

- **Short-Range (SR) Radio Components (AN/VRC-87A/D/F):** Consists of RT-1523/A/B/C/D/E, Mounting Base (MB) (MT-6352/A), Vehicular Amplifier Adapter (VAA) (AM-7239/A/B/C/D/E), Vehicular Antenna (AS-3900/3916), Handset (HS) (H-250), Loudspeaker (LS) (LS-671), Cable (W4) that connects RT to VAA, Antenna Cable (CG-3856), Loudspeaker Cable (CX-13292), and Power Cable.

AN/VRC-87A/D/F

- *Short-Range Radio with Dismount (SR-D) Components (AN/VRC-88A/D/F):* Same as Short-Range Radio, plus Dismount (Manpack) Radio.

AN/VRC-88A/D/F

- *Long-Range (LR) Radio Components (AN/VRC-90A/D/F):* Consists of RT-1523/A/B/C/D/E, Mounting Base (MB) (MT-6352/A), Vehicular Amplifier Adapter (VAA) (AM-7239/A/B/C/D/E), Vehicular Antenna (AS-3900/3916), Handset (HS) (H-250), Loudspeaker (LS) (LS-671), Power Amplifier (PA) (AM-7238/A/B), Cable (W2), connects RT ANT to PA, Cable (W4), connects RT to VAA, Antenna Cable (CG-3856), Loudspeaker Cable (CX-13292), and Power Cable.

- **Short-Range/Long-Range Radio Components (AN/VRC-89A/D/F):** Consists of 2 RT-1523/A/B/C/D/E), Mounting Base (MB) (MT-6352/A), Vehicular Amplifier Adapter (VAA) (AM-7239/A/B/C/D/E), Vehicular Antenna (AS-3900/3916), 2 Handsets (HS) (H-250), 2 Loudspeakers (LS) (LS-671), Power Amplifier (PA) (AM-7238/A/B), Cable (W2), connects RT ANT to PA, 2 Cables (W4), connect RTs to VAA, 2 Antenna Cables (CG-3856), 2 Loudspeaker Cables (CX-13292), and Power Cable.

AN/VRC-89A/D/F

- **Short-Range/Long-Range Radio with Dismount Components (AN/VRC-91A/D/F):** Same as Short-Range/Long-Range Radio, plus Dismount (Manpack) Radio.

- *Long-Range/Long-Range Radio Components (AN/VRC-92A/D/F):* Consists of 2 RT-1523/A/B/C/D/E), Mounting Base (MB) (MT-6352/A), Vehicular Amplifier Adapter (VAA) (AM-7239/A/B/C/D/E), Vehicular Antenna (AS-3900/3916), 2 Handsets (HS) (H-250), 2 Loudspeakers (LS) (LS-671), 2 Power Amplifiers (PA) (AM-7238/A/B), Power Amplifier Mount (PA Mt) (MT-6353), Cable (W2), connects RT ANT to PA, 2 Cables (W4), connect RTs to VAA, 3 Cable (CG-3856), 1 connects PA to antenna (5') (2 are in installation kit), Cable (CX-13291), connects RT-B PA Mt to VAA, Cable (CX-13298), connects RT-A to RT-B for RXMT, Cable (CX-13303), connects RT-B PA Mt to MB, and 2 Loudspeaker Cables (CX-13292).

AN/VRC-92A/D/F

Planning Ranges

The ranges shown in the accompanying chart are based on line-of-sight and are average for normal conditions. Range depends on location, sighting, weather, and surrounding noise level, among other factors. Use of OE-254 antenna increases range for both voice and data transmissions. Enemy jamming and mutual interference conditions degrade these ranges. In data transmissions, use of a lower baud rate will increase range.

VOICE TRANSMISSION MAXIMUM PLANNING RANGES:

TYPE RADIO	RF SWITCH POSITION	PLANNING RANGES
Manpack/Vehicular	LO (low) M (medium) HI (high)	200 M – 400 M 400 M – 5 KM 5 KM – 10 KM
Vehicular Only	PA (power amplifier)	10 KM – 40 KM

DATA TRANSMISSION MAXIMUM PLANNING RANGES:

TYPE RADIO	BAUD RATE USED	RF SWITCH POSITION	PLANNING RANGES
Manpack/Vehicular (Short Range)	600 – 4800 BPS 16,000 BPS (16 KBPS)	HI (high) HI (high)	3 KM – 5 KM 1 KM – 3 KM
Vehicular (Long Range)	600 – 2400 BPS 4800 BPS 16,000 BPS (16 KBPS)	PA (power amp) PA (power amp) PA (power amp)	5 KM – 25 KM 5 KM – 22 KM 3 KM – 10 KM

Loading Frequencies

The procedure for loading single-channel (SC) frequencies requires setting the proper switches, pressing the correct number keys for the frequency you wish to load, and storing the load in RT permanent memory by pressing the STO (storage) button. Loading secure frequencies requires special COMSEC devices that transmit the proper "FILL" data to the radio, including frequencies, FH data, secure transmission data, and other necessary information. The current device is called and AN/CYZ-10. The AN/CYZ-10 automated net control device (ANCD) is a handheld device capable of receiving, storing, and transferring data between ANCDs, or between ANCD and a SINCGARS or ASIP radio. The primary application for this device is to fill the ASIP with FH data, time, communications security (COMSEC), and loadset information. Correct operating instructions may be obtained from various technical manuals and the unit signal officer.

ANCD KEYPAD

AN-CYZ-10 Automated Net Control Device (ANCD)

Key Operator Tasks

Many tasks are needed to become completely proficient with the SINC-GARS and they would fill a good portion of this guide. However, two important and basic operator tasks follow:

1. **Select RT Preparation Settings from MENU.** The tasks listed below are necessary to get the radio in operation.

a. Set RT Volume	1. Press MENU	Press MENU to display VOL level
	2. Press Digit (1–9) for VOL	Display reads WHSP if 0 selected
	Setting (0) for Whisper Mode	
b. Set RT Channel	1. Press MENU (until CHAN)	Display reads (1–6), (Q) for CUE, (M) for Manual
	2. Press Digit (1–6) for Channel desired: (0) for MAN, (7) for CUE	
c. Set RT Power	1. Press MENU (until PWR)	Display reads (LO, M, HI, PA)
	2. Press CHG for desired PWR setting	
d. Set RT Mode	1. Press MENU (until MODE)	Display reads (SC, FH, FHM)
	2. Press CHG for desired MODE	
e. Set COMSEC	1. Press MENU (until CMSC)	Display reads (PT, CT, TD, RV)
	2. Press CHG for desired CMSC setting	
f. Set Backlight	1. Place RT in SQ ON	Backlight lights (4 settings Low to High, then OFF)
	2. Press FREQ/Backlight	
	3. Press CHG until desired setting	

Default settings are: VOL (5), CHAN (1), PWR (LO), MODE (FH), COMSEC (CT).

2. **Load Single-Channel (SC) Frequency into ASIP Radio.** The ASIP operator is required to perform this task in preparation for the employment of single channel communications, use of the CUE (key the radio), and ERF (electronic remote fill) methods of late net entry, and for single channel frequency updates. The operator determines the required frequencies from the ANCD or another source. These frequencies are then loaded into the radio by use of the receiver-transmitter (RT) keyboard. The steps are:

a. Prepare to perform task	1. Obtain proper freq from ANCD	(Load CUE freq only if directed)*
b. Load SC freq	2. Set RT controls:**	RT display shows "GOOD"
	COMSEC to PT	(or see unit maintainer)
	Mode to SC	
	FCTN to Z-FH, TST, and then to LD	
	CHAN to MAN, CUE, or 1–6	
c. Store SC freq	1. Press: [FREQ]	Display shows [00000] or [30000]
	2. Press: [CLR]	Display shows [_____]
	3. Enter 5-digits SC freq	Display shows SC [XXXXX]
d. Prepare to communicate	Press STO (within 7 sec)	Display blinks once (data is stored)
e. Set COMSEC	1. Repeat: Step b-1 for each freq needed	(As directed by NCS or unit SOP)
	2. Set: FCTN to SQ ON complete	Loading of SC freq is complete

*Only NCS and Alt NCS will load a CUE frequency.
**RT settings for ASIP are set via MENU.

FIELD EXPEDIENT ANTENNAS

Expedient antennas are temporary antennas designed and constructed by the user to increase the range of tactical radio sets. Antennas that are components of tactical radio sets are, for the most part, vertical antennas, resulting in the signal being radiated equally in all directions. Expedient antennas increase the operating range of a given radio set, providing increased efficiency through the use of an antenna specifically designed for the operating frequency in use, elevation of the antenna above the ground, or concentration of the radiated signal along a given direction. Field expedient antennas are easily constructed from field wire using poles on trees for support. Whatever antenna is used, remember that the most important considerations are site location and location of the radio set. Before deciding to construct a field expedient antenna, other considerations or operating hints that may improve communications are as follows:

- Use a headset to receive weak signals.
- Speak slowly and distinctly, directly into the microphone or handset.
- Use an RC-292 antenna, if available.
- Use continuous wave (CW) in place of voice for increased range on AM radios.

Steel wires should be clipped off, leaving only the copper wires. The copper wires are twisted together and placed into the center hole of the auxiliary antenna connector or the antenna connector, making sure the wires do not touch any other part of the radio set.

If the whip antenna of your radio becomes damaged, try a piece of communication wire tied to a broomstick or a tree limb. Insert the end of the wire in the antenna connector. If you hold the stick or limb in a vertical position, you should be able to communicate. It will not be as effective as with the whip antenna, but it is better than no antenna at all.

Vertical Antennas

Vertical field expedient antennas improve radio set performance by virtue of height above the ground. The most effective height above the ground is equal to one-half the wavelength of the operating frequency in meters. Elevation above this height requires ground plane elements.

Improvised Whip Antenna

Whip Antennas may become broken during use, with no replacement antenna readily available. If this should happen, it is possible to improvise a satisfactory replacement by using telephone cable WD-1/TT or by lashing the broken antenna pieces together.

Emergency Repair of Whip Antenna Using Field Wire WD-1/TT

Emergency Repair of Whip Antenna Using Broken Antenna Sections

Patrol Antenna

The patrol antenna is used primarily with FM radios. It can be used extensively in heavily wooded areas with the portable radio sets to increase line-of-sight communications. Antenna performance increases with height above the ground up to 13 meters.

Length in meters	$^1/_2$ wavelength of operating frequency
Height	Variable (lead-in not over 13 meters)
Radiation	360 degrees

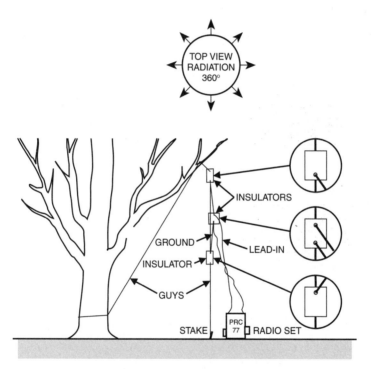

Patrol Antenna

To determine length of antenna in meters, divide 142.5 by your operating frequency.
Example: constant = 142.5 divided by op. freq. 45.0 = 3.17 meters.
Or, constant = 468 divided by op. freq. 45.0 = 10.4 feet.

Field Expedient RC-292 Antenna

The field expedient 292 antenna is used with FM radios. It is used in place of the RC-292 when such an antenna is not available. Principal parts consist of:

- 65 feet of gutted 550 cord
- 5 insulators
- Four 6.5-foot lengths of antenna elements (16 gauge copper wire, see note 2)
- Three 1-foot-long gutted 550 cord (see note 3)
- 50 feet of coax cable (RG-58 or RH-174)
- Solderless BNC connector (see note 4)

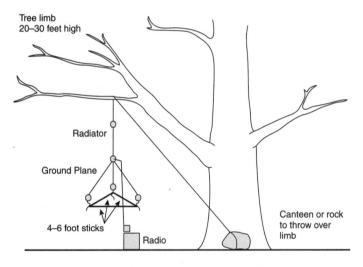

Field Expedient RC–292 Antenna

Notes:
1. Insulators should be made of a semiflexible plastic (i.e., spoons, flashlight lenses, etc.).
2. Use wire from GRA-50 dipole antenna for the radiator element.
3. The 550 cord end is tied in a loop to create a slip knot to put ends of sticks through during execution.
4. Once coax is connected, use electrical tape to secure and cover bare wires.

Construction:

Blowup of Field Expedient RC-292 Antenna

Horizontal Antennas

When the situation does not require mobility and the antenna group RC-292 is not available, you can get greater distance by using the long-wire horizontal antenna. The physical length in meters of one wavelength for a given operating frequency can be computed as follows:

$$\text{length (meters)} = \frac{285}{\text{operating frequency (MHz)}}$$

All horizontal antennas described here are fed by connecting the receiver-transmitter to one end of the antenna.

Horizontal Antenna for Use with AM and FM Radios

Long-Wire Antenna

The long-wire antenna is used with both AM and FM radios to increase the range. It is normally used in open terrain where installation can be accomplished with ease.

Length	5 or 7 wavelengths of operating frequency
Height	3 meters
Range	Up to 2 to 3 times the operating range of set
Resistor	400–700 ohms
Radiation	Without resistor—from both ends
	With resistor—off resistor end only

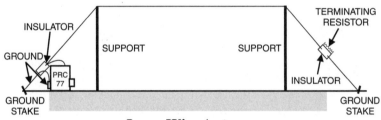

Long-Wire Antenna

Vertical Half-Rhombic Antenna

The vertical half-rhombic antenna has the advantage of being smaller in physical size than the horizontal antenna and requires only one pole for construction. It can be made directional with the use of a resistor. The principal disadvantage is that if the angle between the antenna wire and surface of the earth is too small, the signal will be radiated at an upward angle that may be above the intended receiver. A typical vertical half-rhombic antenna consists of 100 feet of field wire WD-1/TT, erected over a single 30-foot support base. One leg of the antenna terminates at the resistor; the other end is connected from the insulator to the radio by a 5-foot lead-in wire.

Length	2 wavelengths of operating frequency, with a 5-foot lead-in
Height	20 meters
Range	Up to 2 to 3 times operating range of set
Resistor	400–700 ohms
Radiation	Without resistor—equally off both ends
	With resistor—off resistor end only

Note: A counterpoise is used as an additional ground in everyday climates. When the counterpoise is used, it is placed on top of the ground and is installed from one ground stake to the other, and then to the battery case clip. If the counterpoise is not used, the ground lead-in is connected from the ground stake to the battery case clip. The insulators and the resistor are installed approximately knee high.

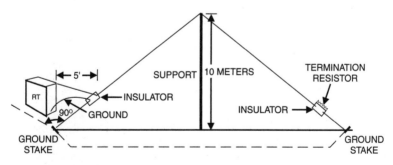

Vertical Half-Rhombic Antenna

19

Field Expedient Antiarmor Devices

There are many weapons you can use to destroy a tank or an armored personnel carrier. The weapons most frequently used are the light antitank weapon (LAW), the M47 man-portable, antitank weapon (Dragon), the heavy antitank missle (TOW), mines, and high-explosive, dual-purpose rounds of the M203 grenade launcher. There may be times, however, when you will not have these weapons available. In such cases, you may have to use field expedient devices. In order to construct some of these devices, you must know how to prime charges, electrically and nonelectrically.

FLAME DEVICES
Flame devices are used to obscure the vision of a vehicle's crew and to set the vehicle afire.

Molotov Cocktail
A Molotov cocktail is made with a breakable container (usually a bottle), a gas and oil mixture, and a cloth wick. To construct it, fill the container with the mixture, and then insert the cloth wick into the container. The wick must extend both into the mixture and out of the bottle. Light the wick before throwing the container. When the container hits the vehicle and breaks, the mixture will ignite, burning both the vehicle and the personnel around it.

Eagle Fireball
An eagle fireball is made with an ammunition can, a gas and oil mixture, a white phosphorus

WICK

GASOLINE
AND OIL
MIXTURE

Molotov Cocktail

341

grenade wrapped with detonating cord, tape, a nonelectric blasting cap, a fuse igniter, and a grapnel (or rope with bent nails).

To construct an eagle fireball, fill the ammunition can with the mixture. Wrap the grenade with detonating cord, and attach a nonelectric firing system to the end of the detonating cord. Place the grenade inside the can with the time fuse extending out. Make a slot in the can's lid for the fuse to pass through when the lid is closed. If available, attach a rope with bent nails or a grapnel to the can. When you throw the can onto a vehicle, the bent nails or the grapnel will help hold the can there. Before throwing the can, fire the fuse igniter.

Eagle Fireball

Eagle Cocktail

An eagle cocktail is made of a plastic or rubberized bag (a waterproof bag or a sandbag lined with a poncho), a gas and oil mixture, a smoke grenade, a thermite grenade, tape, string, and communications wire or cord.

To construct an eagle cocktail, fill the bag with the mixture. Seal the bag by twisting its end and then taping or tying it. Attach the

Eagle Cocktail

thermite and smoke grenades to the bag using tape, string, or communications wire. When attaching the grenades, do not bind the safety levers on the grenades. Tie a piece of string or cord to the safety pins of the grenades. Before throwing the eagle cocktail, pull the safety pins in both grenades.

EXPLOSIVE DEVICES

Towed Charge

A towed charge is made of rope or communications wire, mines or blocks of explosives, electrical blasting caps, tape, and electrical firing wire.

To construct a towed charge, link a series of armed antitank mines together with a rope or communications wire. If mines are not available, use about 25 to 50 pounds of explosives attached on a board (sled charge). Anchor one end of the rope on one side of the

Towed Charge

road, and run its other end to a safe position from which the charge may be pulled onto the road. Attach an electric firing system to each mine (or to the explosive), and connect those systems to the firing wire. Tape the firing wire to the rope running to the position from which the charge is pulled onto the road. At that position, conduct a circuit check, and then connect the firing wire to a blasting machine.

Just before a vehicle reaches the site of the towed charge, pull the charge onto the road so that it will be run over by the vehicle. When the vehicle is over it, fire the charge.

Pole Charge

A pole charge is made of explosives (TNT or C4), nonelectric blasting caps, time fuse, detonating cord, tape, string or wire, fuse igniters, and a pole long enough for the mission. Prime the desired amount of explosives with two nonelectric firing systems, and attach the explosives to a board or some other flat material. The amount of explosives you use depends on the target to be destroyed. Tie or tape the board with the explosives to the pole. The time fuse should be only about 6 inches long. Before putting a pole charge on a target, fire the fuse igniters.

Some good places to put a pole charge on a vehicle are under the turret, over the engine compartment, in the suspension system, and in the main gun tube (if the charge is small enough to fit in the tube).

Pole Charge

Satchel Charge

A satchel charge is made of explosives (TNT or C4), nonelectric blasting caps, time fuse, detonating cord, tape, fuse igniters, and some type of satchel. The satchel can be an empty sandbag, a demolitions bag, or other material. To construct the device, fill the satchel with the amount of explosives needed for the mission. Prime the explosives with two nonelectric firing systems. Use only about 6 inches of time fuse. Seal the satchel with string, rope, or tape, and leave the time fuse and igniters hanging out of the satchel. Before throwing a satchel charge onto a target, fire the fuse igniters.

Satchel Charge

WEAK POINTS OF ARMORED VEHICLES

To use expedient devices, you must know the weak points of armored vehicles. The following are some of the common weak points:

- Suspension system
- Fuel tanks
- Ammunition storage compartments
- Engine compartment
- Turret ring
- Armor on the sides, top, and rear (normally not as thick as that on the front)

Weak Points of Armored Vehicles

DEAD SPACE VISUAL AND WEAPON

Dead Space

BUTTONED-UP ARMORED VEHICLES

If an armored vehicle is "buttoned up" and you have no antiarmor weapons, fire your rifle at the vision blocks, at any optical equipment mounted outside the vehicle, into the engine compartment, at any external fuel tanks, or at the hatches. That will not destroy the vehicle but may hinder its ability to fight.

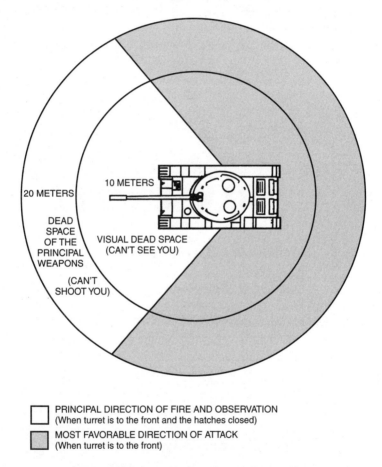

PRINCIPAL DIRECTION OF FIRE AND OBSERVATION
(When turret is to the front and the hatches closed)

MOST FAVORABLE DIRECTION OF ATTACK
(When turret is to the front)

Dead Space, 10 meters and 20 meters

Appendix A

Armored Vehicle Recognition

In the recent past, armored vehicle identification was usually just a matter of distinguishing between vehicles manufactured by Warsaw Pact nations and those manufactured by NATO nations. Even in those days, it was sometimes difficult distinguishing between vehicles on a simple friend-or-foe basis. In 2003 and 2004, several former Warsaw Pact nations joined NATO bringing much former Warsaw Pact equipment with them. In addition, changes in international relations have made it more likely that we will meet a third world nation's troops such as experienced in our operations in Iraq and Afghanistan. Most third world nations do not manufacture their own combat vehicles, but buy them from other countries. As a result, many of them have vehicles from nearly every manufacturing nation in the world.

As a result, one of the best ways to identify armored vehicles is to compare the observed vehicle characteristics with four known vehicle attributes or characteristics. Most, but not all armored vehicles have all four characteristic areas:

1. **Track and suspension system:** Many tanks can be recognized by their track and suspension systems unless grass, dirt, terrain, dust, or other factors are obscuring the tracks. To identify the track and suspension system, check to see whether it has support or return rollers.

- Most former Warsaw Pact vehicles have a flat (Christie) suspension system, without support or return rollers, without torsion bars, and unevenly spaced road wheels.

- Most NATO vehicles have a suspended track, support or return rollers, torsion bars, shock absorbers, and evenly-spaced road wheels.

2. **Turret:** Most turrets can be grouped into three categories:
   - Big, bulky turrets—older models
   - Well-sloped turrets—newer models
   - Streamlined turrets—newer models
3. **Main gun:** Armament varies from machine guns to large cannons. In turreted vehicles, normally the heaviest armament is in the turret. Look for the main gun, the main gun bore evacuator, and its relative location on the main gun.
   - Types of main guns:
     — Smooth main gun, without bore evacuator or blast deflector
     — Main gun with bore evacuator
     — Main gun with bore evacuator and muzzle brake or blast deflector
   - Types of muzzles:
     — Single-baffle
     — Double-baffle
     — Multibaffled
4. **Cupolas:** The cupola is a small, turretlike projection normally on top of the turret. It is used by the vehicle commander and usually mounts a machine gun.

Studying these various characteristics will assist you in remembering unique attributes about various armored vehicles and ultimately allowing you to identify most vehicles by nomenclature. The following pages contain common NATO and former Warsaw Pact armored vehicles.

NATO Armored Vehicles

CHIEFTAIN—BRITISH
    Large shallow turret with long, sloping front
    Long gun tube with bore evacuator in center
    High, flat engine decks
    6 road wheels with skirting plates covering support rollers

CENTURION—BRITISH
    Large square turret
    Bore evacuator $2/3$ down from muzzle
    6 road wheels with skirting plates covering support rollers

CHALLENGER—BRITISH
Center-mounted turret and fighting compartment
6 road wheels (space between third and fourth); 4 return rollers
5 smoke dischargers each side of main gun
Steel skirting covering upper track

MCV 80—BRITISH
High rear deck
Small, shallow turret
Flat engine decks
6 road wheels

AMX30—FRENCH
Large squat turret
Long gun tube, no bore evacuator
Flat engine decks
5 road wheels with support rollers

AMX10—FRENCH

Large cupola set to the left
Long thin gun (20 mm)
Flat hull with long, sloping front plate
5 road wheels with support rollers

LEOPARD—GERMAN

Large rounded flat turret
Bore evacuator $^2/_3$ from muzzle
Long sloping-sided hull with horizontal exhaust louvres at rear
7 road wheels with support rollers

LEOPARD II—GERMAN

Large squared turret
7 evenly-spaced road wheels
Bore evacuator $^2/_3$ from muzzle
Grenade launchers on rear side of turret
Jagged track skirting

MARDER—GERMAN
Small turret placed centrally on hull
Gun mounted on turret
Long hull with inward-sloping sides, domed cupola at rear
6 road wheels with support rollers

M60—UNITED STATES
High rear deck; prominent cupola
Tortoiseshell-shaped turret
6 road wheels with 3 support rollers

M60A1—UNITED STATES[1]
Wedge-shaped turret
Bore evacuator $^2/_3$ down from muzzle, no blast deflector
6 road wheels with support rollers

---

[1]Drawing from Alan K. Russell, *Modern Battle Tanks and Support Vehicles:* Greenhill Books, London, and Stackpole Books, Mechanicsburg, PA.

M60A3—UNITED STATES
Wedge-shaped turret
Large thermal sleeve $^2/_3$ down from muzzle
Thermal sight and laser range finder mounted at body end of gun
   (not shown)
6 road wheels with 3 support rollers

M113—UNITED STATES
.50-cal MG, pintle mounted
Rectangular, box-shaped hull
Track—5 road wheels, no support rollers

M109A61—UNITED STATES
Self-propelled howitzer with long gun tube
7 evenly-spaced road wheels
Large, boxy turret mounted rear of center

M1 ABRAMS—UNITED STATES
Low, boxy
Low turret—no cupola
7 road wheels covered with skirt

M2 BRADLEY—UNITED STATES
High profile
Distinctive turret in center with tow launcher on left side
6 road wheels, space between third and fourth road wheel
Skirt over road wheels

Former Warsaw Pact Vehicles

PT 76

> Cone-shaped turret set well forward
> Short gun with evacuator at center, muzzle brake at end
> Wide, long, square hull
> Narrow back, 6 road wheels, no support rollers

T54/55

> Dome-shaped turret mounted over third road wheel
> Long gun with bore evacuator at muzzle
> Sloped, low-silhouetted hull
> 5 road wheels with gap between first and second
> No support rollers
> Infrared searchlight for gun

T62

Smooth, round (pear-shaped) turret
Long gun with evacuator $1/3$ down from muzzle
Flat engine deck
5 road wheels, with large gaps between third, fourth, and fifth, no
  support rollers

T64

Turret centrally mounted on chassis
Support rollers and six road wheels
Glacis has four steel ribs and V-shaped splash guard
Infrared searchlight mounted to left of the main armament
125-mm main gun with midtube bore evacuator

T72

Turret centrally mounted on chassis
Support rollers and 6 road wheels
V-shaped mud deflector on front slope
Infrared searchlight mounted to left of gun tube

T80

Rounded turret mounted midway on tank
Single snorkel mounted on left side of turret
Long gun with bore evacuator $^1/_3$ distance from muzzle
6 evenly spaced road wheels with 3 support rollers
Sharply sloped upper glacis with V-shaped splash guard

T-10

Turret round, well forward, well sloped
Long gun tube, bore evacuator near end of muzzle break
Hull, narrow; splash guard, wide
7 road wheels, 3 support rollers

ZSU 23-4
    Shallow and square-sided turret
    4 antiaircraft guns
    Square-sided hull
    6 road wheels, no support rollers

BMD
    Same turret and armament as BMP (see below)
    Driver's hatch centered below main gun
    5 road wheels, 4 support rollers
    Found with airborne units

BMP
    Circular and cone-shaped turret
    Short gun with missile mounted above
    Low, wide hull
    6 road wheels with support rollers

BTR 60P

May have small turret
Machine gun toward front
Large, boatlike hull with sharp square nose
Wheeled—4 large wheels each side

BRDM

No turret
Armament may vary from pintle-mounted machine gun to antitank missiles
Long, sloping hood and raised troop compartment
4 wheels

BRDM-2

    Small, cone-shaped turret, centered on hull
    Machine gun mounted in turret
    Square-shaped hull with distinct undercut at nose
    Wheeled—2 each side

SAU 122

    PT-76–type chassis with 7 road wheels
    Turret location is rear of center
    Infrared searchlight top left of turret
    Double-baffle muzzle brake and bore evacuator

Appendix B

Operational Graphics

Operational graphics (map symbols) depict control measures and friendly and enemy units and equipment. These symbols are normally written on graphical overlays, which fit to the individual map scale, to help leaders better identify the battle plan and the placement of units and equipment applicable to the battle.

RULES
Operational graphics depict both the operational and support roles of the battle and have certain rules.

Control Measures
All control measures (obstacles, locations, routes, and lines)—friendly, enemy, neutral, or factional—are drawn using the color green.

Affiliation	Hand-Drawn	Computer-Generated
Friend, Assumed Friend	Blue	Cyan
Unknown, Pending	Yellow	Yellow
Neutral	Green	Green
Enemy, Suspect, Joker, Faker	Red	Red

Unit Symbol Color Defaults

All other friendly graphic control measures are shown in black. All other enemy graphic control measures are shown in red. If red is not available, they are drawn in black with a double line or the abbreviation saying "ENY" placed in at least two locations to avoid confusion. If colors are used to show friendly or enemy (hostile factions), they must be shown in a legend on the overlay describing what the color means.

Unit and Equipment Symbols

Unit and equipment symbols are composed of three components: a frame (geometric border), fill, and icon. Frames are geometric shapes used to display affiliation. The basic affiliation categories are friendly, unknown, neutral, and enemy. The unknown unit frame shape is normally used only for aircraft and ships. The frame shape for suspected friendly, enemy, or neutral is used for ground units not positively identified. The basic frame shapes for units, installations, activities, and logistics sites are shown in the following figure (Unit Installation and Site Symbol Frames).

	Friendly Ground Units	Friendly Sea/Air	Unknown Sea/Air	Neutral	Enemy Units
Surface					
Subsurface					
In-flight					

Unit Installation and Site Symbol Frames

Fill refers to the area within the frame. If color is used in a symbol, it indicates affiliation. Generally, black is used for the frame, icon, and modifiers when symbols are displayed on a light background. White is used for these elements when they are displayed on a dark background. A color fill can be used if an icon is displayed within the area of the frame. The figure (Unit Symbol Color Defaults) shows the color defaults for affiliation used for hand-drawn and computer-generated symbols.

The icon is a "role indicator" that shows the warfighting function the unit performs either on the ground, in the air, or at sea. An example is the crossed rifles, which represent an infantry unit.

UNIT SIZE

Squad/crew	Smallest unit/UK section	▭ •
Section or unit larger than a squad but smaller than a platoon	Unit larger than a US squad/UK section but smaller than a platoon equivalent	▭ ••
Platoon or detachment	Platoon/troop equivalent	▭ •••
Company, battery, or troop	Company/battery/squadron equivalent	▭ ı
Battalion or squadron	Battalion equivalent	▭ ıı
Group or regiment	Regiment/group equivalent	▭ ııı
Brigade	Brigade equivalent	▭ X
Division	Division	▭ XX
Corps	Corps	▭ XXX
Army	Army	▭ XXXX
Army group or front	Army group/front	▭ XXXXX
Special size indicator for a nonorganic or temporary grouping	Battalion task force	▭ with ⊔ıı
	Company team	▭ with ⊔ı

UNIT TYPE

Adjutant General (personnel services and administration)	**AG**
Aerial observation	Air Force (surveillance) Army
Airborne (normally associated with another branch symbol)	
Air cavalry	
Air defense	
Amphibious	
Amphibious engineer	
Antiarmor	
Armor	
Armored cavalry	
Army aviation — Rotary wing	
Fixed wing	
Attack helicopter	
Bridging	

UNIT TYPE *(Continued)*

Cavalry or reconnaissance		
Chemical (NBC)		
Chemical (NBC decontamination)		
Chemical (NBC reconnaissance)		
Chemical (smoke generator)		
Civil affairs (US only)		CA
Data processing unit		DPU
Dental		
Engineer		
Electronic warfare		EW
Field artillery		
Finance/pay		
Infantry		
	Light	

UNIT TYPE *(Continued)*

	Mechanized APC	
	BIFV (mounted)	
	BIFV (dismounted)	
	Motorized	
Maintenance		
Medical		
Military intelligence (at corps and below, insert is CEWI)		MI
Military police		MP
Motorized		
Mountain		
Ordnance		
Petroleum supply		
Psychological operations		
Quartermaster		

UNIT TYPE *(Continued)*

Ranger	RGR
Rocket artillery	
Service	SVC
Signal/communications	
Sound ranging	
Special forces	SF
Supply	
Supply and maintenance	
Supply and transportation	
Support	SPT
Surface-to-air missile	
Surface-to-surface missile	
Transportation	
Unmanned air reconnaissance (RPV, etc.)	

WEAPONS AND EQUIPMENT

Select the appropriate weapon symbol.

(light automatic weapon)   (gun)

Add horizontal bars (one for medium or two for heavy) to denote the size.

(medium machine gun)   (heavy gun)

If a weapon has a high trajectory, a **o** is placed at the base of the shaft.
If a weapon has a flat trajectory, a ⌒ is placed at the base of the shaft.

(medium mortar)   (light antitank gun)

If the weapon is primarily for air defense, a ◠ is placed at the base of the shaft.

(air defense missile)   (air defense gun)

If the weapon is rocket launched, a ⌃ is placed at the head of the shaft. If a weapon
is also a tracked, self-propelled vehicle, a ⌂ is placed below the weapon symbol.

(rocket launcher)   (tracked, self-propelled
                                         medium howitzer)

WEAPONS AND EQUIPMENT *(Continued)*

	LIGHT	MEDIUM	HEAVY
Air defense gun			
Antitank gun			
Antitank missile, self-propelled			
Antitank rocket launcher			
Flamethrower	portable	vehicular	
Gun in air defense role, self-propelled			
Gun in antitank role			
Howitzer			
Machine gun/automatic weapon			
Mortar			
Multibarrel rocket launcher			
Surface-to-air missile			
Surface-to-surface missile			

VEHICLES

Armored personnel carrier (APC)	
Armored engineer vehicle	
Armored vehicle launch bridge (AVLB)	
Bradley infantry fighting vehicle (BIFV)	
Cavalry fighting vehicle (CFV)	
Tank	LIGHT MEDIUM HEAVY

LOCATIONS

A solid line symbol represents a present or actual location.	
A broken line symbol indicates a future or projected location.	
Basic symbols other than the headquarters symbol may be placed on a staff that is extended or bent as required. The end of the staff indicated the precise location.	

POINTS

	OWN	ENEMY
General or unspecified point (Exact location is the tip at the bottom of the symbol)		
Coordinating point (Exact location is the center of the symbol)	⊗	⊗
Contact point		
Start point	SP	SP
Release point	RP	RP
Strongpoint (May be combined with unit size symbol)	SP 6 SP 5	SP 2
Checkpoint	8	
Linkup point	● 8	
Passage point	PP 8	
Point of departure	PD	
Pop-up point	⋈ PUP	
Rally point	RALLY	
Rendezvous point (Letter in circle appears in alphabetical sequence for number of points required)	A RDVU	

LINES

Front lines	Own present	
	Own planned	
	Enemy present	
	Enemy anticipated or suspect	
General tactical boundary	Own present	
	Own planned	
	Enemy present	
	Enemy anticipated or suspect	
Obstacle line (Tips point toward the enemy)		
Fortified line		

ROUTES

Attack General symbol for main attack—double arrowhead	
General symbol for other than main attack—single arrowhead	
Double arrowhead for direction of main attack and axis of advance for the main attack	
Single arrowhead for supporting direction of attack and supporting axis of advance	
Axis of advance Actual	ALPHA
Proposed with date and time effective	RED EFF 040530Z NOV
Axis of advance for unit designated to conduct main attack	TF 2-7
Bypass Bypass easy	
Bypass difficult	
Bypass impossible	
Direction of attack Direction of attack is shown graphically as an arrow extending from the line of departure. The arrow is not normally labeled.	LD X OBJ RED LD X
Follow and support mission	

OBSTACLES

Abatis	
Booby trap	
Nonexplosive antitank	
Trip wire	
Wire	
Point Planned abatis reinforced with antipersonnel mines	
Executed or fired demolition reinforced with antitank mines	
Booby-trapped nonexplosive antitank obstacle with target serial number	
Linear Antitank ditch (A rectangle need not be used when the obstacle is drawn to scale on the overlay. Teeth point toward the enemy.)	Under preparation Completed
Unspecified	
Wire (enemy under preparation)	

Minefields
  Indicators
    Antipersonnel mine	

Antitank mine	

OBSTACLES *(Continued)*

Antitank mine with antihandling device	
Mine cluster	
Mine, type unspecified	
Conventional A planned minefield consisting of unspecified mines	
A completed minefield consisting of unspecified mines	
Scatterable minefield (DTGs used for self-destruct mines)	
Conventional row mining (outline drawn to scale)	
Nuisance Nuisance minefield	
Phony Phony minefield	
Protective Protective minefield	
Antitank ditch reinforced with antitank mines	
Tactical Tactical minefield of scatterable antitank mines, effective till 101200Z	
Completed antitank minefield (drawn away from the location and connected by a vector)	

FIRE PLANNING

Basic Concentration/point	
Linear concentration/line	
Rectangular target	
Target reference point (TRP)	X1300Z
Concentrations and barrages Linear concentration	AG ✕ 1201
Targets and final protective fires Friendly targets (not enemy) are represented by one of the following symbols, as appropriate. Targets for friendly fires are normally designated using two letters followed by four numbers.	
A linear concentration, target number 1201, on a friendly target effected at 100700Z.	1201 AT100700Z
Final protective fire (identified by unit designation)	A/1-3

NBC

(Height of burst in meters)   (Target number)

(Delivery unit and time on target)   (Weapon type and yield)
(For chemical weapons, type of agent is written here)

Appendix C

Minefields and Minefield Recording

Mines are one of the most effective tank and personnel killers on the battle-field. Minefields that an infantry platoon or squad most commonly emplace are the hasty protective, point, and phony.

U.S. policy regarding the use and employment of antipersonnel land mines (APLs) outlined in this guide is subject to the *Convention on Certain Conventional Weapons* and executive orders. Current U.S. policy limits the use of non-self-destructing APLs to (1) defending the U.S. and its allies from armed aggression across the Korean demilitarized zone and (2) training personnel engaged in demining and countermine operations. The use of the M18A1 Claymore in the command-detonation mode is not restricted under international law or executive order. Note, however, that some countries employ antihandling devices (AHDs) on antipersonnel (AP) mines, but U.S. forces are not authorized to employ AHDs on any type of AP mine.

HASTY PROTECTIVE MINEFIELD
In the defense, platoons and squads lay hasty protective minefields to supplement weapons, prevent surprise, and give early warning of enemy advance. A platoon can install hasty protective minefields, but only with permission from the company commander. Hasty protective minefields are reported to the company commander and recorded on DA Form 1355-1-R. The leader puts the minefield across likely avenues of approach, within range of and covered by his organic weapons. If time permits, the mines should be buried to increase effectiveness, but they may be laid on top of the ground in a random pattern. The minefield should be recorded before the mines are armed. The leader installing the minefield should warn adjacent platoons and tell the company commander of the minefield's location. When the platoon leaves the area (except when forced to withdraw by the enemy),

it must remove the minefield or transfer responsibility for the minefield to the relieving platoon leader. Only metallic mines are used in hasty protective minefields. Booby traps are not used; they delay removal of the mines. The employing platoon must make sure that the minefield can be kept under observation and covered by fire at all times. The following example describes how to lay a hasty protective minefield.

After requesting and receiving permission to lay the minefield, the platoon leader and squad leaders reconnoiter to determine exactly where to place the mines. The leaders determine a need to use antitank mines to block enemy vehicles at the bridge and the ford. The leaders decide that antipersonnel mines are needed to protect the antitank mines and to cover the likely avenues of approach of enemy infantry.

While the soldiers are placing the mines, the platoon leader finds an easily identifiable reference point in front of the platoon's position. The platoon leader records the minefield using a reference point. The row of mines closest to the enemy is designated A and the succeeding rows are B, C, and so on. The ends of a row are shown by two markers. They are labeled with

**Antipersonnel and Antitank Mines
in a Hasty Protective Minefield**

the letter of the row and number 1 for the right end of the row and number 2 for the left end of the row. The rows are numbered from right to left, facing the enemy. The marker can be a steel picket or a wooden stake with a nail or can attached so that it can be found with a metallic mine detector.

From the base reference point (concrete post), the platoon leader measures the magnetic azimuth in degrees and paces the distance to a point between 15 and 25 paces to the right of the first mine on the friendly side of the minefield. This point, B-1, marks the beginning of the second row. The platoon leader places a marker at B-1 and records the azimuth and distance from the concrete post to B-1 on DA Form 1355-1-R.

Next, from B-1 the platoon leader measures the azimuth and distance to a point 15 to 25 paces from the first mine in row A. He places a marker at this point and records it as A-1. The platoon leader then measures the distance and azimuth from A-1 to the first mine in row A and records the location of the mine. He then measures the distance and azimuth from the first mine to the second, and so on until all mine locations have been recorded as shown. The platoon leader gives each mine a number to identify it in the tabular block of DA Form 1355-1-R. When the last mine location in row A is recorded, the platoon leader measures an azimuth and distance from the last mine to another arbitrary point between 15 and 25 paces beyond the last mine. He places a marker here and calls it A-2. The platoon leader follows the same procedure with row B.

When the platoon leader finishes recording and marking the rows, he measures the distance and azimuth from the reference point to B-2 to A-2, and records them. If antitank mines are being used, it is recommended that they be used at the A-2/B-2 markers, because their large size facilitates retrieval.

The platoon leader now ties in the reference point with a permanent landmark that he found on the map. He measures the distance and azimuth from this landmark to the reference point. The landmark might be used to help others locate the minefield should it be abandoned. Finally, he completes the form by filling in the tabular and identification blocks.

While the platoon leader is tying in the landmark, the soldiers arm the mines nearest the enemy first (row A). The platoon leader reports that the minefield is completed and keeps DA Form 1355-1-R. If the minefield is transferred to another platoon, the gaining platoon leader signs and dates the mines transferred block and accepts the form from the previous leader. When the minefield is removed, the form is destroyed. If the minefield is left unattended or abandoned unexpectedly, the form must be forwarded to the company commander. The company commander forwards it to battalion to be transferred to more permanent records.

DA FORM 1355-1-R
HASTY PROTECTIVE MINEFIELD RECORD
(FM 20-32)

Marking and Recording Minefield

When retrieving the mines, the soldiers start at the reference point and move to B-1, using the azimuth and distances as recorded. They then move from B-1 to the first mine in row B. However, if B-1 is destroyed, they move from the reference point to B-2 using that azimuth and distance. They will have to shoot the back azimuth from B-2 to the last mine. The stakes at A-1, B-1, A-2, and B-2 are necessary because it is safer to find a stake when traversing long distances than to find a live mine. Some rules to remember:

- The minimum distance between rows of antitank (AT) mines is 8 meters.
- In Korea (only), the minimum distance between any row and a row containing AP mines is 15 meters.

SCALE
2 CM = 25 PACES

ROW	TYPE	ACTUATION	MINE NUMBER
A	M6A1	TRIP WIRE	1.2.7.
	M21	PRESSURE	3.4.5.6.
B	M16A1	TRIP WIRE	1
	M18A1	CONTROLLED	2.3.4.

REMARKS LAND MARK IS ROAD
JUNCTION AT NA 12343409

UNIT 2ND PLT, A CO I-4TH 1ST INF DIV	
REF PT	
CONCRETE POST BY ROAD	
REMARKS POINTS A1 + A2, B1+B2	
ARE MARKED WITH 2"x 2" STAKES	
MAP & SHEET NO TALBOT 5568	
NAME OF OIC LT. ALLAN	
Signature R. Allan	Hour & Date 8-JUL-75
MINES REMOVED	
MINES TRANSFERRED	

DA FORM 1355-1-R, 1 JULY 75,
REPLACES DA FORM 1335-7, 1 MAR 68, WHICH IS OBSOLETE

Hasty Protective Minefield Record

- The distance between the start row marker and the first mine in a row is the mine spacing for that row.
- Start and end row markers are permanent markers and must be made of detectable material.
- The spacing between mines is at least 4 meters to prevent sympathetic detonation. There is no maximum distance between mines within the row.

- The minefield must be fenced on all sides if M18A1 AP mines are employed and the minefield will be in place for more than 72 hours.
- The minefield has at least one landmark that is located to the rear, never to the extreme side or front.
- Measurements are in meters.
- AHDs, nonmetallic mines, or low-metallic mines are not used.

POINT MINEFIELDS

Point minefields disorganize enemy forces and hinder their use of key areas. Point minefields are of irregular size and shape and include all types of anti-tank and antipersonnel mines and antihandling devices. They should be used to add to the effect of existing and reinforcing obstacles, or to rapidly block an enemy counterattack along a flank avenue of approach.

PHONY MINEFIELDS

Phony minefields, used to degrade enemy mobility and preserve friendly mobility, simulate live minefields and deceive the enemy. They are used when lack of time, personnel, or material prevents the use of actual mines. Phony minefields may be used as gaps in live minefields. To be effective, a phony minefield must look like a live minefield, which is accomplished by either burying metallic objects or making the ground look as though objects are buried.

Appendix D

Platoon and Squad Organization

All infantry platoons and units acting as infantry use the same basic doctrinal principles in combat, but some differences exist between organizations. Most units operate from a modified table of organization and equipment (MTOE) based on their organization, mission, and location. Rifle platoons are organized as light infantry, mechanized infantry, infantry, air assault infantry, airborne infantry, or ranger infantry. The importance of organizing units for combat cannot be overemphasized. All military units regardless of classification as combat arms, combat support, or combat service support, should have a fighting organization. The enemy doesn't care what your specialty is; if you are a cook, mechanic, or other noninfantry element, you need to have a fighting battle roster for those times when you will need to defend yourself. The war in Iraq and the war on terrorism in Afghanistan and around the world have proven to us that there is no safe military occupational duty specialty. Every unit needs to have the minimum ability to fight and defend itself as a collective fighting force.

The most common organization is that of the light infantry platoon, and it is the easiest to duplicate with soldiers who are not used to being infantry. It consists of three rifle squads and a platoon headquarters with two machine

PLATOON LEADER
PLATOON SERGEANT
PLATOON RATELO
2 MACHINE GUNNERS
2 ASSISTANT MACHINE GUNNERS

Light Infantry Platoon Organization

gun teams (if available). Each machine gun team has a gunner and an assistant gunner. The antiarmor weapons are distributed evenly throughout the squads and are usually assigned to more seasoned soldiers.

The most common rifle squad has nine soldiers. It fights as two rifle teams. The squad has one squad leader, two rifle team leaders, and (if weapons are available), two automatic riflemen (M249 SAW), two riflemen (M16), and two grenadiers (M203).

ORGANIZING FOR COMBAT

In order to organize your unit as a fighting infantry platoon or fighting force, you have to take a look at and analyze your personnel and equipment. Organize your force based on the amount of personnel you have. If you only have 13 people, you might consider just replicating a large infantry squad with 3 fire teams (you can also have two larger fire teams) or one infantry squad

Light Infantry Squad Organization

with a machine gunner and an antiarmor specialist. Additionally, you have to look at your available weapons and determine who is best at utilizing weapons such as the machine gun or antiarmor weapons if you have them available. Often soldiers are assigned more than one weapon, such as an M16 rifle, while they may also be responsible for a crew-served machine gun that is mounted on the vehicle. You will want to assign someone the duties of machine gunner in the event your element has to dismount and fight. There is no right or wrong way to organize your element; just ensure your personnel know their assigned duties and their assigned weapon system(s). When time presents itself, conduct the necessary individual and unit training that is most critical to your survival in the event you get into a fire fight.

Duties and Responsibilities

The *Rifle Squad Leader* is responsible for the squad. He is a tactical leader and leads by example. He controls the movement of his squad and its rate and distribution of fire. He controls two fire teams in the offense; selects each fighting position in the defense; and gives the commands and signals to commence, cease, and shift fires. He briefs the squad on orders, trains the squad, manages the squad's administrative and logistical needs, is responsible for accountability and maintenance of personnel and equipment, and keeps the squad fit to fight.

The *Team Leader* controls the movement and fires of the fire team. He assists the squad leader in tactical control of the squad and in training team members on individual and collective tasks and battle drills. The team leader sends reports as requested to the squad leader when his team makes contact. The team leader controls fire and distribution for his team by designating and marking targets.

The *Grenadier* is equipped with an M203 weapon system consisting of an M4/M16 rifle and an attached 40-mm grenade launcher. The M203 allows him to fire high-explosive rounds to suppress and destroy enemy infantry and lightly armored vehicles. He also can employ smoke to screen and cover his squad's movement, fire, and maneuver. During night and adverse weather conditions, the grenadier also may employ illumination rounds to increase his squad's visibility and mark enemy or friendly positions. The grenadier provides the fire team with an indirect fire capability out to 350 meters.

The *Automatic Rifleman's* primary weapon is the M249 squad automatic weapon (SAW). Each infantry squad has two automatic weapons. The M249 provides the squad with a high volume of sustained long-range suppressive and lethal fires far beyond the range of the M16/M4 rifle. The gunner employs the SAW to suppress enemy infantry and bunkers, destroy enemy automatic rifle and antitank (AT) teams, and to enable other teams and squads to maneuver. If a unit does not have a SAW, the next best thing is to designate the automatic riflemen in the squad and have them use the burst mode on their rifles to accomplish rapid fire.

The *Rifleman* is armed with an M4 or M16A2, 5.56-mm rifle. He is employed at the direction of the team leader.

The *Antiarmor Specialist* is equipped with the Javelin AT missile system, M47 Dragon, or even the M136 AT-4. The available AT weapon system destroys enemy armor threats that may impede the platoon's or unit's progress or it can be employed to destroy other targets of opportunity. The Javelin provides the squads, platoon, and company with a lethal, fire-and-forget, man-portable, top-attack antiarmor capability to defeat enemy main battle tanks during day, night, and adverse weather conditions at ranges up to 2,000 meters.

The *Machine Gun Crew* consists of three personnel. The three-man machine gun crew consists of the gunner, assistant gunner, and the ammunition handler. The gunner is the senior member of the crew and responsible for putting the gun in and out of action. The assistant gunner supports the gunner and replaces the gunner in his absence. The ammunition handler carries the spare barrel and additional ammunition for the machine gun and provides local security for the machine gun crew with his assigned rifle.

Appendix E

Organic and Supporting Weapons

ORGANIC WEAPONS

Organic weapons are weapons that are assigned to the platoon over which the platoon leader has direct control. All leaders must know how to employ these weapons effectively in all tactical situations. Additionally, the infantry platoon routinely uses antiarmor weapons, hand grenades, and mines. The following tables outline some of the key organic weapon systems available to the modern infantry platoon:

WEAPON CAPABILITIES	M9 Pistol	M16A2	M249 MG	M203	M4
WEIGHT (lbs)	2.6	8.7	15.5	11	7.5
LENGTH (in)	8.5	39	41.1	39	29.75 closed; 35 open
MAXIMUM RANGE (m)	1,800	3,600	3,600	400	3,600
ARMING RANGE (m)	N/A	N/A	N/A	14	N/A
MINIMUM SAFE RANGE (m)	N/A	N/A	N/A	31	N/A
RATE OF FIRE (rounds per minute)					
CYCLIC (rpm)	N/A	700–800	800	N/A	700–900
RAPID (m)	N/A	N/A	200*	35	N/A
SUSTAINED	60	16	85	35	12/15
EFFECTIVE RANGE					
AREA (m)	N/A	800	800	350	600
POINT	50	580	600	160	500
MOVING (m)	N/A	200	N/A	N/A	N/A
AMMUNITION					
TYPE	BALL	BALL, TRACER, DUMMY, PRACTICE, and BLANK	BALL, TRACER, DUMMY, PRACTICE, and BLANK	HE,WP, CS, ILLUM, TP, and BUCKSHOT	
EXAMPLE LOAD (rds)	30	210	600		

* With barrel change

M870 ARMY SHOTGUN

LENGTH OF SHOTGUN	39 INCHES, APPROXIMATELY
LENGTH OF BARREL	20 INCHES
MAGAZINE CAPACITY—ROUNDS	4
SHELL (GUAGE)	12
AMMUNITION	12 GUAGE, 2 3/4 INCH 00 BUCK, MILITARY RD
SAFETY	CROSSBOLT TYPE
FORE-END	PLAIN BEAVER-TAIL STYLE

Organic Weapons

TECHNICAL SPECIFICATIONS	M72 LAW	M136 AT4	JAVELIN
WEIGHT (lbs)	5.1	14.8	49.5
LENGTH (in)	24/36	40	47.2
MAXIMUM RANGE (m)	1,000	2,100	2,500
ARMING RANGE (m)	10	10	65
MINIMUM SAFE RANGE (m)	10	30	65
EFFECTIVE RANGE			
STATIONARY(m)	200	300	2,000
MOVING (m)	165	300	2,000
BACKBLAST(m)	50	60	25 at 60 degree angle

Antiarmor Weapons

GRENADE SPECIFICATIONS	FRAGMENTARY	WP	THERMITE	CONCUSS
WEIGHT (oz)	14	27	32	15.6
RANGE (m)	35	30	25	40
(Thrown by average soldier)				
PACKING (box)	30	N/A	16	20
BURST RADIUS (m)	15	35		2
		60-sec. burn	40-sec. burn	

MINE SPECIFICATIONS	M21 ANTITANK	M18A1 AP (Claymore)	M14 AP Toe Popper*	M16A1 AP Bouncing Betty*
WEIGHT (lbs)	18	3.5	3.6	3.5
PACKING (box)	4 mines 4 fuses	6 mines with accessories	90 mines 90 detonators	4 fuses, trip wire
BURST RADIUS (m)	N/A	100 (eff); 250 (max)	1 individual	30

*U.S. policy regarding the use and employment of this mine is subject to the convention on Certain Conventional Weapons and Executive Orders. Current U.S. policy limits the use of non-self-destructing mines to (1) defending the U.S. and its allies from armed aggression across the Korean demilitarized zone and (2) training personnel engaged in demining and countermine operations. The use of the M18A1 Claymore in the command-detonation mode is not restricted under law of Executive Order.

Hand Grenades and Mines

SUPPORTING WEAPONS

Supporting weapons provide the platoon and squad leaders additional fire-power. They must know how to effectively integrate the fires of these weapons with the fires of their organic weapons. The following tables out-line some of the key supporting weapon systems available to the modern infantry platoon:

SPECIFICATIONS	M2 (.50 CAL) MG	MK 19	M202 FLASH	M3 RAAWS
WEIGHT (lbs)	84	72.5	26.7	22
LENGTH (in)	65.1	43.1	34.7	42.6
MAXIMUM RANGE (m)	6,767	2,200	N/A	
ARMING RANGE (m)	N/A	15 to 30	N/A	
MINIMUM SAFE RANGE (m)	N/A	28	20	50 (HEAT)
				500 (illum)
				250 (HE)
				50 (SMOKE)
				50 (TNG)
RATE OF FIRE				
CYCLIC (rpm)	500	375	N/A	
RAPID (rpm)	40*	60	N/A	
SUSTAINED (rpm)	40*	40	N/A	6
EFFECTIVE RANGE				
AREA (m)	1,830	2,200	750	200–1,300
POINT (m)	1,200	1,500	200	
STATIONARY (m)	N/A	N/A	N/A	700 (HEAT)
MOVING (m)	N/A	N/A	N/A	250
BACKBLAST (m)			50	60
BURST RADIUS (m)		30	20	
AMMUNITION				
TYPE	BALL, AP, TRACER, API, API-T, INCEN, and BLANK	HEDP, HE	FLAME	HEAT, ILLUM, HE, HEDP, SMOKE, TP, and TNG

* with barrel change

Supporting Weapons

| | AMMUNITION | | (meters) MIN | MAX | RATE |
WEAPON	MODEL	TYPE	RANGE	RANGE	OF FIRE
M224	M720/M888	HE	70	3,490*	30 rounds per minute
60-mm	M722	WP	70	3,490	for 4 minutes**, then
	M721	ILLUM	200	3,490	20 rounds per minute,
	M302A1	WP	33	1,630	sustained.
	M83A3	ILLUM	725	931	
	M49A4	HE	44	1,930	
M252	M821	HE	83	5,608	30 rounds per minute
81-mm	M889	HE	83	5,608	for 2 minutes, then
	M819	RP	300	4,875	15 rounds per minute,
	M853	ILLUM	300	5,100	sustained.
M120	M57	HE	200	7,200	16 rounds per minute
120-mm	M68	WP	200	7,200	for 1 minute, then
	M91	ILLUM	200	7,100	4 rounds per minute,
	M933	HE	200	7,200	sustained.
	M934	HE	200	7,200	
	M929	WP	200	7,200	
	M930	ILLUM	400	6,900	

*Bipod mounted, charge 4 (maximum range handheld is 1,340 meters).
**Charge 2 and over, 30 rounds per minute can be sustained with charge 0 or 1.

Mortars

	M119	M198	M109A6
CALIBER	105-mm	155-mm	155-mm
MAXIMUM RANGE (for HE) (m)	14,000	24,000	24,000
PLANNING RANGE (m)	11,500	14,600	14,600
MINIMUM RANGE (m)	DIRECT FIRE	DIRECT FIRE	DIRECT FIRE
DANGER CLOSE RANGE (m) at Planning Range	600	600	600
RATE OF FIRE			
MAXIMUM (rpm)	6 rpm for 3 min.	4 rpm for 3 min.	4 rpm for 3 min.
SUSTAINED (rpm)	3	2	1
PROJECTILE			
TYPE	HE, M760, ILLUM, HEP-T, APICM, CHEM, RAP	HE, WP, ILLUM, SMK, CHEM, NUC, RAP, FASCAM, CPHD, AP/DPICM	HE, WP, ILLUM, SMK, CHEM, NUC, RAP, FASCAM, CPHD, AP/DPICM
FUSES			
TYPE	PD, VT, MTSQ, CP, MT, DLY	PD, VT, CP, MT, MTSQ, DLY	PD, VT, CP, MT, MTSQ, DLY

LEGEND:

AP — Armor Piercing	MIN — Minute
APICM — Antipersonnel Improved Conventional Munitions	MO — Multioption—VT, PD, DLY
	MT — Mechanical Time
CHEM — Chemical	MTSQ — Mechanical Time Super Quick
CP — Concrete Piercing	NUC — Nuclear
CPHD — Copperhead	PD — Point Detonating
DLY — Delay	RAP — Rocket Assisted Projectile
DPICM — Dual Purpose Improved Conventional Munitions	RD — Round
	RP — Red Phosphorus
FASCAM — Family of Scatterable Mines	RPM — Rounds per Minute
HE — High Explosive	SMK — Smoke
HEP-T — High-Explosive Plastic Tracer	TIME — Adjustable Time Delay
ILLUM — Illumination	VT — Variable Time
	WP — White Phosphorus

Field Artillery

Appendix F

Acronyms and Abbreviations

AA	assembly area; avenue of approach
ACL	allowable cargo load
ADA	air defense artillery
AG	Adjutant General
AH	attack helicopter
ALICE	all-purpose lightweight individual carrying equipment
AMC	at my command
ANCD	automated net control device
AO	area of operations
APC	armored personnel carrier
AR	automatic rifle
ASL	assistant squad leader
AT	antitank
ATGM	antitank guided missile
AVLB	armored vehicle launch bridge
BAS	battalion aid station
BCS	battery computer system
BDU	battle dress uniform
BFV	Bradley fighting vehicle
BIFV	Bradley infantry fighting vehicle
BMP	a Soviet infantry fighting vehicle
BOS	battlefield operating systems
BP	battle position
BRDM	a Soviet vehicle used by reconnaissance units
BTR	a Soviet wheeled vehicle
C^2	command and control
CAS	close air support
CASEVAC	casualty evacuation
CCD	camouflage, concealment, and decoys
CCP	casualty collection point

CEWI	combat electronics warfare and intelligence
CFV	cavalry fighting vehicle
CH	cargo helicopter
CLU	command launch unit
CNR	combat net radio
COA	course of action
CP	command post
CS	combat support
CSS	combat service support
CW	continuous wave
DEW	directed-energy weapon
DLIC	detachment left in contact
DTG	data time group
DZ	drop zone
EA	engagement area
EMP	electromagnetic pulse
EPW	enemy prisoner of war
ERP	enroute rally point
EW	electronic warfare
EZ	extraction zone
FA	field artillery
FAC	forward air controller
FDC	fire direction center
FDO	fire direction officer
FEBA	forward edge of battle area
FFE	fire for effect
FFU	friendly forward unit
FH	frequency hopping
FIST	fire support team
FLOT	forward line of own troops
FM	frequency modulation; field manual
FO	forward observer
FPF	final protective fire
FPL	final protective line
FRAGO	fragmentary order
FSO	fire support officer
GD	ground distance
GL	grenade launcher
G-M	grid-magnetic
GPS	global positioning system
GS	general support

HE	high explosive
HEAT	high-explosive antitank
HEDP	high-explosive, dual purpose
HHC	headquarters and headquarters company
HQ	headquarters
ICM	improved conventional munition
ICOM	integrated communications security
IEDK	individual equipment decontamination kit
IR	infrared
IRP	initial rally point
ISR	intelligence, surveillance, and reconnaissance
ISU	integrated sight unit
IVIS	intervehicular information system
KIA	killed in action
km	kilometer
LAW	light antitank weapon
LBE	load-bearing equipment
LC	line of contact
LCSS	lightweight camouflage screening system
LD	line of departure
LD/LC	line of departure/line of contact
LMG/COAX	light machine gun/coaxial
LOGPAC	logistics package
LZ	landing zone
MAW	medium antitank weapon
MBA	main battle area
MCS	maneuver control system
MD	map distance
MDMP	military decision-making process
MEDEVAC	medical evacuation
MEL	maximum engagement line
METT-TC	mission, enemy, terrain and weather, troops available, time available, and civil considerations
MG	machine gun
MOPP	mission-oriented protective posture
MOUT	military operations in urban terrain
MRE	meal ready to eat
MTOE	modified table of organization and equipment
NAI	named area of interest
NATO	North Atlantic Treaty Organization
NBC	nuclear, biological, chemical

NCO	noncommissioned officer
NLT	not later than
NVD	night vision devices
OBJ	objective
OCOKA	observation, cover and concealment, obstacles, key terrain, avenues of approach
OH	observation helicopter
OP	observation post
OPCON	operational control
OPLAN	operations plan
OPORD	operations order
OPSEC	operations security
ORP	objective rally point
OT	observer target
PAC	personnel and administration center
PCC	precombat check
PCI	precombat inspection
PD	point of departure
PDF	principal direction of fire
PIR	priority of intelligence requirement
PL	phase line; platoon leader
PMCS	preventive maintenance checks and services
POSNAV	position navigation
PSG	platoon sergeant
PSYOP	psychological operations
PUP	pop-up point
PW	prisoner of war
PZ	pickup zone
R&S	reconnaissance and security
RATELO	radiotelephone operator
RDVU	rendezvous point
REDCON	readiness condition
RF	representative fraction
ROE	rules of engagement
ROI	rules of interaction
RP	release point
RPV	remotely piloted vehicle
RRP	reentry rally point
RS	road space
RSTA	reconnaissance, surveillance, and target acquisition
RT	receiver-transmitter

SALUTE	size, activity, location, unit, time, equipment
SAW	squad automatic weapon
SBCT	stryker brigade combat team
SC	single-channel
SE	spot elevation
SF	special forces
SINCGARS	single-channel ground and airborne radio system
SITREP	situation report
SL	squad leader
SOI	signal operation instructions
SOP	standing operating procedure
SP	start point
SPOTREP	spot report
TACP	tactical command post
TF	task force
TL	team leader; time length
TLP	troop-leading procedure
TOT	time on target
TOW	tube-launched, optically tracked, wire-guided
TRP	target reference point
UAV	unmanned aerial vehicle
UH	utility helicopter
UO	urban operations
VA	vertical angle
VT	variable time (fuse)
WARNO	warning order
WIA	wounded in action
WP	white phosphorus
WRP	weapons reference point
XO	executive officer

Appendix G

References

FM 3-0   *Operations*, 14 June 2001

FM 3-06   *Urban Operations*, 1 June 2003

FM 3-22.68   *Crew-Served Machine Guns, 5.56-mm and 7.62-mm*; 31 January 2003

FM 3-7   *NBC Field Handbook*, 29 September 1994

FM 3-100   *NBC Operations*, May 1996

FM 20-3   *Camouflage, Concealment, and Decoys*, 30 August 1999

FM 20-32   *Mine, Countermine Operations*, 1 October 2002

FM 21-75   *Combat Skills of the Soldier*, August 1984

FM 22-100   *Army Leadership*, 31 August 1999

FM 4-25.11 (FM 21-11)   *First Aid*, 23 December 2002

FM 3-90   *Tactics*, 4 July 2001

FM 3-90.1   *Tank and Mechanized Infantry Company Team*, 9 December 2002

FM 6-30   *Tactics, Techniques, and Procedures for Observed Fire*, 16 July 1991

FM 3-21.71(FM 7-7J)   *Mechanized Infantry Platoon and Squad (Bradley)*, 20 August 2002

FM 3-21.8 (FM 7-8) Draft   *The Infantry Rifle Platoon and Squad*

FM 7-10   *The Infantry Rifle Company*; Change 1, 31 October 2000

FM 7-20   *The Infantry Battalion*; Change 1, 29 December 2000

FM 21-18   *Foot Marches*, 1 June 1990

FM 101-5-1   *Operational Terms and Graphics*, 30 September 1997

FM 3-90.1 (FM 71-1)   *Tank and Mechanized Infantry Company Team*, December 2002

GTA 05-08-001	*Survivability Positions*, 1 August 1993
GTA 07-06-001	*Fighting Position Construction: Infantry Leader's Reference Card*, 1 June 1992
STP 21-24-SMCT	*Soldier's Manual of Common Tasks, Skill Level 2, 3, and 4*, August 2003
STP 21-24-SMCT	*Soldier's Manual of Common Tasks, Skill Level 1*, August 2003
Call Handbook No. 03-15	*The Radio Telephone Operator (RTO) Handbook*, June 2003
TM 11-5820-890-10-8	*SINCGARS Ground Combat Net Radio (ICOM)*, February 1995

Index

STACKPOLE BOOKS

Military Professional Reference Library

Air Force Officer's Guide
Airman's Guide
Armed Forces Guide to Personal Financial Planning
Army Dictionary and Desk Reference
Army Officer's Guide
Career Progression Guide
Combat Leader's Field Guide
Combat Service Support Guide
Enlisted Soldier's Guide
Guide to Effective Military Writing
Guide to Military Installations
Guide to Military Operations Other Than War
Job Search: Marketing Your Military Experience
Military Money Guide
NCO Guide
Reservist's Money Guide
Servicemember's Legal Guide
Servicemember's Guide to a College Degree
Soldier's Study Guide
Today's Military Wife
Veteran's Guide to Benefits
Virtual Combat

Professional Reading Library

Fighting for the Future: Will America Triumph?
by Ralph Peters

Roots of Strategy, Books 1, 2, 3, and 4

Guardians of the Republic: History of the NCO
by Ernest F. Fisher

Vietnam Order of Battle
by Shelby L. Stanton

No Gun Ri
by Robert L. Bateman

Stackpole Books are available at your Exchange Bookstore or
Military Clothing Sales Store or from Stackpole at
1-800-732-3669 *or* **www.stackpolebooks.com**